PORTUGAL'S WINES
AND
WINE-MAKERS

PORTUGAL'S WINES
AND
WINE-MAKERS

Port, Madeira and Regional Wines

Richard Mayson

Here's to the Aussie Wine Makers!

Richard Mayson

8th June 1993

EBURY PRESS
LONDON

First published in 1992 by Ebury Press
an imprint of the Random Century Group
Random Century House
20 Vauxhall Bridge Road
London SW1V 2SA

Text copyright © 1992 Richard Mayson
Maps and diagrams copyright © Malcolm Porter
Designed by Rowan Seymour

A Jill Norman Book

A catalogue record for this book is available from the British Library

ISBN 0 09 177156 0

Filmset in Garamond by SX Composing, Rayleigh, Essex
Printed and bound in Singapore by Kyodo Printing

Contents

Acknowledgements

All books have to start somewhere. This one dates back to a lunch given in February 1980 by Jorge Ferreira, then a director of the port house A. A. Ferreira. Looking out through the plate glass windows at the grey city of Oporto with a glass of old tawny on hand, I remember thinking that it would be a good idea to take more of an interest in wine.

A large number of people have helped me since and I am indebted to all the wine-makers in Portugal who, over the years, have given up their time and wine to produce this book. A few deserve special mention. In Oporto and the Douro: the Bergqvist family at Quinta de la Rosa, Jeremy Bull of Cálem, David Baverstock, the Australian wine maker working for the Symington group; Miguel Champalimaud (Quinta do Côtto), Peter Cobb (Cockburns), Jorge Ferreira, Bruce Guimaraens (Fonseca), his brother Gordon Guimaraens (Cockburns), twins João and Ricardo Nicolau de Almeida (Ramos Pinto), father and son Rolf and Dirk van der Niepoort, Alastair and Gilly Robertson, impeccable hosts at Taylor's Quinta de Vargellas; David Sandeman, the Symington family, especially James, Peter and Paul, and brother and sister Cristiano and Teresa van Zeller, owners of Quinta do Noval. On Madeira, Manuela de Freitas (Barbeito), José Teles of the Portuguese Government Trade Office and Antonio Serra Alegre (Madeira Wine Company) were especially forthcoming with information.

Elsewhere in Portugal, a number of dedicated producers have been particularly helpful: another Australian, Peter Bright of João Pires, Luis Pato and his wife who makes a wonderful *Leite Creme* pudding, brothers Antonio and Domingos Soares Franco (José Maria da Fonseca Succrs.), Manuel Sousa Pinto (Sogrape) and Antonio Vinagre, owner of Quinta do Tamariz. I owe special thanks to Christopher and

Elizabeth Gotto who helped me enormously when I first began researching this book in July 1989. Without them, the task would have been much less pleasurable.

Back in Britain I owe a great deal of gratitude to João Henriques of the Portuguese Government Trade Office who has supported the book from the start. My former employers, the Wine Society, deserve a vote of thanks along with all my friends and wine trade colleagues. Raymond Reynolds, formerly wine-maker for Taylors and now a UK wine importer specializing in Portuguese wines, helped me with the technical details in Chapter 3. Antonio Macedo of Vinhos de Portugal and Richard Pass of RS Pass Wines Ltd and wine-writer Charles Metcalfe have also provided me with up-to-date information. Jane Hunt M.W., James Suckling of the *Wine Spectator*, his wife Catherine Scott and Bill Warre M.W. and Tim Stanley-Clarke of Fells have all shared some good bottles of wine with me when the chips were down. My editor Jill Norman has been a constant source of encouragement. I am grateful to her for her patience and advice.

Finally I must thank my parents who have been on hand at many a time when I felt that this book would never be finished. It is thanks to them that I have been able to spend so much time pursuing an interest in wine.

Richard Mayson,
London,
January 1992

Preface

At a time when Cabernet Sauvignon and Chardonnay sound less like the names of grapes and more like international brands, Portugal is a find. This small, rectangular country on the prow of Europe has continually bucked global trends and is proud to make wine her own way.

Yet Portugal is changing. A revolution in the mid-1970s woke the Portuguese from their slumbers and brought them rudely into the late twentieth century. A revolution in wine-making is following in its wake. The thirsty Portuguese, who previously kept most of the wine for themselves, are making a determined effort to improve their wines and capture new markets.

Despite flourishing sales coupled with a significant improvement in quality, few people seem to know what really lies behind the curiously unpronounceable names that are steadily appearing on the lists and shelves of wine merchants and supermarkets world wide. I find from my own experience that even the wine trade seems to have a sketchy understanding. In fact behind names like the Douro, Madeira, the Alentejo, Bairrada, Dão and Vinho Verde lie some of the most interesting developments in European wine-making. There is also a captivating country.

Books have been written separately about Port and Madeira but few put these two great wines in their national context. Other books have lumped Portuguese wines with those of Spain when in reality the differences between the two countries outweigh their similarities.

My aim in writing this book is to explain why Portuguese wines are different. The reasons are both good and bad. The book starts by bringing the country up-to-date, tracing the traditions that have kept Portugal's wines and wine-makers separate from the rest of Europe. It continues by unravelling the wealth of largely indigenous grape varieties growing in Portuguese vineyards; some with mysterious names like 'dog strangler' and 'tail of the cat' that are never likely to be the subject of varietal worship. Over a hundred different grapes are listed in Chapter 2 along with quality assessments. Moving from the vineyard to developments in the winery, production methods are explained in Chapter 3, highlighting some of the differences between theory and practice. This sets the scene for the main part of the book which is a journey around Portugal uncovering the wines and the people who make them. Port and Madeira are joined for the first time by over forty different wine regions, many of which have only just received official recognition. Each chapter follows a similar format with an introduction to the region, a description of the wines and an alphabetical guide to significant wine-makers. A short section at the end of the chapter provides a guide for anyone intending to visit the vineyards. The book concludes with some crystal-ball gazing and a glance at some of the possibilities that may lie ahead.

Portugal's Wines and Wine Makers has been written both for members of the trade and enthusiasts interested in finding out about wine either at home or on the spot. Above all, it is written by a wine drinker for the wine drinker who wants to find out why Port, Madeira and Portuguese regional wines taste the way they do. For anyone tiring of world-wide Cabernet and Chardonnay-mania, it is an exciting time to discover Portugal.

I

Bringing Portugal up to Date

The Portuguese are a nation of traders. Ever since its borders were first established, this small, rectangular country surrounded on two sides by a large and often hostile neighbour has looked out to sea for trade and prosperity. Portugal has developed an island culture on the continent of Europe.

The British are often labelled 'a nation of shopkeepers' – an independent-minded, island race frequently at odds with their continental neighbours. This may explain why the Portuguese and the British have nearly always been in tune with each other. Overseas trade first with Britain, then with America and France, certainly helps to explain the evolution of Portugal's wine-making up to the present day.

Early Wine-makers

The roots of Portugal's wine industry go back to the days before the nation was established. It seems likely that the marauding Phoenicians were Portugal's first wine-makers, and the Romans continued the tradition, fighting off the Celts and bringing civilization to the land they christened Lusitania. There is evidence that the Romans brought *amphorae*, the descendants of which survive in the form of the *anforas* that are still used for making wine in parts of southern Portugal.

When the Romans left, Iberia was overrun by successive tribes of Suevi, Visogoths and Moors. The Christian Suevi and Visogoths occupied the north while, at the beginning of the eighth century, the Moors advanced rapidly from the south, taking over the whole peninsula. The Moslems turned a blind eye to wine-making and left the Christian smallholders to tend their own vines.

The Birth of the Wine Trade

Portugal emerged in the twelfth century when the Christians drove the Moors south
along the Atlantic seaboard with one hand, fending the Castilians off with the other.
By the middle of the thirteenth century the last of the Moors had been expelled, and
Portugal's borders have remained virtually unchanged ever since.

Trade with Britain began soon afterwards. Portuguese wines were exchanged for
bacalhau (salt cod) and wool. According to H. Warner Allen, in his largely historical
book *The Wines of Portugal*, the first recorded Portuguese wine to be exported was
Osey, a dessert wine probably from the Algarve. Anglo-Portuguese trading links
were sealed by the Treaty of Windsor, which pledged perpetual friendship between
the two countries in 1386. The Treaty has been invoked on a number of occasions
since, most recently during the Second World War. The 600th anniversary of the
Treaty of Windsor was celebrated in London and Lisbon in 1986.

By the end of the fifteenth century Lisbon was one of the world's great trading
centres. The empire-building that followed the epic voyages of Prince Henry the
Navigator, Gil Eanes, Bartolomeu Dias and Vasco da Gama put Portugal on the map
and expanded her trading network to include Africa, India and Brazil. British traders
continued to visit Lisbon, taking sugar, spice and wine in exchange for more
mundane products from northern climes. In *Henry VI, Part 2*, Shakespeare mentions
a wine called Charneco, which Warner Allen attributes to Bucelas, close to the
outskirts of Lisbon (see page 151).

British Merchants

During the fourteenth and fifteenth centuries the British developed a taste for French
wine, and exports of Portuguese wines declined. From the middle of the seventeenth
century, however, relations between England and France were jeopardized by a tariff
war. Imports of French wines were prohibited for a time, and in 1693 William III
began to impose punitive levels of taxation. Edmund Penning Rowsell, in *The Wines
of Bordeaux*, records that while the duty on Iberian wines stood at £21 12s 5d a tun,
the levy on French wines rose steadily to £51 2s – over a shilling a bottle.

This drove merchants to Portugal. At first they settled in the extreme north,
buying wine in the Monção district (see page 118), which they shipped from the port
of Viana do Castelo. To begin with, trade in the wine they called 'Red Portugal'
looked promising. Vines grew with vigour in the warm, damp Atlantic climate and
there was an abundance of cheap wine. But the quality was disappointing. Vines were
cultivated, much as they are today, as a secondary crop, and the thin, astringent red
wines spoiled before they reached the British Isles.

Looking for more robust wines, the merchants travelled up the River Douro.

Although they were only 70 kilometres or so from the coast, the early merchants found that the wines were the opposite of those they had left behind. Fast and furious fermentation at high temperatures produced dark, austere red wines that quickly earned them the name 'Black-strap'. In a determined effort to make sure that these wines arrived at their destination in good condition, merchants often added a measure of brandy to stabilize them before shipment.

The Demand for Port

These red wines, however, were nothing like the sweet, rich, fortified Port wine that we enjoy today. The discovery of Port is credited to a Liverpool wine merchant who, in 1678, sent his two sons to Portugal to learn about wine. At Lamego, in the mountains high above the Douro, they found a monastery where the abbot was adding brandy to the wine during the fermentation, killing off the active yeasts and so producing an intensely sweet, alcoholic wine. The name of the abbot goes unrecorded but he certainly deserves the fame of Dom Perignon, the monk at Hautvillers who invented Champagne.

Relations with France were broken altogether with the outbreak of the War of the Spanish Succession in 1702, and a year later Britain and Portugal signed the Methuen Treaty, which laid down tariff advantages for Portuguese wines. Portugal's wine-makers were to benefit from this discrimination in their favour for over 150 years, until it was finally dropped by Gladstone in 1860.

By the time the Methuen Treaty was signed, a number of foreign merchants were already well established in Oporto. A German, Christiano Kopke, began trading as early as 1638, followed by the firm of Warre, founded in 1670. Croft, Quarles Harris and Bearsley (the forerunner of Taylor's) were all trading by 1700. The Methuen Treaty brought an era of prosperity to Douro wine-makers, and between 1703 and 1750, Morgan Bros., Offley, Hunt Roope and Burmester all began trading.

Pombal and Early Regulations

Not everyone appreciated Port. Scribblers in London taverns wrote poems despising it, perhaps in much the same way as today's writers criticize wines and expose the occasional scandal in magazine and newspaper columns. There is no doubt that by the 1730s there were plenty of scandals to expose. Sugar was being added, and elderberry juice was used to give more colour to wine overstretched by poor-quality spirit. This unprincipled over-production brought about a slump in the Port trade and prices came crashing down. In 1750 the price of a pipe of Port fell to just 7 escudos, from the 60-70 escudos it had been fetching a few years before. The downturn became a crisis.

Prompted by a threatening letter from wine merchants in England, the shippers contacted the ruthless Prime Minister of the day, Sebastião José de Carvalho e Melo, better known as the Marquês de Pombal. He quickly stepped into the fray, seizing the opportunity to manipulate the potentially lucrative Port trade to his own advantage. In 1756 he founded the Companhia Geral da Agricultura dos Vinhos do Alto Douro. Its charter aimed at re-establishing the good name of the wines by controlling their production so that both growers and shippers would obtain a reasonable return, without price fluctuations damaging demand on one hand and farmers abandoning the land on the other. In short, it was to bring stability back to the Port trade. But Pombal also granted the company a trading monopoly with Brazil and the exclusive right to sell wine in and around Oporto. Riots broke out, which Pombal was quick to blame on the English shippers, and had it not been for Britain's involvement in the Seven Years War with France and Spain, Anglo-Portuguese trade might have come to an end. In the event, William Pitt was anxious to remain on good terms with Portugal and turned a deaf ear to the shippers' complaints.

The establishment of the company was accompanied by a series of measures to regulate Port production. A commission was set up to draw a boundary around the Douro region restricting Port production to vineyards within the demarcation. This was marked out with sturdy granite posts (over 100 of which still stand) setting out two zones: a zone for table wines, and a zone producing high-quality wines for export called the *Feitoria*. In an effort to stamp out fraud, all elderberry trees were uprooted and every vineyard was registered. Production quotas were issued, based on an average of the previous five years' yields. Any contravention of the rules was to be met with severe financial penalties. Besides this, Pombal gave the company the exclusive right to sell the brandy needed to make Port, a right which the Portuguese government retained until recently.

There is no doubt that the company was a lucrative exercise for Pombal, who often flouted his own rules, selling wine from his vineyards at Carcavelos near Lisbon (see page 154) for blending with Port. But Pombal's far-reaching measures were equally far-sighted, providing the basis for the legislation that operates in the Douro today.

Pombal's influence spread far and beyond the Douro, with his orders to uproot vineyards in regions as far apart as the Minho, Bairrada and Ribatejo to leave more room for the cultivation of wheat. But after Pombal fell from power in 1777, many of his rules were either relaxed or abolished. British Port shippers were once again free to compete and exports doubled in the last two decades of the seventeenth century, rising to 98,000 pipes (over 500,000 hectolitres) in 1799. Over 60 per cent of this went to Britain, earning Port the epithet, 'the Englishman's wine'.

Madeira and the Americas

Madeira, on the other hand, was doing well out of trade with the other side of the Atlantic. Vineyards were established on the island by Prince Henry the Navigator, who is thought to have introduced Malvasia vines from Crete and planted them for the benefit of the early settlers. By the beginning of the sixteenth century, the Portuguese discoveries in Africa and the east had made Madeira into an important trading post and there was a constant demand for wine from passing ships. With the colonization of America in the seventeenth century, Madeira started to export wine, establishing an important market on the east coast. Noel Cossart, in his book *The Island Vineyard*, records that in 1680 there were thirty wine shippers on Madeira. At about the same time that brandy was being added to wines from the Douro, alcohol (probably distilled from cane sugar) was added to Madeira in order to help the wine survive a long sea voyage.

In the latter part of the seventeenth century, ships *en route* to India called regularly at Funchal to pick up casks of wine for the journey. It was soon discovered that Madeira wine tasted better after pitching and rolling across the tropics, and a fashion developed in America for *vinho da roda*: wines that had benefited from the round voyage.

With American independence in 1776 and the return of the colonial troops, a market opened up in Britain. Merchants began to look for ways to simulate the long, tropical sea voyages that had proved to be so beneficial by heating the wine up in *estufas* (hothouses) at home (see page 58). There was much abuse of the *estufa* system to begin with, and for a short period at the beginning of the nineteenth century the practice of *estufagem* (heating) was banned. But in 1835 *estufas* were again legalized, founding the system that is used to make Madeira today.

The east coast of the United States continues to be a significant market for quality Madeira. The Madeira Club at Savannah, on the coast of Georgia, survived prohibition and still meets regularly, over 200 years after it was founded.

Wine and Wellington

The French marched into Lisbon in 1807. The Portuguese invoked the Treaty of Windsor, and Sir Arthur Wellesley (later Duke of Wellington) was sent with an expeditionary force to drive them out. The war in Portugal lasted until 1811, after three years of battle in the country around Torres Vedras, north of Lisbon. Wellington's officers drank the local wine, starting a vogue for Bucelas, Carcavelos and a wine that nineteenth-century merchants simply called 'Lisbon'. Henry Vizetelly, writing in 1877, devotes two chapters of his book *Facts about Port and Madeira* to wines from the Lisbon region, though significantly he bemoans the fact that 'Lisbon wines have gone completely out of fashion in England.' He talks about the world-famed Torres Vedras, and speculates that it would be so much better if the wines were imported direct rather than mixed with 'the undrinkable *vins verts* of our enterprising French neighbours'.

The Wine Society, now Britain's largest and oldest wine club, was founded in 1874 with a number of casks of Bucellas (archaic spelling) left over after an international exhibition at the Albert Hall. They listed the wine at 19s per dozen bottles until 1886.

Disease and Devastation

In the mid nineteenth century Portuguese vineyards suffered the dual blow of oidium and phylloxera. Oidium (powdery mildew) arrived in the Douro in 1848, imparting 'a strange bitter flavour' to that year's wine, according to Henry Vizetelly. Between 1851 and 1856 it devastated the region, killing off vines and reducing yields to half what they had been in the 1840s. On Madeira, where grapes were the island's principal crop, oidium ruined the economy, reducing yields from 50 million hectolitres to just 600 in three years. Of the seventy British shippers on Madeira, thirty-five left for Spain. Desperate growers tried a number of different remedies, among them coal tar, sulphate of potash and phosphate of lime, but none had any effect. The disease was finally brought under control by dusting the vines with sulphur, and by the 1860s the vineyards were being replanted.

There was worse to come, however. Just as production was returning to normal, phylloxera arrived. This tiny louse was discovered in a Hammersmith greenhouse in 1863, having been carried across the Atlantic. It quickly rampaged through Europe, feasting on the roots of *Vitis vinifera* vines until the plants withered and died. Phylloxera reached Portugal in 1868 and chewed its way through most of the country's vineyards over the next ten years. In the Douro, whole hillsides were abandoned as farmers fled from the region, and some terraces have never been replanted. On Madeira, where phylloxera arrived four years later, it ruined the island's economy for the second time in twenty years. Henry Vizetelly visited Portugal when phylloxera was at its height and describes the lengths to which growers were prepared to go to combat the louse. He mentions a substance called *kainit*, a mixture of sulphate of potash, natural magnesia, Aylesbury sewage, and vine ashes, which is sown into the ground around the base of the vine. On Madeira, Vizetelly visited a vineyard belonging to a Mr Leacock, who was uprooting his vines and painting them with 'a kind of varnish . . . which has succeeded in restoring most of the diseased vines to a comparatively healthy condition'.

Restocking the Vineyards

We now know that neither Mr Leacock's nor any other remedy was successful in eradicating phylloxera from European vineyards. To this day the only effective way of controlling the louse is to graft cuttings of *Vitis vinifera* on to phylloxera-resistant American vines. None of these are suited to making quality wine. *Vitis labrusca* in particular produces wine with an odd musky aroma and flavour, but *V. berlandieri* is particularly good at standing up to phylloxera. By crossing *berlandieri* with other vine species like *riparia* and *rupestris*, hybrids have been developed as rootstock.

In Portugal, the restocking of vineyards following phylloxera's feast was a slow and costly procedure. For a time the government prohibited the importation of American vines, believing them to be a cause of phylloxera rather than a cure. The ban was lifted in 1883 following pressure from the growers and shippers, but grafted vines take between five and eight years before they reach full production and it was not until the turn of the century that output returned to pre-phylloxera levels.

In the meantime, many small growers took short cuts to return to normal production. *Labrusca* hybrids like Isabella, Jacquet and Cunningham, planted on their own roots, were found to grow quickly and produce large quantities of grapes. Whole tracts of vineyard were replanted with direct producers or hybrids, most growers happy that high yields and resistance to disease more than made up for the low quality of the wine. Farmers grew accustomed to drinking *vinho americano* and so the hybrids stayed. Since phylloxera, two-thirds of production on Madeira has come from these grapes and, today, smallholdings on the island and in the Minho, Dão and the Oeste are still riddled with hybrid vines. The European Community forbids the export of wines made from hybrid grapes and a programme of vineyard reconversion has begun, with subsidies available to help eradicate direct producers. But many growers on Madeira and in the Minho seem proud of their hybrid varieties and have no intention of handing over their right to their glass of *vinho americano* to the authorities in Brussels. In many parts of the country, more than 100 years after the phylloxera epidemic, the government's programme of *Boa vinha, melhor vinho* (good vines, better wine) seems to be falling on deaf ears.

Nineteenth-century Wine-makers

In spite of the havoc wreaked on Portugal first by war, then by oidium and phylloxera, the wine industry continued to expand throughout the nineteenth century. Over twenty new Port shippers were established, among them the well-known names of Graham (1814), Cockburn (1815), Càlem (1859), Delaforce (1868) and Ramos Pinto (1880). A rapid increase in exports to Brazil and the colonies brought a period of prosperity to growers. New vineyards were planted and production increased to 4 million hectolitres by the end of the 1880s, over half of which was exported. Merchants set up in business, buying, blending and ageing the best table wines made by thousands of small farmers. José Maria da Fonseca, Sandeman, Wynn & Constance, Camilo Alves and Carvalho, Ribeiro & Ferreira became important shippers of wines from the Lisbon region. A lucrative but dishonest trade was established with France: wines from the Oeste and Ribatejo were sent for blending with wines from Bordeaux (see page 139). This lasted until the mid-1920s when, after a number of attempts to establish a *modus vivendi* with Portugal, France prohibited imports of Portuguese wine.

Twentieth-century Upheaval

The halcyon days were short-lived, and by the turn of the century Portugal's wine industry returned to a state of turmoil. Production continued to increase, reaching 7 million hectolitres in 1908, while exports fell.

This coincided with a period of chronic instability. Mounting political pressure during the latter part of the nineteenth century finally ruptured the nation in the first decade of the twentieth. King Carlos I was assassinated in 1908 and the monarchy ended two years later, when Manuel II bowed to the republican tide, abdicated and left Portugal for England. However, one of the last acts of the government, under the monarchist dictator João Franco, was to follow the example set by Pombal and demarcate five wine-producing regions: Colares, Carcavelos, Moscatel de Setúbal, Dão and the country producing Vinho Verde. The boundaries of the Douro were redefined and it was established that Port could be legally exported only via the mouth of the River Douro or the port of Leixões. Lists of authorized grape varieties were drawn up and the planting of new vineyards were prohibited, in a brave attempt to improve quality and limit production.

Early republican governments continued to pursue the same course. Bucelas and Madeira were demarcated in 1911 and in 1913 and a credit fund was set up to help growers establish co-operatives. But the political infighting grew worse and for sixteen years the country drifted directionless through a succession of governments. Between 1910 and 1926, Portugal was ruled by forty-nine different administrations with no less than sixty-three Ministers of Agriculture. Corruption was rife and governments were too weak to enforce the laws they passed. The outbreak of the First World War precipitated an economic crisis which left Portugal seriously in debt. The army stepped in, putting an end to the liberal republic in 1926. Almost no one took any notice when, in a last-ditch attempt to balance the books, the military President appointed António de Oliveira Salazar, the son of a Dão smallholder, to the post of Finance Minister, giving him complete control of Portugal's purse-strings.

Wine and the Strong Arm of the State

By pruning expenditure and raising new taxes, Salazar accomplished what had previously been thought to be a mission impossible: turning a massive deficit into a budgetary surplus in his first year and repeating it annually. Due to his financial prudence, Portugal survived the world slump of 1929-31 almost unscathed and in 1932 he was appointed Prime Minister.

Salazar had no time for playing politics and quickly established a new constitution which put him at the head of a one-party, corporate state, founded on tiers of 'voluntary' *federações* (federations) and *gremios* (guilds). One of Salazar's first acts was to knock some shape into the chaotic wine industry. Rather like Pombal, Salazar was not afraid of using the strong arm of the state. He set up the Casa do Douro in 1932 to 'discipline and protect the production' of Port, followed by the Instituto do Vinho do Porto (Port Wine Institute) and the Gremio dos Exportadores (Guild of Exporters) a year later (see page 69).

In 1933 the government established regional Federações dos Vinicultores (Wine Growers' Federations) to oversee wine-making in Portugal. They were charged with improving the quality of production, the creation of co-operatives and the regulation of the market for Portuguese wines. The federations were joined by another *gremio* which was put in charge of the sale and export of wine.

These bodies were used to enforce a rash of government legislation relating to wine. In 1937 the system of control was streamlined further by the creation of the Junta Nacional do Vinho (National Wine Junta), an all-powerful regulatory body which superseded the federations in all but the regions of Dão, Vinho Verde and the Douro. *Selos de garantia* (seals of guarantee) were awarded to wines from the demarcated regions that met with the required standard of the federations and the Junta (JNV).

The Co-operative Movement

Salazar rightly attributed the chaotic state of Portugal's wine industry to the fragmented land holdings in north and central Portugal. Until the end of the 1930s, the wine trade was a *laissez-faire* balancing act between the growers on the one hand and merchants, who bought in, bottled and marketed wines under their own labels, on the other. The mid-thirties financial crisis in Brazil upset this fragile state of affairs and the government took positive steps to impose a structure on the wine industry in line with its own corporate thinking.

The JNV began a programme of co-operativization. Adegas Co-operativas (co-operative wine cellars) were set up to buy grapes from local farmers, making wine in large central wineries instead of small private cellars. The first co-op was founded at

Muge in the Ribatejo in 1935, but the programme was slow to make an impact and in 1947 the JNV calculated that 90 per cent of Portugal's 330,000 wine-makers were still producing less than 10 pipes (5,500 litres) of wine.

The co-operative movement really began to take off after the Second World War. In 1953 the Minister of Economics, Ulisses Cortês, gave the go-ahead to a JNV plan for 127 co-operatives with a total capacity for nearly 2 million litres of wine, accounting for around a quarter of Portugal's total production. At the same time, taxes were levied on wine to help finance the programme.

During the late 1950s and the 1960s, co-operatives sprang up all over the country. They were all built to a similar, state-approved plan and furnished with the most modern equipment available. At the time they were hailed as a significant advance, but the system imposed by central government was too inflexible and the standard of Portuguese wine-making undoubtedly deteriorated. In Dão and Colares laws were passed to protect the co-ops from private competition, handing them a virtual monopoly. Wine-making techniques soon became outdated, and the moribund quasi-state bureaucracy was incapable of providing either the money or the initiative to improve the quality of co-operative wine-making. In many co-ops, cement fermentation vats are actually a part of the structure of the building, making it almost impossible to replace them with more modern stainless steel.

Big Brands

Portugal remained neutral in the Second World War and, in the period that followed, while other European countries were counting the cost of conflict, Portugal was awash with inexpensive wine. Sensing the opportunity presented by British and American troops returning home from France with a taste for wine, Portugal became the ideal launch-pad for the first popular brands. Mateus and Lancers both took off in the 1950s when post-war austerity ceased to bite. The combined exports of the two brands (joined by 100 or more look-a-likes) rose to nearly 3 million litres – over a quarter of Portugal's total production. The story of the rise and fall of the rosé phenomenon is told on page 199.

Revolution

The Portuguese are obsessed with dates. There seem to be streets named after every day of the year, but one day, 25 April 1974, is engrained on people's minds more than any other. This was the day that the Salazar regime was overthrown by a military coup, and the popular uprising that followed changed the course of Portugal's history.

Salazar had died in 1970, after suffering a stroke when his deckchair collapsed two years earlier, and his successor, Marcelo Caetano, was incapable of delivering much-needed reform. Portugal had been waging war in the colonies since the beginning of the 1960s and the country was physically and financially drained. Tension built up in the army and there was little resistance when the tanks finally rolled into Lisbon, overthrowing fifty years of totalitarian rule.

The post-revolutionary government promised the restructuring of wine production. All *gremios* were abolished and a commission was set up to liquidate the Casa do Douro, which was viewed as a political instrument of the previous regime. But Portugal ran out of control and in the *verão quente* (hot summer) of 1975 attempts were made to establish a left-wing military dictatorship. Much of the economy was taken into state control, and stories abound that the Port trade was on the point of being nationalized. Apparently the dismissal of the pro-communist general who was Prime Minister at the time prevented the papers from being signed. Two Port firms, Royal Oporto and Borges & Irmão, were nationalized, however, and a spate of occupations and strikes hit the wine industry. In the Alentejo (see page 174) whole estates became co-operatives as farm-workers took control. For a time an army captain took over the management of the Casa do Douro announcing progressive taxation to favour small growers.

The backlash that took place in the conservative north of the country in the autumn of 1975 threatened civil war but, in 1976, the revolution ended peacefully with the first free elections for over fifty years. The political bickering left the economy in tatters, however, and Portugal's wine-makers had lost an important market with the hurried decolonization of the overseas territories. Interest rates were high and foreign investment was lacking, leaving little scope for growers to improve their wine-making to match the standards being demanded by the markets of the United States and northern Europe. In 1977, seeking both political and economic stability, the government took the first important step to become a part of Europe.

Wine and Europe

Portugal joined the European Community in 1986. With 360,000 hectares of vines producing 10 million litres of wine (2.7 per cent of total Community output), she did not present the same increase in the wine lake as Spain, which joined at the same time. But Brussels insisted on a number of conditions to bring Portugal into line with other European wine-making countries. Among the most important were the liberalization of domestic trade, the prohibition of irrigation and a survey and classification of grape varieties. In return Portugal would receive grants to help growers uproot hybrid vines and improve the quality of their wine-making.

In 1985, anticipating entry into the community, the Portuguese government

D.O.C. Regions

1 Vinhos Verdes
2 Port and the Douro
3 Dão
4 Bairrada
5 Bucelas
6 Colares
7 Carcavelos
8 Setúbal
9 Lagoa
10 Lagos
11 Portimão
12 Tavira
13 Madeira

I.P.R. Region

14 Chaves
15 Planalto - Mirandês
16 Valpaços
17 Encostas da Nave
18 Varosa
19 Lafões
20 Castelo Rodrigo
21 Cova da Beira
22 Pinhel
23 Alcobaça
24 Encostas d'Aire
25 Óbidos
26 Almeirim
27 Cartaxo
28 Chamusca
29 Coruche
30 Santarém
31 Tomar
32 Alenquer
33 Arruda
34 Torres
35 Arrábida
36 Palmela
37 Borba
38 Portalegre
39 Redondo
40 Reguengos
41 Vidigueira
42 Granja-Amareleja
43 Moura
44 Évora

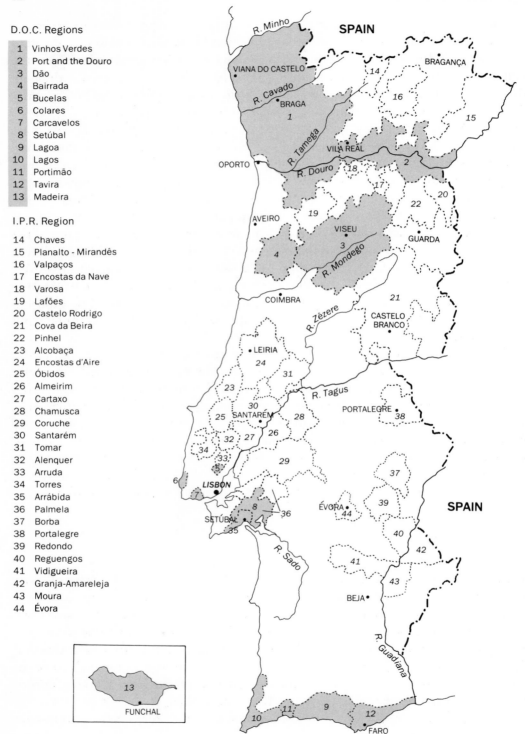

drew up a list of 'authorized' and 'recommended' grapes for every demarcated region in the country. The legislation is full of anomalies and includes some strange grapes like Medock (*sic*) and Branco Sem Nome (white without name), but it is a significant step towards sorting out the muddle in Portuguese vineyards. The Junta Nacional do Vinho was abolished in 1986 and replaced by a new administrative body with a much more friendly name: the Instituto da Vinha e do Vinho (Vine and Wine Institute or IVV). Under the new organization, numerous protective monopolies set up by Salazar were abolished and wine-makers have slowly been freed from the shackles of state control.

European Community grants are transforming the landscape. Communications are being improved, helping to open up some of Portugal's most remote wine-making regions to outside investment. Horizontal presses, stainless steel vats and refrigeration machines are being hauled into place and cellars are being given a much needed lick of paint. But a lack of skilled wine-makers, especially in co-operatives, hampers progress, and it is among the large privately owned firms that most of the recent improvements are to be found.

RDs, DOCs, VQPRDs and IPRs

The Portuguese have a habit of referring to things by their initials and this extends to wine regions. The eight Regiões Demarcadas (Demarcated Regions or RDs, listed above) established early this century were joined by Bairrada and Algarve in 1979. On joining the European Community in 1986, the government announced a list of VQPRDs (Vinhos de Qualidade Produzidos em Regiões Determinadas). These entered the statute books in 1989/90 as IPRs (Indicacões de Proveniência Regulamentada). There are now thirty-one IPRs all over the country, from Chaves in the north to the Alentejo in the south. Portugal's RDs have recently been re-designated Denominacâo de Origem Controlada, Controlled Denomination of Origin or DOC. For the moment, however, wine-makers are able to use either RD or DOC on their labels (see map, opposite). Confused? So is the Portuguese government, which has had difficulty in deciding on the names for all the new regions (see map, opposite). More information on Portugal's IPRs can be found on pages 140, 158, 166, 176, 189 and 193.

Single Quintas

The merchants and co-operatives that have dominated the production of Portuguese wines for most of the twentieth century have recently been joined by a band of single *quintas* or estates. Instead of selling grapes to a shipper or co-op, a number of enterprising growers have started to make and market wines from their own vineyards. Growers in the Douro were given the green light to export their own wine with the lifting of restrictions in 1987 (see page 69), and a number of Vinho Verde producers found a voice through APEVV (Associação dos Produtores-Engarafadores de Vinho Verde) in 1985 (see page 121). The growth of single *quintas* throughout Portugal can only help to increase the diversity of wines which, in regions dominated by co-operative wine-making, have become standardized over the past forty years.

Portugal up to Date

An estimated 380,000 hectares of vines are currently farmed in Portugal by 180,000 growers, 87 per cent of whom produce less than 100 hectolitres of wine. Between 35 and 40 per cent of all growers deliver their grapes to 117 co-operatives, over 100 of which are in the country north of the River Tagus. With production averaging 8.5 million hectolitres over the 1980s, Portugal is the world's seventh largest producer of wine.

Between 1981 and 1989, the total volume of wine exported increased from 1.4 to 1.6 million hectolitres while its value soared from 13.4 million to over 53 million escudos. The United States and Angola top the league table of principal markets, followed in order by the United Kingdom, Germany, Switzerland and Denmark. Port sales amount to 800,000 hectolitres, 700,000 of which are exports. Sales of Madeira add up to 40,000 hectolitres, 38,000 of which are exports.

The Portuguese themselves are a thirsty nation, with an annual per capita consumption of between 60 and 70 litres. This compares with 109 litres in 1965 and, in common with other European wine-producing countries, the consumption of wine continues to decline.

2

Vineyards, Grapes and Wines

Portugal is fortunate in having a wide array of different grapes, many of which are unique to the country. Only a handful of vines have travelled into Portugal, leaving it like a viticultural island. This is refreshing at a time when the French Cabernet Sauvignon and Chardonnay grapes seem set to take over the world. With the Portuguese justly proud of their own vines, it will take more than mere persuasion for most growers to uproot their native vines and replace them with foreign interlopers.

What is less refreshing is the way in which many Portuguese vineyards still remain an unknown not just to outsiders but, in many cases, to the growers themselves. Traditionally vines have been planted in a haphazard manner, with different grape varieties mixed up together on the same vineyard plot. In older vineyards there may be as many as ten or fifteen different grape varieties side by side, simply planted in the proportions that were felt to be suitable for the type and quantity of wine that the owner of the vineyard wished to make. Hybrids and direct-producing vines intended for use as rootstock after last century's phylloxera epidemic are still common in some parts of Portugal. In these jumbled vineyards it is a slow and difficult process to weed them out.

This muddled cohabitation of different vines is still a feature of vineyards all over Portugal. It means that different varieties are often harvested and fermented together, and it restricts more innovative wine-makers in their experiments to determine which grapes have the best properties for the style of wine they want to make. Mixed vineyards also make it difficult to pick grapes at their optimum ripeness, as varieties ripen at different times. Consequently, must from overripe and underripe grapes is often pumped into the same vat.

Vineyard husbandry tends to be fairly rudimentary. All too often vines are grown for yield rather than for the quality of the grapes that they produce. A few more kilos per hectare means a few more escudos for the farmer when he delivers his grapes to the local co-operative to be turned into wine. Yields of over 100 hectolitres per hectare are not uncommon in parts of the Minho and the Oeste (see pages 114 and 139).

Irrigation, which tends to promote yield, is in theory forbidden now that Portugal belongs to the European Community, but legislation from Brussels does not seem to stop a farmer diverting a water channel in the direction of his vines. In the drier parts of the central south of Portugal there is a strong case for allowing irrigation, provided that it is carefully controlled. Vines growing through a rainless summer often suffer from water stress, which causes uneven ripening if the drought is prolonged. But under the present EC law, which was designed around France and Germany, vines may be watered only if they have 'experimental' status. If some of the drier parts of southern Portugal are to develop their vineyards successfully, there will be a large amount of 'experimental' planting.

Many Portuguese vineyards have an upkempt look in comparison with the neat rows of box-hedge vines that you see when travelling through the major vineyard regions of France. Vines are frequently allowed to sprout in all directions, turning the countryside into a riot of greenery. In the north-west of Portugal, high training systems actively promote vigour and large yields of acid grapes, low in sugar and extract (see page 114). Further south, training systems are lower. Most of the vineyards in central Portugal are trained on wires and pruned according to the French double or single Guyot system. A few traditional growers, however, still choose to trail their vines up individual canes, bending the branches into elaborate shapes. Franco Esteves Gonçalves, in his book *Portugal – A Wine Country*, lists sixteen different regional methods of *envidilha* or vine-propping, some with names like 'rabbit's tail', 'ring and fly's wing' and 'bridled horse'. Few are now in general use, though some growers in Bairrada and the more remote regions inland still use their own highly idiosyncratic methods for training vines.

In the Alentejo and the deep south of the country, large swathes of stubby vines grow free-standing and are pruned according to the *taça* or *gobelet* method used in the Rhône and the south of France. The south is also the flattest part of the country, where holdings are much more extensive than those in the north and lend themselves easily to mechanization. *Gobelet* pruning, however, makes it almost impossible to harvest by machine. To date there are only two mechanical harvesters working in Portuguese vineyards, both on large agricultural estates close to Lisbon.

But there is a revolution taking place in the world's vineyards, one which Portugal is finding it difficult to escape. First of all, the European Community has had some harsh words to say to Portugal about all the hybrid and direct-producing vines that are still being grown in some parts of the country, particularly in the Oeste and on Madeira. These are phylloxera-resistant vines yielding large quantities of fruit which makes wine with a distinctly unpleasant musky taste. They were introduced to Portugal after the phylloxera epidemic that wiped out most of the country's vineyards and are planted, mostly on their own rootstock, by lazy farmers looking for quantity rather than quality. Laws now technically forbid the export of wines made from hybrid grapes, though many Portuguese have developed a taste for wine made from these direct producers. In an attempt to sort out the muddle, a programme of rationalization of Portugal's vineyards has begun, with grants available to farmers wishing to uproot their hybrid vines and replace them with approved stock.

Words like 'clonal selection' have crept into the vocabulary of only the most advanced grower – wine-makers cultivating a few foreign grapes. Before growers can start to think about selecting the best disease-resistant strains of indigenous varieties, most need to take the basic step of looking more closely at the gamut of different grapes that they have been growing for all these years.

Newly planted vineyards are now being set out with different vines in plots, so that grape varieties may be harvested when they are ripe. Different varieties can be fermented separately too and so, at long last, Portugal is at the beginning of a massive viticultural awakening.

It will be a slow and sometimes painful operation. Until very recently, little research had taken place for nearly a century since Villa Maior and Cincinnato da Costa surveyed Portugal's vineyards in two academic tomes published in 1875 and 1902. After travelling around Portugal early this century, Pedro Bravo and Duarte de Oliveira (1916) list around 900 grape varieties growing in Portuguese vineyards. They admit that many of these are in fact the same varieties given different names in different places, and complain about the lack of research to date.

There is still a lack of knowledge, although enormous strides have been made in the Douro with the establishment of ADVID, a viticultural research institute at Vila Real University sponsored by a number of major Port companies. But vines planted in the north of Portugal still turn up in the south masquerading under a completely different name, while another with the same name in two places turns out to be two completely different grapes. This complicates research into Portuguese varieties. Even the European Community (which has made valiant attempts to sort out the confusion caused by so many different synonyms) seems to have been defeated in some areas of its research. A survey of Portugal's grape varieties undertaken by the Instituto de Gestão e Estruturacão Fundaria in 1986 is riddled with errors. At the end of the twentieth century, little has changed in most Portuguese vineyards since vines were replanted after phylloxera took its toll over 100 years ago.

This is highlighted in a courageous study of eighty-five different Portuguese grapes by Professor Truel of the French Viticultural Research Station at Montpellier University. It is on this and on information gleaned from some more knowledgeable growers that the following attempt to untangle Portuguese vineyards, the grapes and the wines they make is based.

Asterisks, up to a maximum of three, are awarded according to quality, with brackets signifying where there may be untapped potential.

Native White Varieties

Alva
The name Alva turns up in the north of the Alentejo, where it is the local name for Roupeiro (see below). **

Alvarinho
This thick-skinned, low-yielding grape is authorized only around Monção in the very north of the country, where it makes a unique varietal Vinho Verde. Alvarinho wines have more body than most Vinhos Verdes, typically achieving levels of alcohol around 12 or 13° compared with the 9 or 10° wines more common in north-west Portugal. The wines tend to be fragrant, with little or no sparkle, and have an appley aroma and taste. The keep better in bottle than other Vinhos Verdes, although Alvarinho wines are at their best in the eighteen months after the harvest. Because of their rarity and relatively low levels of production, Alvarinho wines can be expensive. Production at the Palácio de Brejoeira, the most famous of all Alvarinho vineyards, barely reaches 40 hectolitres per hectare, low by Portuguese standards. These wines are also highly prized in Galicia in Spain, where the same grape is called Albariño. ***

Antão Vaz
This grape makes bland white wines in the south of the Alentejo around Reguengos and Vidigueira. Domingos Soares Franco of José Maria da Fonseca thinks that it may have potential in the hot, dry Reguengos region. *(*)

Arinto
Acidity is Arinto's main hallmark. As Padernã in Vinho Verde and Arinto in Bucelas, where it must account for at least 75 per cent of the blend, Arinto has the remarkable capacity to hang on to its acidity even after a run of 30°C summer days. Potentially one of Portugal's better white grapes, Arinto is rarely given the opportunity to prove its true worth. Bucelas is the closest Arinto comes to making a varietal wine, but there it is usually blended with the ferociously acidic 'dog strangler', Esgana Cão. Primitive wine-making has also hidden its real qualities, so until someone comes up with a well-made wine the true quality of Arinto will continue to be something of an

unknown. Until now Arinto has simply made lemony, acidic wines that last well in bottle.

The link between the Arinto and Riesling grapes conjectured by some writers does not stand up to scientific scrutiny. *(**)

Arinto do Dão

Not to be confused with the Arinto growing in Bucelas (see above), Arinto do Dão makes large quantities of ordinary alcoholic wine in Dão and around Pinhel. It is sometimes called Assario Branco. *

Assario

This name, sometimes encountered in the Alentejo and Dão is, according to Truel, sometimes the French Listan but at other times a different grape variety altogether. *

Avesso

This white Vinho Verde grape, planted in warmer country inland along the Douro around the towns of Baião and Resende, makes wines with good aroma, slightly higher levels of alcohol and less acidity than most Vinhos Verdes. The same grape is called Jaen Blanco in central Spain. *(*)

Azal Branco

This Vinho Verde grape, grown in the centre of the region around Amarante and Penafiel, ripens late, making typically crisp, acidic wines. *

Batoca

A secondary Vinho Verde grape, possibly the same as the Alvadouro, which is found inland to the south around Pinhel. This vigorous vine produces large bunches of grapes that are sensitive to rot in the Minho's damp climate. *

Bical

Used in Bairrada mainly for the production of sparkling wines, Bical can make scented dry whites with some quality. It is known as Borrado das Moscas in Dão (see below). *(*)

Boal

Cincinnato da Costa identified five different varieties of Boal or Bual in Portugal: Boal Cachudo, Boal Carrasqueenha, Boal Branco, Boal de Alicante and Boal Bonifacio (also called Vital). On Madeira Boal Cachudo is the most common, though it has become rare, accounting for less than 1 per cent of the island's total crop. Most Bual wines have in fact been made from Tinta Negra Mole. It is planted mostly around Camara de Lobos, where at low altitudes it yields small quantities of sweet grapes and makes rich, concentrated wines. Now that the European Community insists that a wine labelled Bual should be made from Boal grapes, more should be planted in future. ****

Borrado das Moscas

Dão's 'fly droppings' grape is the same as the Bical in neighbouring Bairrada (see above). In the Dão it makes wines that combine high levels of alcohol with high acidity. *(*)

Cerceal do Dão

This is not the same grape as the better-known Sercial in Madeira, but a productive variety used for white Dão. It has the capability to retain its acidity while making a wine that is low in alcohol in the Dão's warm climate. Due to the confusion involved with the Sercial name, it is not known how widely planted this vine is. *(*)

Códega

This grape variety, planted in the Douro for white Port, is thought to be the same as the Roupeiro, which is used increasingly successfully in the Alentejo for table wines. It is found all over the Douro and Trás-os-Montes, where it tends to ripen early, making flat-tasting wines that are low both in alcohol and in acidity. In the Pinhel region to the south, Truel estimates that it accounts for around half the region's white wine production. Here it is known as Codo Siria. *(*)

Crato Branco

Grown in the Algarve, Crato Branco is planted around Lagoa where it makes a nutty, dry, fortified wine. There are no references to this grape growing elsewhere under another name. *

Diagalves

This table grape, grown widely in the Alentejo, may be good to eat but it is certainly not up to much when it gets into a bottle. Its large, productive bunches of ripe grapes make flat, flabby white wines. There are moves to forbid its use in wine-making. *

Douradinha

The 'small golden one' grown in Dão is susceptible to rot and makes wines that are low both in alcohol and in acidity. *

Encruzado

This low-yielding grape is probably the best white grape in Dão, where it is capable of making balanced, aromatic wines. More planting is being encouraged. ***

Esgana Cão

Such are the levels of acidity in this grape that even the dogs won't touch it. So the saying goes, and hence the name: Esgana Cão or 'dog strangler'. This is in fact the mainland name for Madeira's Sercial, which is also well known for its acidity (see below). Esgana Cão in Portugal goes into Vinho Verde, white Port and Bucelas as and when its fierce levels of acidity are needed. It may even be used in Setúbal's sweet dessert wines. *(**)

Esganoso

In Vinho Verde country the 'dog strangler' becomes plain 'strangler', but it's the same acidic grape making thin wine in the cool Atlantic climate of northern Portugal. *(*)

Fernão Pires

This is one of Portugal's most adaptable white grapes, making everything from sparkling wines in the Bairrada to a rich, oak-aged dry white and a sweet botrytized wine in the Ribatejo. As a result it is the most widely planted white variety, ripening fairly early and producing reasonable yields. It makes aromatic, sometimes almost peppery wines, which can be good if cleanly made. Fernão Pires turns up with a sex change as Maria Gomes in the Bairrada. **(*)

Folgosão

This is an early-ripening grape planted in the Douro, Trás-os-Montes and Beira Alta. *

Galego Dourado

Grown on the Atlantic coast in the Oeste and Carcavelos, Galego Dourado makes high-alcohol, low-quality wines. It is sometimes called Olho de Lebre ('eye of the hare'), or just Pedro where it is found in Australia. *

Gouveio

The Verdelho in Madeira (see page 213) is called the Gouveio in the Douro, where it is important for white Port. It yields large quantities of sweet, sugary grapes and is therefore well suited to the production of fortified wines. **

Jampal

Found in vineyards around Torres Vedras and the Ribatejo, where it may be called João Paulo, Jampal is supposed to be able to produce reasonably good wine, but primitive white wine-making in both these regions means that it rarely gets the chance. *(*)

Loureiro
This quality variety has traditionally been grown for blending with Trajadura and Padernã to make Vinho Verde but is now being used successfully on its own to make a varietal wine. Well-made Loureiro Vinhos Verdes tend to be low in alcohol and high in acidity. Terpenes in the grape skin produce fresh, floral, aromatic wines sometimes reminiscent of Riesling. Loureiro performs best in the cooler districts around Barcelos, Braga and near the coast, where it can yield up to 100 hectolitres per hectare. It is also gaining favour in Galicia in northern Spain. ***

Malvasias
'Malvasias', in the plural, covers a variety of different grapes that are rightly or wrongly called Malvasia all over Portugal. The best-known form of Malvasia is Madeira's Malmsey but even there the term covers a number of different varieties, including grapes that have nothing to do with Malvasia at all. Malvasia Candida is the best Malvasia and was used for Madeiras labelled 'Malmsey'. It is now almost extinct, and Tinta Negra Mole makes most of these intensely rich, sweet wines. Malvasia in fact accounts for just over 2 per cent of Madeira's vines. ***

Back on mainland Portugal the Malvasia Rei (thought by some to be the same as the Palomino in Jerez) is grown in the Douro, where it makes pale, neutral wine for white Port. It is also grown in Beira Alta and the Oeste, where it is called Seminario and produces large quantities of very ordinary table wine. *

The Malvasia Corada planted in Dão is the same as the Vital grown in the Oeste (see below) and a grape called Malvasia Fina in the Douro. Other grapes called Malvasia are used to make the fat white wines of Colares and the deliciously ripe white Buçaco.

Manteudo
Well adapted to the hot, dry conditions of southern Portugal, fat Manteudo grapes make large quantities of bland white wine in the Alentejo and the Algarve. *

Maria Gomes
This is not the name of a girl but of a grape growing in Bairrada's vineyards, mainly for the production of sparkling wines. It turns up again in the south of Portugal as Fernão Pires (see above). **(*)

Padernã
The Arinto grape, when planted in the Minho for Vinho Verde, is called the Padernã. True to form, it makes light, acidic wines, usually for blending with Loureiro and/or Trajadura. (See Arinto, above.) *(*)

Pé de Perdiz

The 'foot of the partridge' is thought to be the same as the Murrão, which is found planted for Vinhos Verdes around Penafiel. *

Rabigato

A certain amount of confusion surrounds the identity of this north country ('cat's tail') grape, which is the same as the Rabo de Ovelha grown all over the south of Portugal (see below). This Rabigato, which is used for Vinhos Verdes, is thought to be different from the Rabigato do Douro which is sometimes a constituent of white Port. *

Rabo de Ovelha

Called the 'ewe's tail' because of the elongated shape of the bunch, this grape is found all over Portugal, where it is also known as the Rabigato (see above). Large bunches of sweet, early-ripening grapes make fat, alcoholic wines in the warm southern sun. *

Roupeiro

Called Códega in the Douro, the Alentejo's Roupeiro is capable of making fresh, fragrant honeyed white wine in a hot climate. The trick is to drink it young. Around Portalegre, in the north of the Alentejo, the same grape is called Alva. **

Seminário

This ordinary grape, which makes vast amounts of ordinary wine in the Oeste, is christened in some parts of Portugal with the name of Malvasia Rei, which it plainly does not deserve. *

Sercial

Sadly something of a rarity in Madeira, despite all the wines masquerading under the name, Sercial is in fact more common on mainland Portugal, where it is called Esgana Cão or 'dog strangler' (see above). In Madeira, Sercial is a late-ripening grape planted at high altitudes or on the cooler north side of the island, and makes good, dry, often rather acid wines that age well. Madeiras labelled 'Sercial', though often not made from the Sercial grape, are the driest and most delicate of the island's wines. Most are made from the ubiquitous Tinta Negra Mole.

Like the Arinto (see above), Sercial is sometimes thought to be related to the German Riesling, although this appears not to be the case. ***

Tamarez

The name Tamarez crops up in Bairrada and all over the south of Portugal but no one is really clear if it is the same grape. Tamarez d'Algarve is probably Roupeiro (see above). Tamarez d'Azeitão is also called Trincadeira das Pratas.

Terrantez do Dão
A minor Dão grape, not to be confused with the Terrantez in Madeira. *

Terrantez
This Madeira grape is now rarely seen. It makes wines that are at once both sweet and astringent. At one time it was so highly prized that poems were written about it:

> *As uvas de Terrantez*
> *Não comas nem as des*
> *Para vinho Deus as fez.*

'Terrantez grapes: don't eat them or give them away. God made them for wine.' It rhymes in Portuguese! ***

Trajadura
This productive, disease-resistant variety is often used to fill out Vinhos Verdes. It ripens rapidly and loses acidity fast if not picked early, but gives alcohol and weight to acidic 'green' tasting wines. **

Uva Cão
Dogs seem to have a rough time in Portugal. The Uva Cão or 'dog grape' is permitted in Dão where it ripens late, producing fiercely acidic wine. It is not widely planted. *

Verdelho
After being promoted to the 'noble' category from being merely 'good' early this century, Madeira's Verdelho vines are now scarce. Planted on the cooler north side of the island, Verdelho's small, hard grapes manage to produce high sugar levels while retaining their acidity. Verdelho wines tend to be medium dry but most are not in fact made from Verdelho grapes.

Verdelho has been used with some success for making peachy dry white table wines in Australia. It is also planted in the Douro, where it is called Gouveio, although the Madeirans don't believe that it is the same grape. **(*)

Verdelho do Dão
No relation to Madeira's Verdelho, the Verdelho do Dão makes ordinary, acid wines. *

Viosinho
Viosinho is grown in the Douro and Trás-os-Montes, where it is capable of making some fresh-flavoured dry white table wines. *(*)

Vital

Known as Malvasia Corado in the north of Portugal and Vital in the Oeste, this widely planted variety ripens early, making bland wines with low acidity. *

Native Red Varieties

Alfrocheiro Preto

This variety gives colour to red wines in Bairrada, the Ribatejo, the Alentejo and more particularly in the Dão. Depending on the year, it is also capable of high levels of alcohol. Peter Bright of João Pires finds it a useful grape making a sweet, ripe-flavoured red at Herdade de Santa Marta, near Moura in the Alentejo. *(*)

Alvarelhão

A quality grape making relatively light, balanced reds all over the north of Portugal, chiefly in the wilds of Trás-os-Montes, the Alto Douro and Dão. The grapes are red rather than black in colour and the wines retain good levels of acidity. Alvarelhão is thought to be the same as the Brancelho sometimes grown for red Vinho Verde. **

Azal Tinto

This is one of the principal varieties used for making astringent red Vinhos Verdes. It is planted all over the north-west of Portugal and is especially important around the town of Amarante, in the centre of the Vinho Verde region. Azal ripens with difficulty, producing purple, acidic, mouth-puckering wines for early drinking. *

Baga

Baga accounts for around 80 per cent of the Bairrada's vineyards, making this one of Portugal's most-planted red grape varieties. The name means 'berry', which well describes this small, dark, thick-skinned grape. As a consequence of the high proportion of skin to pulp, wines made from the Baga grape tend to be deep in colour and almost undrinkably astringent when young. This is often not helped by the continuing practice of fermenting crushed grapes with stalks as well, to make numbingly tannic wines that will never soften. Underneath all these layers of tannin, though, there is often a flavour of good, ripe blackcurrant fruit. Though wild and untamed when young, well-made Baga wines like those from Caves São João (see page 136) soften and develop a rustic but almost claret-like depth of character with age. The best will last twenty or more years.

Baga is also planted extensively in the Dão, especially around the town of Oliveira do Hospital, and in the Ribatejo, where it is called the Poeirinha. **(*)

Bastardo

The Trousseau in the French Jura is burdened with the ignoble name of Bastardo in the north of Portugal. This grape must have something of an identity crisis, for wherever it travels it gains another name, from Gros Cabernet in South Australia to Pinot Gris de Rio Negro in Argentina. This vigorous, early-maturing variety was once important for Port, though its only attributes are low acidity and high levels of sugar. As a consequence of recent viticultural research, the Bastardo has been excluded from new Douro vineyards, though it is still allowed to make up to 60 per cent of a Port blend. In Dão, to the south, it is allowed up to 80 per cent, though it is almost never used in such quantity. It is called Abrunhal in parts of Beira Alta.

Small amounts of Bastardo are encountered in Madeira, although there is some doubt as to whether it is the same grape as on the mainland. *(*)

Borraçal

This vigorous vine climbs trellises all over north-west Portugal. It ripens late to make acidic wine, low in alcohol, for blending with other red Vinho Verde grapes – Vinhão, Espadeiro and Azal. The same grape is called Caiño in the Orense province of northern Spain. *

Brancelho

This is planted in the Minho, where it makes pale-coloured wines. It is thought to be the same as the Alvarelhão (see above). *

Camarate

Growers in the Oeste are proud of a grape they call Camarate but none of them seem to be quite sure what it is. Australian wine-maker Peter Bright thinks it is a fancy synonym for a red-fleshed *teinturier* variety otherwise called Castelão Nacional or Castelão Português. Truel lists it as an alternative name for the white grape Fernão Pires in the Ribatejo. *

Castelão Francês

This, one of the most widely planted grapes in southern Portugal, also travels around under the names of João de Santarém and Trincadeira, although, to add to the confusion, the latter is sometimes used as a synonym for the Douro's Tinta Amarela. But Castelão Francês is probably best known by its nickname, Periquita ('small parrot'). This originates from a small vineyard planted with cuttings of Castelão Francês by a certain José Maria da Fonseca in the middle of the last century. The site, on the north-facing slopes of the Arrábida hills, was called Cova de Periquita and, because of the success of the wine produced there, the name Periquita (sometimes Piriquito/a) stuck. The grape is referred to throughout this book as Castelão Francês or by the regional name of João de Santarem (Chapter 11) and Periquita (Chapter 12).

Today Castelão Francês is found in different guises in Oeste, the Ribatejo, the Alentejo and on the Setúbal Peninsula. In warm climates it ripens well, making wines that start off firm and raspberryish when young and sometimes take on a tar-like quality with age. *:*

Complexa

This was introduced to Madeira in the 1960s as an alternative to Tinta Negra Mole. Complexa is classified as a 'good' rather than a 'noble' grape, and makes a darker and rather less astringent Madeira base wine than Negra Mole. *(*)

Cornifesto

A secondary grape confined to the Douro and Trás-os-Montes, where it produces wines that are light and low in alcohol. *

Doçal

An extremely vigorous vine that is really suited only to the high-culture systems of north-west Portugal. It is no longer planted and is therefore only found mixed in older vineyards. The name, 'doce' meaning sweet, suggests that it is capable of high sugar content. *

Espadeiro Tinto

A productive variety planted in Vinho Verde country, where it ripens with difficulty to make a light, fragrant red. Usually blended, though at Quinta do Tamariz (see page 123) António Vinagre has experimented with a varietal Espadeiro wine that smells and tastes remarkably like an underripe Pinot Noir. The grape sometimes referred to as Espadeiro Tinto in the Lisbon region is not the same but is in fact the Douro's Tinta Amarela. *(*)

Jaen

The Spanish name is used for a productive Portuguese grape planted in the Dão, where it makes wines with low acidity but reasonable colour. It is sometimes used for blending with more astringent reds in Bairrada. *

João de Santarém

A name used in the Ribatejo for Castelão Frances (see above), which is also commonly known by the nickname Periquita. *:*

Monvedro

This grape, occasionally called Bonvedro, used to be widely grown around Lisbon but has now fallen out of favour. With other names like Lambrusco do Alentejo and Tintureiro suggesting colour and little else, there is probably a good reason why it is no longer planted. *

Moreto
This grape is widely grown south of the Tagus, where it makes rather thin, pale wines even after days of hot sunshine. *

Mortágua
A local name for Castelão Francês (see above) in the Oeste or Touriga Nacional in the Ribatejo. ***

Mourisco Tinto
A hermaphrodite Douro grape that gained its reputation resisting phylloxera. Its big, fat grapes make firm but pale acidic wines and the vine is therefore rarely planted in newer vineyards. It is, however, still an officially 'recommended' Port grape. João Nicolau de Almeida of Ramos Pinto considers it to be better as a table grape than for making wine, although Gordon Guimaraens at Cockburn's likes the wine for its staying power in lighter blends. Mourisco is a big producer provided it pollinates successfully. It does better when planted on warm sites, mixed in with other varieties.

In the Pinhel region it is known as Marufo and in the Alentejo as Tinta Grossa. *(*?)

Mureto do Dão
This Dão variety makes deep-coloured, low-alcohol wines which some wine-makers believe to be an essential component in blends. It is sometimes confused with the more widely grown Moreto, which Truel considers to be a different grape. *(*)

Pedral
Confined to the Monção area in the northernmost part of Portugal, this vigorous variety makes light reds that are low in alcohol. *

Periquita
This is a nickname for the grape known variously over the south of Portugal as Castelão Francês, João de Santarém, Mortágua or Trincadeira. Periquita is also a brand name for a José Maria da Fonseca wine made mainly, though not entirely, from the Castelão Francês or Periquita grape. For more information on Periquita see Castelão Francês above, or page 165. ***

Poeirinha
Bairrada's Baga (see above) is called the 'small dusty one' in the Ribatejo, where it also makes tannic reds. *(*)

Rabo de Ovelha Tinto

The red 'ewe's tail' grape grown for Vinho Verde is the same as the Douro's Tinta Amarela. It is found especially in the high Basto sub-region. *

Ramisco

How sad it is that one of the world's unique grape varieties should be confined to a few shrinking vineyards on Portugal's Atlantic coast. Ramisco is the grape that grows ungrafted in the sand dunes to make Colares (see page 147). It is not found anywhere else and is probably the only *Vitis vinifera* variety never to have been grafted. The few hectares of gnarled old vines that remain produce tiny quantities of small, thick-skinned grapes. The wines are often hard and astringent when young and need time to reveal the scented blackcurrant fruit of Ramisco. Primitive wine-making doesn't help today's Ramisco wines. **(*)

Rufete

This productive, early ripening Douro variety is thought to be the same as Tinta Pinheira in Dão (see below). *

Sousão

This black grape is grown widely in the Douro, where it is used to give colour to young Port which then drops out after a fairly short time. Although considered to be a high-yielding producer of rather rustic, raisiny reds, it is used in Quinta do Noval's legendary Nacional wine, where it can account for up to 25 per cent. It is also planted in California and South Africa for their own 'Port' wines. Vinhão, which is grown throughout the Minho, is thought to be the same grape (see below). *(**?)

Tinta Amarela

Planted extensively in the Douro around the turn of the century, this grape has subsequently fallen out of favour, probably due to its susceptibility to bunch rot. It is a productive variety, making wines with good colour and aroma which Bruce Guimaraens, wine-maker at Taylor and Fonseca, likens to China tea. It is also found in the Dão and in other parts of Portugal, where its names include Rabo de Ovelha Tinto, Trincadeira Preta and Espadeiro. **

Tinta Barroca

This Port grape is well suited to the Douro's extreme conditions, providing a good yield of dark, sweet grapes even on cooler north-facing slopes. Gordon Guimaraens at Cockburn's rates Barroca highly, though he believes that the wines lack some length. It is also planted extensively in South Africa, where it makes 'Port'-style wines and a few robust table reds as well. **(*)

Tinto Cão

This high-quality Port variety probably deserves more attention since low yields have pushed it out of Douro vineyards towards extinction. It is widely acknowledged for its ability to make excellent wines, and now that it is counted among the top five Port grapes Tinto Cão is beginning to make a welcome return. ***

Tinta Carvalha

Widely grown throughout Portugal, this variety produces enormous amounts of pale washed-out wine. It is mostly found in Dão, the Ribatejo and the Alentejo. *

Tinta Francisca

Once thought to be the same as Pinot Noir, Tinta Francisca is grown in the Douro, where it tends to make wines that are sweet but lacking in concentration. It does not therefore count among today's favoured few. *

Tinta da Madeira

In spite of its name, this variety is no longer widely planted in Madeira. It is, however, well adapted to making fortified wines in hot climates and is planted in California for 'Port'. Truel, though, uses the name Tinta da Madeira for Tinta Negra Mole, in order to distinguish it from the Algarve grape of the same name. *

Tinta Negra Mole

This is now the most planted *vinifera* variety in Madeira, where it has taken hold (along with all the hybrids and direct producers) since phylloxera ravaged the island in the last century. Negra Mole ('soft black') is a productive vine, its fat grapes making plenty of fairly thin, pale red wine. Classified as 'good' rather than 'noble', in Madeira it is a versatile vine planted all over the island. It produces everything from rich, sweet wines at lower altitudes to wines that are more delicate and acidic on the higher slopes. Young wines labelled anything from 'Sercial' to 'Malmsey' are made predominantly from Negra Mole, though they rarely achieve the complexity of wines made from noble grapes. **

A grape called Tinta Negra Mole is also grown extensively in Algarve but this is thought to be completely different. Here it makes rather pale, washed-out, alcoholic reds. *

Tinta Pinheira

This productive vine is grown widely in Dão and in vineyards in the Douro, Bairrada, Oeste and Alentejo. It makes large amounts of pale, dull wine. *

Touriga Francesa

Not to be confused with the lesser-quality Tinta Francisca, Touriga Francesa is among the top five varieties recommended for Port production. Found throughout the Douro and Trás-os-Montes, where it stands up well to long, hot, dry summers, Touriga Francesa makes scented, fruity reds that are less weighty than wines made from Touriga Nacional, with wonderful length of flavour. Its dependability makes it a popular grape with farmers. ✻✻✻

Touriga Nacional

Everyone agrees that Touriga Nacional is one of Portugal's very best grapes. It heads the league table for Port and is slowly regaining its pre-eminence in Dão. It grows fairly vigorously in the hot, dry Douro climate, resists disease, but produces very little fruit. The individual grapes are small and black, making deep-coloured, powerful, tannic wines that retain their fruit with age. This makes it the perfect variety for vintage Ports, which are black and numbingly tough and tannic when young but reveal their complexity and concentration with age. In the Douro, only the Sousão (see above) makes deeper, darker wines.

A programme of clonal selection backed by the Port trade is working towards increasing the yields of this top-quality Portuguese grape. This should help Touriga Nacional to gain recognition from growers all over the north of Portugal. ✻✻✻

Trincadeira

The name refers to the Tinta Amarela or the Castelão Francês grapes, depending on where they are grown (see entries above).

Verdelhos

A number of different red Verdelhos have been identified in the Vinho Verde region, especially around Ponte de Lima. These include Verdelho Tinto, used in Madeira, and Verdelho Feijão. ✻

Vinhão

Planted widely in Vinho Verde country, the Vinhão is thought to be the same as Sousão in the Douro, where it produces similarly deep-coloured though less astringent reds (see also Sousão). ✻

Foreign White Varieties

Alicante Branco

This productive variety grows all over Iberia and in North Africa. It grows prolifically in the Oeste for the production of bulk table wines, where it does nothing for quality. Farana or Boal de Alicante are local synonyms. The latter has no connection with Madeira's Boal. *

Chardonnay

The grape that has travelled the world from its native Burgundy vineyards has made few inroads into Portugal. There are isolated Chardonnay vineyards making appley dry whites in the Douro, Bairrada and Oeste, while on the Setúbal Peninsula a combination of an Australian wine-maker, oak and ripe Chardonnay grapes makes something approaching the rich 'buttery' New World style. It has now become an authorized grape for Arrábida's new DO wines. A small amount of Chardonnay also goes into Raposeira's sparkling wines. ***

Gewürztraminer

Gewürztraminer grows in one vineyard in the Douro and on the Setúbal Peninsula, where it is blended with Riesling and Muscat to make wine closest to the spicy Alsatian style. **(*)

Listrão

Thought to be the same grape as Spain's Palomino, Listrão is planted on the Atlantic island of Porto Santo, where under arid conditions it makes a flabby base wine used for inexpensive dry Madeiras. *

Moscatel de Setúbal

The Muscat of Alexandria which is planted all over the south of Iberia is called Moscatel de Setúbal, and makes Setúbal's rich, sweet dessert wines. It is more productive than the world's other chief variety of Muscat, the Muscat à Petits Grains, but tends to make coarser, more raisiny wines. Nevertheless, anyone who has tasted some of José Maria da Fonseca's remarkable old wines will know that Setúbal wines gain in depth and character with age. Moscatel de Setúbal also makes the popular grapey João Pires dry Muscat. **

Padeiro Branco

The ubiquitous Trebbiano or Ugni Blanc is called Padeiro Branco or Douradinha when it is used for Vinho Verde, and Talia in the south of Portugal. Douradinha in the Dão region seems to be a different grape. *(*)

Perrum

This Alentejo grape has long been thought to be the same as Spain's Palomino, although no one is quite sure. In most cases it makes a similarly neutral white wine, though Domingos Soares Franco of José Maria da Fonseca thinks it may have potential. *(*?)

Riesling

Though usually associated with cool climates, Germany's Riesling is planted in tiny quantities in the Douro and on the Setúbal Peninsula. Blended with Muscat and Gewürztraminer in Setúbal, it makes a fragrant, floral wine. **

Sauvignon

There are small plots of French Sauvignon grape on the Setúbal Peninsula and in the Douro and Trás-os-Montes. So far no one has made a successful wine from this cool climate grape. *

Sémillon

A small amount of Sémillon in the vineyard at Casa da Insua in Dão is about the only instance of this grape in Portugal. Blended with local varieties, it makes a ripe, buttery white. **

Talia

The vine that is called Trebbiano in Italy and Ugni Blanc in France is called Talia in the south of Portugal. It is widely grown in the Ribatejo, where it makes typically neutral wine (see also Padeiro Branco above). *(*)

Foreign Red Varieties

Alicante Bouschet

This dreary red-fleshed grape turns up in pockets in the Alentejo. The French have realized that it is of little worth other than for its colour and are uprooting it in favour of better varieties. In Alentejo, however, to give this much denigrated variety its due, it does go into some good if rather rustic red wines. *

Aragonez

Tempranillo in Spain, alias Tinta Roriz in the Douro, doesn't quite eschew its Spanish connections with the name Aragonez in the Alentejo. It is the only Spanish grape to be planted in any quantity in Portugal, where it is used for Port (see Tinta Roriz below) and table wine. In the Alentejo it makes deep-coloured reds more akin to the Duero wines in Spain than to Rioja. It is, however, almost always blended with other local varieties. Aragonez also acknowledges its Spanish origins on the Setúbal Peninsula, where it turns up as Tinto de Santiago. **(*)

Cabernet Sauvignon

The grape that makes the finest clarets has probably travelled the world more than any other, yet there are only a few scattered Portuguese vineyards growing Cabernet vines. There is some in Bairrada, where it is being blended with Baga to soften tannic reds, and there is more around Setúbal, where it is being grown successfully to blend both with Portuguese grapes and with Merlot. While Cabernet must be seen as an inevitable but welcome addition to Portugal's vineyards, it would be a pity if it were to take over from some of the other, more interesting, native red grapes. Cabernet is now officially permitted in eight new IPR regions: Almeirim, Cartaxo, Santarém and Coruche in the Ribatejo, Redondo and Reguengos in the Alentejo and Palmela and Arrábida on the Setúbal Peninsula. *:*

Canica

The hybrid Canica or Cunningham is grown extensively on Madeira, where its pale red juice was at one time used as the basis for lighter Rainwater style wines. Now that the European Community forbids its use in Madeira wines, it is made into thin red wine for drinking in local cafés. *

Grand Noir

This is another French red-fleshed *teinturier* grape that like Alicante Bouschet (above) adds little but colour and quantity to red wines. In France it is on the way out but in the new IPR region of Portalegre it is one of the 'recommended' vines. *

Isabella

This deceptively romantic name covers for a dreary hybrid grape that crops up in Madeira and throughout Portugal. It is one of the early post-phylloxera hybrids that was intended at first as a rootstock but has now taken hold on its own. It is popular among small growers for its high yields, but the confected strawberry flavour is at odds with our tastes. Some farmers, however, seem to have developed a taste for what they sometimes call *morangueiro* (strawberry plant) wine. Fortunately the European Community hasn't, and poor Isabella is no longer likely to go any further than the local tavern. *

Jacquet

It is somewhat disturbing to find that the 'Black Spanish' or Jacquet hybrid has overtaken the well-known *vinifera* varieties in Madeira's vineyards, making it one of the island's most planted grapes. This is a reflection of the market for Madeira's wines in recent years (see page 210), where the need for cheap, low-quality cooking wines has placed few demands on quality. Though its yields are fairly small, Jacquet's black grapes ripen in the sub-tropical sun to give rich, sugary wines. Now that the European Community has no place for hybrids in wines for export, Jacquet is permitted only for local table wines. Much is now being uprooted and replaced by Tinta Negra Mole. *

Mençia
Found occasionally in Vinho Verde country and more extensively in Spanish Galicia to the north, many growers believe Mençia to be a variety of Cabernet Franc. It makes a rather thin but raspberryish-tasting red. *(*)

Merlot
St Emilion's grape is confined to vineyards on the Setúbal Peninsula, where it is now making some rich, plummy red wines with as much as 14° of alcohol. ***

Moscatel Roxo
There are currently only 2 hectares of this rare pink variety of Muscat, making a rich, amber-coloured Setúbal wine. Because of its colour and the tannin it lends to the wine, it has recently been reclassified as a red grape. Domingos Soares Franco of José Maria da Fonseca is keen to preserve the variety, and 3 more hectares will soon enter into production. ***

Pinot Noir
On the whole, Burgundy's Pinot Noir hasn't travelled around as well as Bordeaux's Cabernet. In Portugal it is confined to two vineyards: one south of the Douro where it is used for Raposeira's sparkling wine (see page 206), and another near Muge in the Ribatejo, where Peter Bright has managed to make a ripe-flavoured wine. *

Seibel
The hybrid Seibel grape is grown in the Azores, where it makes poor, thin red wine. *

Syrah
Although the main quality grape of Rhône and Australia might do rather well in Portugal's warm climate, it is not widely planted. There are pockets of experimental Syrah in Alentejo, but these have not been producing for long enough to draw any firm conclusions. *(**)

Tinta Miuda
The 'small red one' growing in Oeste and Ribatejo is now thought to be the same as the Graciano used for Rioja in Spain and the French Morrastell. If it is, then Tinta Miuda could go some way towards helping to improve the quality of wines in these two bulk wine-producing areas. *(**?)

Tinta Roriz
Spain's Tempranillo turns up as Tinta Roriz in the Douro, where it is one of the most planted of all Port grapes. Even within Spain Tempranillo crops up in various

different guises, making fairly light, strawberry-flavoured wines in the cooler
northern vineyards and big, dark spicy reds on the Duero. Downstream on the
Portuguese Douro it is highly regarded, ripening early to make deep-coloured wines
with good length and finesse. It first turned up in the Douro early this century at
Quinta de Roriz, hence the name. In the Alentejo, Roriz acknowledges its Spanish
background with the name of Aragonez. ***

Vintage Guide

Vintages matter in Portugal. There are few catastrophic years but, in spite of the
generally warm climate, there is a considerable variation in wines from different
harvests. Vineyards in the wetter areas close to the coast and in the mountains of
northern Portugal are much more prone to suffer from the unpredictability of the
weather than regions in the south of the country. The best years for table wine in
Bairrada, Dão and the Douro often correspond closely to 'declared' Port vintages
(see pages 74–77). In the wine-producing regions inland and in southern Portugal,
excessive heat and drought are often a problem. But, with the help of modern
equipment, wine-makers are learning to make the best of these extreme conditions.

Asterisks are awarded according to quality:
*** **good or excellent**
** **average**
* **poor**

1991 ***: Heavy rain fell in the north of the country in the first four months of the
year. The flowering took place in near perfect conditions but a cold June followed by
hot, dry weather in July and August delayed ripening. Rain in the north of the
country early in September helped to swell the grapes but in the south bunches were
less even. Few vineyards suffered from disease and the crop was of average size.
Though many good wines have been made, some are slightly unbalanced and over-
alcoholic.

1990 ***: Heavy winter rains around Christmas 1989 replenished the water table in
much of the country, but a prolonged period of dry summer weather combined with
searing heat quickly brought on a drought in some areas. As a result yields were
down by about 10 per cent in the Alentejo and on the Setúbal Peninsula, though this
is more than made up for by the exceptional quality of the wines. In the north of the
country, two short bursts of rain in August and September helped to swell the
grapes. Growers in Bairrada, Dão and the Douro harvested an average-sized crop of
well-ripened grapes.

1989 *(*): As in so much of Europe, July and August were blisteringly hot throughout Portugal. After the previous year's serious shortfall, a large crop was badly needed by growers all over the country. In the event, drought reduced yields by up to 20 per cent and water stress held back the maturation of the grapes in some parts of the country. In general an early harvest produced ripe fruit, though many wines suffer from a lack of acidity. In Bairrada and on the Setúbal Peninsula red wines tend to be unbalanced, lacking in colour and depth.

1988 * (north), *** (south): Disasters are rare in Portugal, but in 1988 the harvest in much of the country came close to being a catastrophe. It came at a bad time for Portugal's developing wine industry, forcing up prices and reducing the amount of wine available for export. An uneven flowering was followed by rain, which continued to fall until the end of June. Many small growers in the north could not cope and mildew set in before anything could be done. The Minho was particularly badly affected, and yields in some vineyards were as much as 80 per cent down on normal. The south was also hit, and in the Alentejo the harvest was half its normal size. But the catastrophe had a silver lining. Quality comes with low yields, and 1988 was saved from being a complete write-off by a warm, dry summer which continued through the harvest. Outstanding wines were made in Dão, Bairrada, Setúbal and Alentejo. In the Douro, which did not escape the poor spring, most of the year's production was needed to make Port.

1987 *(*): An uneven year, the best wines being made in the Alentejo. In the north, high temperatures in the early summer brought on a serious drought, which slowed down the maturation of the grapes. As a result many wines from Dão and Bairrada are light, astringent and lacking in colour.

1986 *(*): For many wine-makers, 1986 was a year to forget. A warm summer was followed by torrential rain at the time of the harvest. Rot set in quickly, badly affecting Bairrada, Dão and the Baixo Corgo in the Douro. The south of Portugal fared better and some good, well-structured wines were made in the Alentejo and on the Setúbal Peninsula.

1985 **(*): The tables were reversed in 1985. After a wet spring, a late hot summer and a warm autumn produced well-ripened grapes. The perfect summer yielded intense, concentrated wines in Dão, Bairrada and the Douro, with good colour and staying power. In the south of the country, the piercing sun was too much for many vineyards and grapes shrivelled on the vine. High fermentation temperatures were a problem for those *adegas* which were not properly equipped, and many wines suffered from excess volatile acidity.

1984 **: A cool summer followed by rain in early October meant that many growers were caught short waiting for their grapes to ripen. As a result, Dão and Bairrada made thin, astringent red wines, though the Douro did rather better. Further south, vines benefited from a relatively cool year, and good, well-balanced reds were made in the Alentejo and Setúbal.

1983 ∗∗∗: This was an excellent year all over the country. Good weather throughout the spring and summer months ensured a crop of really ripe, healthy fruit. Classic, firm-flavoured reds were made all over the north of the country, the best of which should continue to age well. There is, however, a certain amount of inconsistency due to the difficulties that many wine-makers experienced in coping with rocketing fermentation temperatures. The south of the country, lacking the technology, made unbalanced wines with stewed aromas and flavours.

1982 ∗∗∗: A Portuguese polemic: which is the better year, 1982 or 1983? The summer was hot and most regions harvested early. The Douro, Dão and Bairrada all made robust wines with plenty of ripe fruit. Ferreira's Barca Velha has a chocolate-like intensity about it and Buçaco bottled a concentrated, full-flavoured red. In the south of Portugal, 1982 has the edge on 1983 with some excellent, ripe *garrafeiras* being made in the Ribatejo.

1981 ∗: Another year that many growers would rather sweep under the carpet. A cold spring delayed development, and rain in September induced rot. Many wines taste thin and astringent, lacking in fruit and depth. The upper reaches of the Douro, however, escaped the worst of the rain, and Ferreira made a good, spicy Barca Velha – the only high note in an otherwise dull year.

1980 ∗∗∗: A generally late flowering was followed by a warm summer and a dry autumn. Grapes were harvested late but in perfect condition throughout the country. For many wine-makers, 1980 was the best year of the decade. Balanced wines with plenty of fruit were made in Dão and Bairrada, along with a number of excellent *garrafeiras* in the Ribatejo. Curiously, Ferreira did not make Barca Velha in 1980, preferring to declassify its wine as Reserva Especial.

PREVIOUS YEARS

Wines from earlier vintages are not easy to find and should be treated with caution as they have often been badly stored. Old vintages of Barca Velha and Buçaco are available in Portugal and occasionally at auction in London. Both these wines are covered in more detail on pages 108 and 196. Good years in the rest of Portugal were:

1978: Some Ribatejo *garrafeiras* still standing up well.
1975: The hot summer at the height of the revolution.
1974: A few *garrafeiras* worth looking out for.
1970: Some excellent wines from Dão and Bairrada.
1966: Again, wines from Dão and Bairrada have developed well.

Detailed coverage of Port vintages can be found on pages 74–77.

3

Making Portuguese Wines

The theory behind vinification or wine-making is much the same the world over. It is the practice that so often differs. In Portugal wine production methods are diverse. There are a few state of the art wineries equipped with the most modern technology, and there are tiny private *adegas* which have resisted change and continue to make wine in much the same way today as they did more than a century ago. But it's the morass of wine-making somewhere in the middle of these two extremes that lets the country down. Co-operatives, built since the war, have largely been by-passed by recent improvements in wine-making, leaving them out of step with so much of the rest of Europe. Technology is often crude and ineptly handled by unskilled '*tecnicos*' who, year after year, turn out low-grade wines. For anyone visiting a co-operative at harvest time, it is a tragedy to see ripe, healthy grapes frequently being transformed into undrinkable hooch.

Until the European Community came along, there was little incentive to change. There was no money to invest and anyway people had become used to their own style of wine, so Portuguese *adegas* stood still. Now the authorities in Brussels are making the finance available to improve things and Portugal is at the beginning of its own wine-making revolution. It would be a mistake to think that this will happen overnight. The Portuguese countryside has always been slow to change and there is still a lack of skilled wine-makers and oenologists. But the monopolistic practices that were built into the system to protect co-operatives are being overturned as stainless steel vats and refrigeration plants are being swung into place. This may be happening in Portugal twenty or so years after it should, but so much better late than never.

Making White Wines

The wine-making revolution that is taking place will benefit the production of white wines most of all. Portugal is so often labelled as a 'red country', thought to be unsuitable for making white wines. Without know-how and technology, conditions are not best suited for making crisp, fresh-flavoured dry whites. Grapes ripen fast over the hot summer months and the weather often stays warm right through the harvest. Fermentations overheat, producing flat, flabby, often oxidized wines.

There is a fashionable saying that whereas red wines are made in the vineyard, white wines are made in the cellar. Like all good sayings, this is not strictly true. White grapes need to be picked at the right time and transported carefully to the winery. In Portugal, where co-operatives have been paying for grapes according to their weight and sugar levels, farmers have sometimes been picking as late as they dare to maximize their returns. (There are also plenty of instances where farmers have hidden stones in a load to increase its weight.) The larger private wineries, on the other hand, have been encouraging growers to pick early so that the natural acidity is retained to produce a crisper, fresher wine. In the south of Portugal, around Ribatejo and the Setúbal Peninsula, white grapes are picked as early as late August. Ideally they should be picked cool, early in the morning, and delivered to the winery in plastic cases containing around 15 kilos of grapes. All too frequently they arrive warm, squashed into a trailer by the farmer, who has tried to load up as much as possible in order to reduce the number of journeys that he has to make to the winery. A polythene sheet is often used to prevent the juice seeping out from crushed grapes which may already be starting to ferment.

On arrival, the trailer will be weighed and a probe will be driven deep into the grapes to measure their natural sugar content. These are the parameters against which most farmers are paid, though some enterprising wineries are now offering more money for better varieties. The mass of grapes and juice will then be tipped (or sometimes forked) out into a reception hopper. A horizontal Archimedes screw transports everything through to the press. Ideally the grape reception should be made of inert stainless steel but most hoppers are built of cement with a mild steel screw, painted to protect the grapes from contact with metal. Crushing the berries before pressing is normal, though many of the roller systems are too powerful and often crush the stems and pips as well, releasing bitter-tasting phenols into the must. White grapes are rarely destemmed, as this makes the press more difficult to work.

A portion of the harvest may be destemmed if the wine-maker chooses to carry out skin maceration. This is a fairly new technique, used to extract aromas from the skins of white grapes by macerating them for up to twelve hours in their own juice. Aromatic varieties like Muscat and Gewürztraminer benefit most, but wines made from other indigenous Portuguese grapes like Alvarinho, Arinto and Loureiro might also be improved by skin maceration. At the moment it is practised in Portugal only by a few innovative growers with adequate technology.

It is therefore more normal for grapes to be conveyed straight from the crusher to the press. Most presses in Portugal's privately owned wineries are of the horizontal Vaslin type, with metal plates at either end which slowly squeeze the mass of stalks and grapes. The best juice runs off first, from the earliest and most gentle pressing. This, together with the 'free run' juice released by crushing, should be separated from later, harder pressings which release bitter-tasting tannins from the stems and pips. The gentlest way to separate the different musts is to use an inflatable membrane or Willmes type press. From the outside this looks much the same as any other horizontal press, but instead of metal plates at either end, a huge bag inflates from the middle squeezing everything against the inside of the cylinder and pressing the grapes more gently. Only the most advanced wineries in Portugal are currently equipped with these pneumatic presses. Some are computer-programmed, giving the wine-maker complete control over the separation of different qualities of must.

Many co-operatives still use much more primitive methods for extracting the juice from white grapes. Most were equipped with continuous presses – huge spiral screws which squeeze the grapes hard to extract every last drop of juice. These are much faster than the horizontal presses as they never need to stop, but detract enormously from the quality of the must. The mass of pomace (skins, stems and pips) emerges quite dry. The bitter phenolic compounds that are extracted in the process make unpleasant white wines.

There is no doubt that the cleaner the juice is before fermentation begins, the better the wine. Many co-ops ignore this fact and pump the must straight from the press into a vat to commence fermenting. The best way to clean or clarify it is to leave the juice to stand or decant for a day or so until all the debris from pressing has settled to the bottom of the vat. At this stage the must should be chilled or sulphur dioxide added to stop it from fermenting. Cultured yeasts must then be inoculated to start the fermentation.

Decanting is a slow process, however, requiring plenty of spare capacity, which many wineries lack, especially during the harvest. Many large wineries therefore use centrifuges for bulk production. Those with money to spare have invested in rotary vacuum filters – enormous rotating drums that draw the juice into a vacuum through white earth, leaving the solid particles behind.

The clean must should then be analysed for any shortcomings. In Portugal, lack of natural acidity is usually the most common defect, so wine-makers need to add tartaric acid to correct it. In the south of Portugal, acid balance is a particular problem, but only the larger private wineries seem to make the necessary adjustments to make a fresher-tasting wine. Chaptalization, the practice of adding sugar to the must before fermentation to increase the alcohol content, is forbidden in Portugal. With well-ripened grapes it should never be necessary.

Once the necessary adjustments have been made, the juice is ready to start fermentation. Most co-operatives ferment in concrete vats, which should be lined with tiles or epoxy to prevent the acids in the wine reacting with the cement. Many are not lined at all, while others are badly maintained and difficult to clean. Temperatures are virtually uncontrolled. The temperature of the must rises rapidly at the start of fermentation and, unless the vats are cooled, the wine will continue to ferment rapidly in excess of 25-30°C. This results in the loss of primary aromas – the fruity smells that one associates with an enjoyable glass of white wine.

Clean, fresh, grapey aromas and tastes are better preserved if the wine is made at low temperatures in stainless steel vats. These have the dual advantage that they are simple to keep to clean (wood or concrete can trap dangerous bacteria) and easier to keep cool. Cold water can be run down the outside or through a jacket built into the vat. The temperature now accepted by most wine-makers as ideal is between 16 and 18°C – this is 10° or more below the temperature of fermentation in many Portuguese co-ops.

Some traditionalists point an accusing finger at cold fermentation in stainless steel, holding it responsible for loss of character in white wines. Certainly, if temperatures are kept too low, all wines, no matter what variety they are made from, begin to taste the same. This has been happening in Spain and the south of France, where temperature control has been widely adopted in recent years and has been seized on by many oenologists as a panacea for all the evils of the past. But if fermentation is handled by a knowledgeable wine-maker then temperature control is a considerable benefit. In Portugal's warm climate, it is almost essential.

The fermentation of white wines without temperature control will take less than a week, while cool fermentations will continue for fifteen or twenty days before all the sugar is used up. If the wine being made is to be medium dry or sweet, the fermentation can be curtailed by cooling the wine to below 12° and filtering or centrifuging to remove any remaining yeasts. This is the method that the better producers of commercial Vinho Verde use to retain a small amount of natural sugar in their wine. Others rely on a massive dose of sulphur dioxide to kill the active yeasts, and the wines usually suffer as a result.

Most Portuguese producers continue to rely on wild yeasts to complete the fermentation. Wine-makers with a more international view prefer to use yeast cultures, sometimes brought in from abroad. By knocking out strains of wild yeast and inoculating carefully selected commercial varieties, the wine-maker exercises a greater control over vinification. This reduces the risk of stuck or incomplete fermentations, which are always a danger if temperatures are high.

Once the alcoholic fermentation is complete, most wines will, at some stage, go through a secondary malo-lactic fermentation. This is an acid conversion process where malic acid is transformed to lactic acid by malo-lactic bacteria. For this to happen successfully the temperature of the wine should ideally be around 20°C. In cool northern climates the malo-lactic tends to take place in the spring after the vintage as the wine warms up again in the winery. In Portugal, where it tends to stay warm well into the autumn, the malo-lactic tends to happen straight after the alcoholic fermentation in October and November.

Modern wine-makers working in warm climates will often suppress the malo-lactic, however, preventing the bacteria from converting the pronounced malic acid found in apples and cool-climate grapes into softer lactic acid. Vinho Verde grapes in the north of Portugal contain large amounts of malic acid, and the best single-*quinta* wines do not go through malo-lactic fermentation. The apple-like zest of malic acid is very much a part of the wine's style and the taste.

Further south, many co-operatives let the malo-lactic run its natural course and consequently the wines are denied the shot of acidity that they badly need to taste balanced. Few co-ops have the equipment or know-how to control the malo-lactic and, as a result, many wines pick up dirty or volatile flavours. Keeping the wine cool in stainless steel, followed by tight filtration to remove the active bacteria, is the best way of preventing the malo-lactic from taking place. Adding (another) generous dollop of sulphur is the rather crude method that many wineries use.

After the alcoholic or malo-lactic fermentation, the wine should be racked or run off the sediment that, if left in the wine, could cause it to develop 'off' flavours. This should happen three or four times during the winter, as particles still in suspension settle to the bottom of the vat. Then the wine will need still further clarifying or 'fining'. Tiny particles of protein still in suspension in the wine are precipitated by adding a fining agent, usually bentonite clay. By virtue of its opposite electrical charge, it coagulates with the fine sediment that remains in the wine, so bringing it down as a deposit. Further racking and a rough filtration will remove all traces of the fining agent.

Once this has been carried out, most white wines are ready to bottle, but in Portugal far too many wines are left to age in bulk. In all but a few cases this does far more harm than good, as the wine, stored in badly maintained wood or concrete vats, steadily reacts with the atmosphere and oxidizes, losing any remaining freshness. The law in many of Portugal's wine regions enshrines this practice, and some wine-makers still have to put up with a ridiculous legal minimum maturation period before a wine is allowed to be bottled. Even in newly delimited regions like Arruda, producers must still age their wines for at least six months before they can be bottled. There are, however, a few well-made wines from some of the best producers that do benefit from spending a few months ageing in new oak. This is discussed more fully in the section on making red wines below.

Before bottling, one final treatment is usually necessary, especially now that wines are being bottled earlier than before. Most white wines are chilled to remove naturally occurring tartrate crystals that would otherwise precipitate in the bottle. These are quite harmless but are often unacceptable to wine consumers, who frequently mistake them for sugar crystals or even particles of glass. To prevent this happening, most white wines are cooled down to a temperature below o°C for four or five days, after which most of the tartrates drop out.

After the tartrates have been removed, the wine should undergo final filtration immediately before bottling. Medium dry or sweet wines with sugar remaining should undergo sterile membrane filtration, to remove even the smallest stray yeast or bacteria that could destabilize the wine. More often than not, dry white wines are filtered through sheets of cellulose fibre. This is normally sufficient to remove any remaining sediment from the wine.

Ideally, from the arrival of the grapes to the bottling of the wine, cellars should be equipped with stainless steel. Apart from vats, the pumps, pipes, taps, bottling and filtration equipment should all be made from inert material that is easy to keep clean. In Portugal, with the exception of one or two well-equipped wineries belonging to companies like Sogrape and the Fonsecas, this is rarely the case. Most wine-makers have to make do with conditions that are far from ideal. Co-operatives are especially at fault. Their often unhygienic production is one of the chief reasons why Portugal is rarely taken seriously as a country for making white wine.

Making Red Wines

Good reds can be made more easily in a warm climate without recourse to the ever more sophisticated technology being used for white wine-making. But this is not an excuse for some of the sloppy habits in Portuguese wineries which frequently turn ripe, healthy grapes into very unhealthy wine.

Most grapes are delivered to the winery piled into trailers or, in the case of larger private firms, in steel hoppers which are lent out to farmers for the harvest. Red grapes may be trucked for longer distances than white without damaging the must. On arrival at the winery the procedure is very much the same as for white wine production. The trailer will be weighed and a probe driven into the grapes to measure the sugar content, against which farmers will be paid. Until very recently, few co-operatives paid much attention to individual grape varieties, but now some of the better wineries are offering growers incentives for better-quality grapes. This is giving them the opportunity to start fermenting different varieties separately instead of relying on the hodge-podge of different grapes that the farmer happens to have picked that day.

Individual grape varieties should then be tipped into separate reception troughs or hoppers and conveyed (by Archimedes screw) to a roller-crusher which breaks the skins of the berries, releasing juice. Apart from the *teinturier* varieties like the red-fleshed Alicante Bouschet or Grand Noir, most red grapes yield colourless juice. The depth of colour in a red wine is therefore achieved by macerating the skins with the must during the first part of fermentation.

Whether or not bunches of grapes should be destemmed depends on the style of the wine. In Portugal many co-operatives mangle the stalks when attempting to remove them, releasing bitter-tasting substances into the wine, while small wineries without the equipment still ferment on the stalks. It also leads to the extraction of astringent green tannins as the juice ferments, and is one of the main reasons for the harsh, tannic flavours that are sometimes found in Portuguese red wines, particularly those from Bairrada.

Before fermentation is allowed to begin, a sample of the grape must should be analysed. Sulphur dioxide may be added to kill off wild yeasts, and tartaric acid added if necessary to adjust the acid balance and lower the pH of the must. Just as in making white wines, chaptalization is not permitted. Bags of sugar, seen piled high in some French wineries, should not be needed anywhere in Portugal.

Fermentation vessels for red wines vary widely. The traditional, open stone *lagares* where grapes are trodden by foot are still found widely in the Douro for making Port (see page 52), but are only used in the smallest country *adegas* for making red table wine. Most were replaced in the 1960s by concrete vats. These should be lined with tiles or epoxy paint to prevent the wine from reacting with the cement. All too often, the cement vats in co-operatives are unlined or badly maintained. Cracks in the paint or missing tiles harbour bacteria, which can damage or spoil a wine. The best material for fermenting red as well as white wine is stainless steel. It can be kept clean easily, requires little maintenance and makes the fermentation temperature easier to control.

This last benefit is less critical for red wines than for whites, but high fermentation temperatures can still be dangerous for two reasons. First, a degree of temperature control is necessary to preserve the fruit character and to keep down levels of volatile acidity, which give the wine an acetic taste. Wines allowed to ferment at high temperatures often develop a baked, jammy character; something that can be noted in many of the co-operative made reds in Alentejo and Algarve. The second reason for keeping an eye on the thermometer is that yeasts find the going hard at temperatures above 30°C. This can lead to an incomplete fermentation, with the resulting danger that the wine will turn out unbalanced and unstable.

Wine-makers looking to make lighter, softer red wines should not only control the temperature but also need to monitor the period of contact between the juice and skins. Most wine-makers ferment on the skins for a period of one to two weeks before running off the wine and pressing the remaining mass of skins and sometimes stalks and pips. The quality of the press wine depends on the nature of the press. Continuous presses produce a wine which is dark, rough and tannic. It should be kept separate but more usually it is blended back into the wine at a later stage. Many Portuguese wines suffer from being tough, and too much extraction is usually the root cause. In Bairrada, where the small Baga grape makes especially hard wines that take a long time to soften, extraction is a particular problem.

One or two producers are experimenting with thermo-vinification, a technique which flash-heats the must up to 60-70°C for a few minutes to extract the colour without the harsh tannins that make a wine hard to drink. The problem with thermo-vinification is that it makes wines that are soft and easy to drink when young but, if the process is badly handled, quickly lose their freshness with age. Another technique that is being used widely in France to make fresh, fruity red wines in Beaujolais and the Rhône is carbonic or semi-carbonic maceration. Instead of crushing, grapes are kept whole and the fermentation takes place inside the skins, extracting a limited amount of colour and tannin. The process requires a degree of technology and skill to succeed, but in both Bairrada and on the Setúbal Peninsula there are wine-makers employing carbonic maceration to make wines that are attractive to drink young.

A wine-maker in the north of Portugal looking for maximum colour from his grapes will leave the skins steeped in juice throughout the fermentation. This is difficult, as carbon dioxide generated by the fermenting must will force the 'cap', or *manta* as the Portuguese call it, to the top of the vat. When fermentation took place in *lagares*, men with sticks for some reason called *macacos* ('monkeys') would walk along planks over the vat and physically punch down the cap. Some co-ops fermenting in concrete place a crude slatted wooden grill in the vat to hold down the *manta* while letting the carbon dioxide escape.

A much better way to aid the extraction of colour is *remontage*. This is practised widely in France, but in Portugal (where it translates as *remontagem*) its use is still fairly limited. Instead of holding or punching down the cap, the fermenting juice is pumped from the bottom of the vat and sprayed over the floating cap on top. Autovinifiers, used mainly for Port (see page 54), do this automatically. A number of Portuguese co-operatives use autovinification vats for making red table wines but find it difficult to regulate the extraction of colour and tannin.

Fermentation will last for a maximum of twenty days. At the end, once all the sugar has been fermented out, the wine will be run off and racked from the coarse sediment that is left behind. This should be done a number of times during the winter months. Bulk wines tend to be filtered instead.

Over the winter or in the spring after the harvest, the wine will undergo malo-lactic fermentation, making it softer and more rounded. Some less skilled wine-makers, unable to control the malo-lactic successfully, leave things to chance. There are occasions when it takes place after the wine has been bottled, producing unpleasantly fizzy red wine.

The maturation of wines in Portugal is a controversial subject. Only big, well-structured reds with good concentration of fruit and ripe tannins are really suited to long ageing. Thinner, lighter red wines lose what little fruit they have and dry out if they are kept for too long before bottling. Many co-operatives age their wines for long periods in unlined concrete vats. These are difficult to keep clean and cause bacteriological problems in the wine, particularly when levels of sulphur dioxide are allowed to fall.

Most private wine-makers age their wines in ancient wooden vats, usually made from either oak or chestnut. Unless these are regularly cleaned and the staves are well maintained, old wooden casks and vats will harbour dangerous micro-organisms that can harm the wine. Many casks are kept for too long. After about five years' use, the wood ceases to have any influence on the wine. Ideally, casks should be made of new oak and be used for five but no more than ten years.

The oak itself is a matter for some consideration. French oak from the cool forests of Alliers, Nevers, Limoges or Tronçais is much the best, though few wine-makers can afford it. Many use American oak, which is from a different species. It is coarser-grained and imparts a stronger flavour to the wine. A few producers also use Portuguese oak.

Unlike France, Portugal has none of the extensive oak forests planted in the eighteenth century for the manufacture of furniture and casks. Most Portuguese oak comes from isolated trees planted on the cool mountain slopes of Trás-os-Montes and Beira Alta in the north of the country. The wood is frequently knotty and it can often impart a green, resin-like flavour to wines. Part of the problem is that the staves are not properly seasoned before being made up into casks. Opinions differ. J. P. Vinhos (João Pires), who have their own cooperage, use new Portuguese oak successfully for ageing both red and white wines. José Maria da Fonseca prefer to age their wines in French Limousin and renew 10 per cent of their casks every year.

The authorities in Portugal are keen to stipulate the length of time that a wine should be aged before bottling, but give no guide to how it should be matured. In the Dão, for example, a wine can be bottled only after eighteen months' maturation. Some wines from high-yielding vineyards are unable to stand up to this and would be much better bottled young than being badly treated in a co-op. Even the newly delimited IPR (Indicação de Proveniência Regulamentada) regions have some untenable laws. Arruda, Alcobaça and Encostas d'Aire, all bulk-producing areas in the Oeste, must keep their red wines for at least fourteen months.

Like whites, red wines are fined before bottling, usually with gelatine or bentonite. Egg white is now rarely used, though all the rich cakes and puddings of Portugal are the legacy of a time when the whites were used to clarify the wine and the yolks were discarded. Immediately before bottling, those red wines which are to be bottled young are chilled to remove tartrates then given a final, fairly rough filtration. Wines that have aged in bulk for any length of time will have already deposited tartrate crystals in cask or vat.

Most Portuguese red wines are sold ready to drink, and many producers are therefore obliged to age their wines further in bottle before releasing them for sale. For example, *garrafeiras* must spend a year in bottle having previously spent two years in bulk. This is controlled by the IVV (Instituto da Vinha e do Vinho). Whole stacks of bottles are recorded and then sealed by a government official to prevent them being sold before the requisite maturation period is complete. Wines from the demarcated regions have to comply with all the regulations regarding ageing before they can be awarded the *selo de origem* or seal of origin which is stuck over the cork, underneath the capsule on the neck of the bottle.

Producers are also obliged to set aside samples of each bottling. These are sealed by the IVV and kept back for future reference in case there is any cause for complaint.

Making Rosé Wines

Portugal's rosé wines are given a chapter to themselves later in the book, such is their importance in the economy. They are a fairly recent, money-spinning creation, so wine-making techniques among the major producers are fairly advanced.

Red grapes with between 10 and 12° of potential alcohol usually arrive at the vinification plant in large steel hoppers loaned to the growers by the wine-makers. A probe tests the grapes for their sugar content on arrival and farmers are paid accordingly. A dose of tartaric acid in powder form is often added to reduce pH levels before the grapes are destemmed and crushed. Grapes frequently arrive in poor condition, especially after a wet summer like 1988. Great batteries of stainless steel centrifuges then roll into action, and pectolytic enzymes may be added to clean up the must before fermentation begins. Skin contact lasts for up to twenty-four hours, sufficient for the wine to take on a pale pink colour. Most rosés are now made at low temperatures, fermenting for around two weeks at 18°C. The sweetness common to most Portuguese rosés is achieved by running the wine off before fermentation is complete and centrifuging it to remove active yeasts. The wine will then be dosed with sulphur dioxide and stored until ready for blending and bottling. Reflective white concrete tanks, called *balões* or *mamas* because of their shape, are often used for short-term storage, though stainless steel is better and cleaner.

Wines are blended according to the export market (see page 200), and are adjusted again for sweetness using desulphited or unfermented concentrated grape must. Further adjustments for acidity and sulphur take place before the wine is sterile-filtered and bottled. Wines destined for all except the North American market have a slight *pétillance* or sparkle. In most cases, carbon dioxide is injected into the wine as it is bottled. Lancers, on the other hand, introduce a light natural sparkle by passing the wine quickly through their own recently constructed continuous plant. This is also used to make a white sparkling wine and is described in detail below.

Making Sparkling Wines

Most Portuguese *espumantes* or sparkling wines are made by the champagne or traditional method, as the European Community now tells us to call it. In Portugal the process is much the same as anywhere else. A dry base wine is bottled together with a small quantity of *licor de fermentacão* – a mixture of wine, sugar and yeast culture. The bottle is then fitted with a crown cork, shaken to mix up the liqueur, and laid horizontally in an underground cellar where the wine ferments for a second time, creating a natural sparkle. Cooler cellars slow down fermentations and make better wines. After two or three months all the sugar will have fermented and the carbon dioxide in the bottle will have reached a pressure of around 5 atmospheres. But there is another by-product: a sticky sediment which precipitates as the yeasts ferment the sugar and die. In order to remove this, the wine undergoes *remuage*. The necks of the bottles are placed in vertical wooden racks called *pupitres* (there are no Portuguese translations for the French terms), where they are shaken and gradually up-ended daily until the sediment settles on the crown cork. This is a laborious and lengthy process taking several weeks or months. One or two sparkling wine producers have begun to use gyropalettes to automate *remuage* but in Portugal, where investment is often lacking, these are the exception rather than the rule.

After *remuage*, the wine is ready for *dégorgement* or disgorging to remove the sediment. Before this, most producers choose to stack the wine *sur pointes* to age in contact with the yeast sediment. In theory this gives the wine more character and flavour, though in Portugal many wines are left for too long and taste tired as a result. In all but the smallest cellars disgorging is automated. The neck of the bottle is frozen in a brine bath and the crown cork removed, releasing a plug of wine containing the sediment. The bottle is then topped up with *licor de expedicão* – a mixture of wine and sugar which determines the final sweetness of the wine. Finally, the bottle will be sealed with a mushroom cork and a wire *égraffe*. Once the bottle has been labelled, the wine is ready for sale, though some producers with large stocks still choose to age the wine further, often to the detriment of the taste.

What lets so many Portuguese *espumantes* down is not their method of production but the quality of the base wine. Most of this is made in ill-equipped co-operatives in the north of the country and then bought by independent producers to turn into sparkling wine. The individual wine-makers and their wines are described on pages 204–208.

In complete contrast to some of the rudimentary techniques used in Portugal to make traditional '*método champanhês*' *espumantes*, one producer in the south of the country is revolutionizing sparkling wine production with a new method. J. M. da Fonseca Internacional, at Azeitão on the Setúbal Peninsula, was established in 1970 to produce the Lancers brand of rosé wines. In the 1980s, seeing the danger of relying on one brand, Fonseca began to diversify. They have invested heavily in a new

Sparkling wine: the Continuous Method

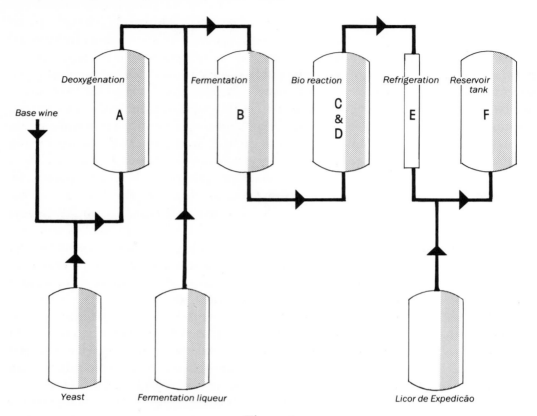

Figure 1

sparkling wine plant, adapted from a system that was first used in the Soviet Union in 1940. It has been patented in the West by the German company Seitz Enzinger Noll, which brought the method to Portugal. The 'Russian Continuous Method', as it is called, is much better than it sounds. A dry white base wine with 10° alcohol is made by cool fermentation from early picked red Castelão Frances (Periquita). It is fined with charcoal to remove any trace of colour. After being stabilized for tartrates and sterile-filtered it is introduced to a series of five stainless steel tanks (Figure 1).

In the first tank (A), a specially prepared active yeast culture of the *Saccharomyces bayanus* strain is injected into the wine. Biological deaeration or deoxygenation takes place as a result of the contact between the yeast and the wine. This is essential, as the second fermentation must take place without the presence of air. The wine then passes into a second tank (B) where sweet *licor de fermentacão* or fermentation liqueur is added. The base wine is mixed with 24 grams per litre of sugar. The fermentation takes place under a pressure of $5 kg/cm^2$ at temperatures between 12 and

15°C. After about nine days only 5 grams of sugar remain, and the now sparkling wine is cooled to around 10°C and moves slowly to the next stage: two bio-reactor tanks (C and D).

Inside, they are packed with sterile wood-shavings. As the wine passes through these they catch the sediment produced by the fermentation, as well as serving to increase the surface area in which the yeast cells are in contact with the wine. The steady autolysis between the yeast and the wine is supposed to contribute the biscuit-like characters that result from the *remuage* and *sur pointes* stages of the 'champagne method' but are not obtained with other bulk processes like the Charmat or *cuve close*. The wood-shavings also filter the wine so that as it leaves the bio-reactor tanks the yeast count is practically nil.

The temperature of the wine is then reduced again to −2 or −3°C (E). As the base wine is stable and tartrates have already been removed, this serves purely to reduce the pressure in the system in order to aid the combination of carbon dioxide with the wine.

Finally it flows into a reservoir tank (F), where *licor de expedicão* is added. At this stage, if necessary, levels of sulphur dioxide can be adjusted and the amount of carbon dioxide can be reduced if it has reached an excess. Before bottling the wine is filtered twice, first through cellulose sheets then through a sterile membrane, to remove any stray yeasts or bacteria.

From the time the base wine enters the system to its emergence at the other end takes just twenty-one days. Apart from the need for occasional maintenance, the process never needs to stop. At Fonseca it functions twenty-four hours a day, seven days a week, producing 50 litres of *espumante* an hour with very little labour. It goes without saying that 'continuous method' is a very much quicker and cheaper way of making sparkling wine than the traditional method of champagne production, but what of the quality of the wine? Well, it is some way from being a Champagne but it is a crisp, clean, slightly yeasty-tasting fizz with a good, reasonably persistent *mousse*. Lancers Método Continuo Espumante is certainly better to drink than nearly all bulk-produced sparkling wines and a good many French and Spanish traditional method wines as well.

The system is also used to put the sparkle into Lancers Rosé. This and the workings of J.M. da Fonseca Internacional are described more fully on pages 202 and 207.

Making Fortified Wines

Fortified wines are so called because they are 'fortified' by the addition of alcohol. In Portugal, *aguardente* or grape spirit is usually added to arrest fermentation before it is complete. By killing off the active yeasts before all the sugar has fermented, this type of fortification leaves a sweet wine, often referred to in general terms as *vinho abafado*. Occasionally spirit may be added after the fermentation to make a dry fortified wine.

This section covers the making of Portugal's two principal fortified wines: Port and Madeira. Carcavelos and Setúbal, two less well-known fortified wines made by a handful of producers, are covered on pages 154 and 166.

Making Port

Port is made in two places. The fermentation takes place in the vineyards up the Douro valley. Then, in the spring after the harvest, most of the wine is shipped 80 kilometres or so downstream to Vila Nova da Gaia near the coast, where it ages in cool *armazens* or lodges.

The most important part of making red Port is the extraction of colour and tannin from the grapes. As the wine is fortified just a few days into fermentation, the juice or must spends only a short time in contact with the skins. For this reason, the maceration that takes place must be as vigorous as possible.

Until the early 1960s all Port was made in much the same way. Every winery or *adega* was equipped with *lagares* – low stone troughs, usually built out of granite, in which grapes were trodden and fermented. Some are still in use, mainly at small privately owned *quintas*.

Grapes are picked and loaded into coarse-woven *cestos da vindima*, baskets holding about 60 kilos of grapes. These are taken to the *adega* and the *lagar* is progressively filled over the course of a day. In the evening, when the *roga* (gang of pickers) can no longer see their way around the vineyard terraces, they put on shorts and jump thigh deep into the slimy, purple mass of grapes in order to tread the must. Most *lagares* hold between 10 and 15 pipes (about 5,500 to 8,250 litres), though one or two large *quintas* have *lagares* with a capacity of 30 pipes. As a rule of thumb, one or two people per pipe are needed to tread a *lagar*.

It takes around two or three hours of treading before the grapes are properly crushed and the *manta* of stalks and skins floats to the top of the *lagar*. This period of treading is called the *corte* or cut. The *roga* stand in line with their arms around each other's shoulders and march methodically backwards and forwards, occasionally to the beat of a drum. At the end of this period *liberdade* or liberty is declared and everyone starts to dance freely in the grapes, usually to the accompaniment of an accordion.

As the grapes are trodden, the must warms up. Wild yeasts on the surface of the grapes are activated and the whole mass of purple skins, stems and juice begins to ferment. As this happens, more and more natural colour is extracted from the skins. After about five hours' continuous treading, the grapes are thoroughly crushed and the *roga* leaves the *lagar*. Planks are run across to enable men with *macacos* (long spiked sticks) to stand above the *manta* and push it down into the foaming must. This is repeated regularly over the fermentation period to keep the skins immersed in the wine.

After between twenty-four and thirty-six hours the level of grape sugar in the must has declined from around 12 or 13° Baume to between 6 and 8°. Depending on the sweetness, the wine-maker will give the go-ahead for the wine to be run off the skins out of the *lagar* and into a *tonel* or vat. This will be waiting, already about one fifth full with 77° *aguardente*. As the spirit is mixed in with the wine, the yeasts are killed and the fermentation is arrested. At this stage the must becomes a young, sweet, spirity, purple Port.

In the Douro, where there are few flat sites anyway, most traditional *adegas* are built on two levels. The *lagares* on the upper level will feed the wooden *toneis* below. The must is simply run off the *lagares* by gravity, leaving behind the mass of stalks and skins. Many *lagares* are equipped with vertical presses, and all that remains will be forked in to extract the last of the juice. This deeply coloured, astringent wine will be run off and fortified separately. It may be blended back again at a later stage or used to bolster the colour in an inferior wine.

Many of the best Ports, destined to be blended into vintage lots, are still made this way. The human foot, for all its many associations, is regarded as ideal for pressing, as it breaks up the grape without crushing the pips. These would otherwise release bitter-tasting phenols into the wine.

But over the last twenty years, treading grapes has become much less widespread. The remote Trás-os-Montes region in the north-east of Portugal has suffered more than any other from mass emigration. Isolated villages which traditionally sent the gangs of pickers to Port *quintas* at harvest-time have lost many of their younger and more able sons and daughters, who have gone to find more profitable work in the cities and abroad. By the mid 1960s many of the larger properties in the Douro were unable to find the manpower necessary to tread their *lagares* and so the shippers were forced to look at other ways of making wine.

A few, notably Cockburn's and Sandeman, adopted a system called the *movimosto* specifically to help small farmers suffering from a shortage of labour. This is a form of *remontage* explained in the section on red wine-making on page 46. Whole bunches of grapes are put through roller crushers before being tipped into *lagares* to ferment. In place of treading, the must is pumped out of the *lagar* and sprayed over the centre of the *manta* to extract colour. The main problem with the system was that the pressure from the pump was usually too weak for the surface area and the *manta* was not broken up sufficiently to ensure good extraction. Consequently, many wines made by the *movimosto* method were lacking in depth of colour and body. The Bergqvists, who own Quinta de la Rosa at Pinhão, have recently taken out their *movimosto* pumps and returned to the traditional *lagares*.

Autovinification

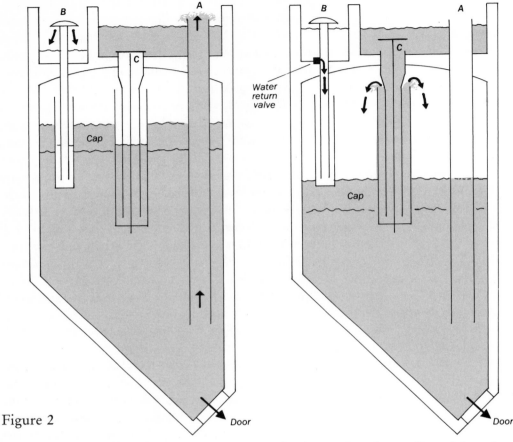

Figure 2

They acknowledge that the system has been detrimental to the quality of the wine in a potentially excellent *quinta*. But Cockburn's, who pioneered the idea in 1966, still use it fairly successfully in their *adega* at Tua. They are the only shippers now using *movimosto* on any scale.

Facing an increasingly serious shortage of labour as conscription in the 1960s took away young men to fight the African colonial wars, most Port producers abandoned *lagares* altogether. Many isolated *quintas* were without electricity, and so from the early 1960s most of the large shippers set about building central wineries. Most of these are equipped with autovinification tanks. These (known as the Ducellier system) were developed in Algeria and have since been adapted for making Port. In most wineries grapes now arrive by road in painted mild steel hoppers with a capacity of about 1,000 kilos. These are weighed on a weighbridge and the grapes are sampled for density to determine the amount of fermentable sugar. Farmers delivering their grapes are then issued with a piece of paper against which they will be paid when the harvest is over.

After weighing, the hoppers are winched up and tipped into the grape reception. A continuous Archimedes screw then conveys the grapes to the crushers. Most wineries use centrifugal crushers which also remove a proportion of the stalks, depending on the year and the style of wine being made. From there the mass of pulp is pumped into autovinification vats which are filled to within 50-75 cm from the top. The vat is then closed and an autovinification unit is screwed into place (Figure 2).

As fermentation begins, carbon dioxide is given off. When the vat is closed, pressure builds up inside. This drives the fermenting must up an escape value (A) which spills out into a trough on the top of the vat. At the same time water is being forced out of a second valve (B) into a separate trough. Once all the water has been forced out, the CO_2 gas escapes and the fermenting must falls back down the central pipe of the autovinificator (C), spraying the floating cap with explosive force. At the same time, the water in the second holding tank on top of the vat gushes back into the valve ready for the pressure to build up and the process to begin again.

At the start of fermentation, the autovinification cycle is fairly slow. But after a few hours, when the fermentation is in full swing, the build-up of pressure inside the vat is such that the cycle takes just ten or fifteen minutes to complete. In a large winery like the Symington's *adega* at Quinta do Bomfim, the sight is spectacular with one vat after another exploding heady carbon dioxide into the air.

Originally most autovinification vats were made of resin-painted concrete, with capacities similar to those of a *lagar*. More modern wineries are equipped with stainless steel vats and a number of significant modifications have been made to aid the process. One of the chief problems with making wine in *lagares* was that in a hot year, the temperature of fermentation could rise quickly to dangerous levels above 32°C. Early concrete autovinification vats suffered from much the same problem, though the must could be pumped out and chilled in a heat exchanger. Must fermenting in stainless steel can be cooled more easily, making the cycle of autovinification much easier to control. The ideal temperature is now at between 25 and 28°C.

Some vats have been modified and equipped with revolving paddles to mix the must and break up the *manta*. This, in the main, has not been successful, as the giant propellers used to stir the vats tend to mash the skins, leaving a large amount of unwanted solids in the wine when it comes to be run off. A better innovation has been the introduction of *remontage*. A few producers use this on its own, though, as with the *movimosto*, extraction is rarely sufficient to make high-quality Port. Others combine *remontage* (page 46) with autovinification. Warre's Quinta da Cavadinha has recently been equipped with state of the art stainless steel vats which use both autovinification and *remontage* to extract colour. By pumping over the must as soon as the crushed mass of grapes enters the vat, colour can be extracted before the autovinification cycle begins. This together with jacket temperature control gives the wine-maker more control over Port vinification than ever before.

Just as in *lagares*, autovinification takes about thirty-six hours for about half the sugar in 12 or 13° Baume grapes to ferment to alcohol. At this point the wine will be run off and mixed with *aguardente*, which arrests the fermentation. Normally 110 litres of spirit are used to fortify 440 litres of must, adding up to a 550-litre pipe of Port. When a very sweet Port is being made, the fermentation is arrested early and a higher proportion of *aguardente* will be used (perhaps 135 litres to 415 litres of must).

The *aguardente* used to fortify Port used to be distilled from wine made in the Douro and central Portugal, especially the Oeste (see page 139). Until 1992, it had to be purchased from the Casa do Douro which set a fixed price and controlled distribution. In recent years, most was of fairly poor quality, distilled from the European wine lake, and in 1990 the shippers ran short due to a hiatus in the government's purchasing system. Ironically, it was Portugal's entry into the European Community that has broken the government's long-standing monopoly and in future Port producers will be able to buy any *aguardente* they choose.

Modern autovinification vats are conical in shape (see Figure 2, page 54). Doors at the base are opened once the wine has been run off, in order to empty the vat of all the *bagaço* – skins, stems and pips that remain after fermentation. This solid mass is then conveyed by Archimedes screw to a press, where the remainder of the juice is extracted before being fortified. The press wine will be set aside for blending with the free-run.

Most white Port is made in much the same way as red, with short skin contact during fermentation. At one time white grapes were trodden in *lagares*, but nowadays most wines are fermented on the skins in cement or stainless steel vats. Fermentation temperatures are frequently too high and the skins impart both colour and tannin to the must, making wines that taste flat and unattractive. A few producers are now using the *bica aberta* method: fermenting in temperature-controlled conditions having first separated the must from the skins. This makes a cleaner, fresher style of white Port.

Nothing is wasted in Port production. New wines are racked off the lees 2-3 months after fortification, and the sediment will be filtered to extract the last few drops of Port. Modern wineries use rotary vacuum filters to clean up this purple sludge, which is then put aside to bolster a basic blend. Even the *bagaço*, left over after having been completed pressed, has some uses. It is often distilled to make the rough *bagaceira* spirit that is drunk in vineyards and cafés all over Portugal. Finally the remains are made into fertilizer and the pips are fed to the chickens.

In the spring, after the harvest, most Port is taken downstream to Vila Nova da Gaia, the town on the opposite bank to Oporto, where the wine is aged. Some stays up in the Douro, where it matures more rapidly in the heat, but this is a technique that is normally used only to speed up the ageing of the most basic wines. Some of these Ports suffer from what the shippers call 'Douro-bake', though this is exacerbated by irregular racking and general neglect.

All Port must age in bulk for a minimum of two years. White Port and basic reds destined for early bottling are often left to age in cement or stainless steel. Better-quality wines are put into lodge pipes between 267 to 630 litres in size, or into wooden vats called *balseiros*, some of which have a capacity of 70,000 litres. Thereafter there is a distinction between so-called 'wood Ports' or wines that gain their character from ageing in bulk, and Ports that mature in bottle. Wood Ports include ruby, vintage character, tawny, late bottled vintage (LBV) and *colheita* wines. They develop their individual style and character from ageing before being bottled. Most (with the exception of a few notable LBVs on page 78) are fined and filtered before being blended and bottled ready to drink. Some basic rubies and tawnies are also flash pasteurized and treated for tartrates in order to ensure that they are completely stable. These wines should not therefore throw a sediment after they have been bottled.

Conversely, vintage, single-*quinta* vintage, crusted and traditional, unfiltered LBV wines will spend a short time ageing in wood (in the case of vintage Port just two years). These wines undergo the minimum of treatment, probably just an occasional racking and certainly no filtration or pasteurization, before bottling. From then on the wine will mature in bottle, losing colour and tannin in the process. This is deposited in the form of a 'crust' or sediment in the bottle.

Further detailed information on the development and style of different categories of Port is included on page 70.

Making Madeira

All the way through this chapter on wine-making, temperature has been of crucial importance. Most wines suffer from being made at too high a temperature and lose primary character as a result. Madeira, on the other hand, actually benefits from being made at high temperatures and most wines are deliberately heated to achieve the desired maderized flavour. The difficulty is that Madeira's wine shippers set about this in so many different ways. There are accepted text-book methods but most producers choose to make wines their own way, often cutting some frighteningly tight corners in order to reduce production costs for more basic wines.

One of Madeira's most serious problems is a lack of good base wine. This is caused in part by a shortage of 'noble' Sercial, Verdelho, Bual and Malvasia grapes (see pages 212–213) as well as some fairly crude wine-making on the part of the Madeira wine producers. At one time the Madeira shippers bought must direct from the growers, who trod grapes by foot in stone *lagares*. The juice was then taken to the shippers in Funchal, who would ferment it in wooden vats or casks. Spirit, which until the 1960s was distilled mostly from sugar cane, was added to arrest the fermentation, leaving residual sugar in the sweeter Verdelho, Bual and Malvasia wines. The juice from Sercial was fermented dry, then fortified to 17 or 18°.

Today few winemakers use *lagares*. The shippers now buy in grapes from the thousands of small farmers all over the island. They are delivered in trailers, which are weighed full as they arrive and empty as they leave. Just as on the mainland, farmers are then paid according to the weight and the potential alcohol of their grapes. The shippers pay more money for relatively scarce 'noble' varieties as opposed to the ubiquitous Tinta Negra Mole. In 1989, the Madeira Wine Company paid 220$00 (escudos) a kilo for Sercial as opposed to 180$00 for Negra Mole. The poor old hybrids like Jacquet fetch only around 40$00 a kilo now that, in theory, they can no longer be used to make Madeira wine.

From the reception hopper, the grapes are crushed and the mass of berries, stalks and skins is pumped into a horizontal, mechanical press. Most producers ferment in 25,000-litre *cubas* made of wood or in huge concrete vats. Interestingly, the Madeira Wine Company (by far the largest producer on the island) has installed stainless steel autovinification vats for the purpose. Although most Madeira is made from red grapes, colour extraction is not of prime importance. Autovinification therefore seems to be unnecessary.

Only the tiny amount of wine made from 'noble' white grapes is pressed and fermented separately in individual lodge pipes or 600-litre oak casks. Malvasia and Bual are traditionally fermented on the skins, while Sercial and Verdelho musts are separated from the skins before fermentation. Few producers ever think of cooling the must and most of Madeira's base wine is made at high temperatures, often around 30°C.

It is at this point that wine-making practices begin to differ. The best wines are made by arresting the fermentation with 95 per cent strength *aguardente* to make a 17-18° wine. Malvasia and Bual will be fortified fairly early on, leaving up to 7° Baume of sugar in the wine, while Verdelho and Sercial are fermented until they are practically dry.

Other wines are made differently. Some producers prefer to let the sugar ferment right out, leaving the fortification until later. This saves them the cost of valuable alcohol, a few degrees of which will be lost with the heating of the wine. These wines are sweetened after fortification according to style: dry, medium dry, medium sweet and sweet. *Vinho surdo* and *abafado* are used to sweeten the better wines. *Surdo* is an intensely sweet wine fortified to 20 per cent just a few hours into fermentation, while *abafado* is a drier wine arrested at a later stage. Cheap wines are adjusted with caramel.

Madeira's *estufa* system (literally meaning hothouse or stove) was developed in the eighteenth century after it was found that Madeiras shipped in cask across the tropics had developed more mature flavours. There are two forms of *estufagem* currently in use. Concrete tanks (*cubas de calor*) ranging in size between 20,000 and

50,000 litres are the most widely used. These are supposedly lined with epoxy resin, tiles or glass (most are not). In the middle of the tank, hot water circulates in a coil made at one time from copper, now from stainless steel. This heats the wine to a temperature of between 40 and 50°C, at which it must remain for a period of at least three months. The greater the heat, the more rapidly the wine develops, but short *estufagem* at high temperatures tends to make wine that smells baked and tastes cooked and stewed. Most of the wine that undergoes this form of bulk *estufagem* has been fermented dry and therefore enters the system unfortified. Although the process is carefully monitored by Madeira's controlling body, the Instituto do Vinho da Madeira (IVM), the damage done to a young wine by heating followed by slow cooling is lasting. Many develop vinegary, volatile flavours as a result.

The second form of *estufagem* is more gentle. Lodge pipes with a capacity of between 600 and 650 litres are filled with wine that has been previously fortified to 18 per cent. These are stored in warm rooms (*armazens de calor*), heated either by the nearby *cubas de calor* or by steam-filled hot water pipes. Temperatures are maintained at lower levels, normally between 35 and 40°C, and the wines develop more slowly over a period of between six months and a year. Consequently they finish up tasting less stewed than wines heated in bulk, and are used for making higher-quality five- and ten-year-old Reserve or Special Reserve blends.

The very finest Madeiras are produced without any artificial heating at all. The wine, made only from the 'noble' grapes, is left to age slowly in 600-litre lodge pipes made from American oak, some of which are over 100 years old. They are stowed under the eaves of lodges in Funchal and heated naturally by the sun. The casks that are closest to the roof mature faster than the wine stored lower down. Some spend 50 or 100 years maturing, topped up at regular intervals to replace wine lost through evaporation. This type of Madeira is called *vinho do canteiro*, after the racks or *canteiros* on which the pipes are stacked.

But you only need to look at Madeira's export figures to find out how the majority of the island's wines are made. In 1989 well over half the island's production was exported in bulk, mainly to France, Germany and Belgium, where it is used in cooking. Not surprisingly, careful wine-making does not feature very high on most shippers' list of priorities in this price-sensitive market and so some fairly crude practices have evolved. Caramel is used unscrupulously both for colouring and sweetening basic Madeiras, and I even heard of one producer using surplus butter to prevent bubbling vats of sugar from boiling over. This subsequently turned rancid and imparted a putrid taste to the wine.

After *estufagem* has been completed, wines start to qualify for age. The cheapest wines are shipped after spending between eighteen months and three years in vat. Better wines are set aside in *lotes* or lots which will be used later for blending. A few *soleras* also exist, though these have been abused by some shippers and are soon to be outlawed in favour of dated blends.

Further information on the different styles and categories of Madeira may be found in Chapter 17, page 214.

A glossary of Portugal's wine-making terms may be found in the final chapter of the book, on page 223.

4

Port and the Douro

The River Douro cuts a gash through the hard, grey mountains of northern Portugal. It rises in Spain, not far from Rioja, starting life as the Duero, a supine stream flowing across the Iberian *meseta*. A short distance downstream from Zamora, the river undergoes a dramatic transformation. Just before it reaches the Portuguese border and becomes the Douro, the River Duero dives like a torrent into a deep gorge, emerging only where it spills into the sea, on the Portuguese Atlantic coast, over 200 kilometres to the west.

Port is made in two places along the course of the Douro. Travelling upstream from the river mouth, the *armazéns* or lodges at Vila Nova da Gaia, where most Port is matured, are separated from the vineyards by 70 kilometres of wild but beautiful country. The Upper Douro, or just 'the Douro' to the Port shippers who make frequent visits to their farms or *quintas*, begins where the river (and the noisy little railway which runs alongside) rounds a bend at Barqueiros near Mesão Frio. A mass of steep terraces suddenly come into view, with vineyards clinging to either side of the narrow river valley like hanging gardens.

This *país vinhateiro* or wine country is shielded from the climatic influence of the Atlantic by the Serra do Marão, a range of barren mountains rising to 1,400 metres above sea level. Rainfall, which averages 1,200mm per annum on the coast, rises to over 1,500mm on the mountains and then diminishes sharply as you travel further inland. The landscape changes progressively. The luxuriance of the damp, green *litoral* is replaced by arid hillsides which turn a deep shade of ochre where the fierce summer heat frequently exceeds 40°C.

It is hard to imagine a more inhospitable place to grow grapes. Salazar, the Prime Minister who ruled Portugal between 1932 and 1968, is on record as saying, 'If

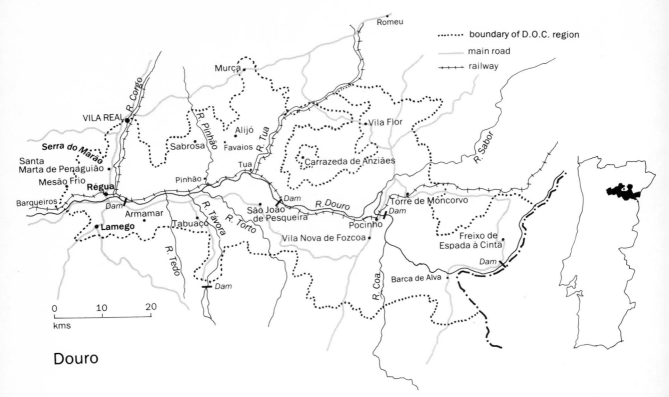

Douro

Portugal exported rock it would be the richest country in the world.' Granite is never very far from the surface in the north of Portugal and it frequently pokes through the thin, poor soils, making much of the land almost unworkable. But in the Upper Douro there is a tract of the country where the geology is different. In the midst of the puce pink which indicates bleak 'eruptive granite' on the geological map of Portugal, there is a narrow patch of green either side of the river. A look at the key shows this to be an outcrop of Pre-Cambrian schist.

This corresponds to Port wine country. The irregular demarcation first drawn around the Douro by Portugal's autocratic but visionary eighteenth-century Prime Minister, the Marquês de Pombal, is closely aligned to the flaky schistous soils that shine almost like steel in the brilliant summer sunlight. This soil is no easier to work than the surrounding granite, though over a period of 300 years it has been worked to much greater agricultural advantage. When labour was plentiful, terraces were hacked from the rock, often with no more than a shovel and a crow-bar giving the vines a metre or two of soil in which to establish a root system. Nowadays bulldozers are frequently seen working the hillsides to prepare the ground for new vineyards, and the uncanny peace and stillness of the valley is shattered from time to time by the sound of dynamite and a small cyclone of dust.

The Douro divides into three officially recognized sub-zones. The Baixo (Lower) Corgo is the most westerly of the three, taking up the portion of the demarcation that lies downstream from the River Corgo, which flows into the Douro close to the town of Régua. It is the coolest and wettest of the three zones, with rainfall at Régua averaging 900mm. The Baixo Corgo therefore tends to produce a lighter style of wine, little of which is ever blended into a high-quality Port. It does, however, account for 18 per cent of the demarcated area, and with over 45 per cent of all the region's vines, it is the most densely cultivated part of the Douro. Most of the wine is used to make standard ruby and tawny Port. These are described more fully on pages 70 and 71.

Upstream from the River Corgo, the Cima (Higher) Corgo is the heart of the demarcated region, centred on the town of Pinhão. Rainfall is significantly lower here (around 700mm) and summer temperatures are a few degrees higher. All the well-known Port shippers own vineyards here and buy in grapes from hundreds of small growers. Although there are a few hillsides that are not planted with vines, principally those abandoned after phylloxera, this is another densely cultivated part of the Douro. Terraces are stacked up the lower reaches of the valleys of the Pinhão and Torto, tributaries of the Douro, and vines crowd into every available space. It is, however, a larger area than the Baixo Corgo, taking up over two-thirds of the Douro demarcation. The Cima Corgo accounts for 40 per cent of all the region's vines and produces most of the quality Port: aged tawnies, LBVs and vintage wines.

The most easterly of the three sub-regions, the Douro Superior, is a relative newcomer. Although it has always been part of the demarcation, it is remote and sparsely populated. Rising labour costs and the need to mechanize viticulture in the Douro have forced many producers to look more closely at the flatter land close to the Spanish border. The Douro Superior is the most arid part of the region. Average rainfall is as low as 400mm at Barca de Alva, and the average temperature is at least 3°C higher than at Régua, fifty kilometres downstream. Allow for the fact that the climate is more extreme, with winters that are often bitterly cold, and the annual average temperature of around 20°C at Barca de Alva disguises oppressive summer temperatures which rise above 40°C. In spite of these climatic extremes, shippers like Cockburn and Ferreira who have pioneered vineyard projects here are happy with the results and are using Douro Superior grapes for high-quality Ports. But the zone, which takes up over 40 per cent of the Douro demarcation, still produces less than 5 per cent of all Port wine.

A total of around 30,000 individual growers farm 33,000 hectares of vines in the Douro. Every vineyard is registered with the Casa do Douro, a quasi-official body which purports to represent the growers. Housed in Régua in a building that looks remarkably like a 1930s cinema, the Casa do Douro keeps a register of the 83,000 individual vineyard sites within the demarcated region. It was set up by the Lisbon government in 1932 as an independent *gremio* or guild to bring order to the Douro region. At the time of writing it still clings on to a number of statutory powers, among them the authorization and grading of vineyards for the making of Port, the distribution of the complicated *benefício* system (see below) and financial support for the twenty co-operatives in the region. The independence of this law-enforcing body has, however, been severely compromised by a business deal whereby the Casa do Douro has bought 40 per cent of the shares in one of the largest Port shippers, Real Companhia Velha (see page 94).

The other shippers protested vehemently and despite a declaration from Portugal's Attorney General that the deal was 'incompatible', the government rubber-stamped the sale. At the time of writing the situation remains confused however. With pressure from Brussels, the Casa do Douro is unlikely to retain its law-enforcing role. A single inter-professional body representing growers, shippers and the government has been mooted to take its place.

Vineyards in the Douro are graded by a complicated points system and classified into six different categories, rated A to F. Twelve different factors are considered, each of which is given a numerical score. The maximum is a positive total of 1,680 points, the minimum a minus score of 3,430. Points are awarded to vineyards on the following criteria:

Altitude: Vineyards situated at an altitude of up to 150 metres are awarded a maximum of 150 points, with a sliding scale allocating a −900 to a vineyard 650 metres or more above sea level. This, together with the locality factor below, effectively rules out Port vineyards on the margins of the demarcated region.

Productivity: A maximum of 120 points is awarded to a vineyard producing less than 600 litres of wine per 1,000 vines, with a negative score of 900 points for a vineyard with a production over 1,800 litres per 1,000 vines.

Nature of the land: 100 positive points for schistous soils, down to −500 for granite and −600 for fertile alluvium. This effectively rules out vineyards planted on any other soil than schist.

Locality: Eighty-four defined sectors of the demarcated region are awarded points, from a positive score of 600 in the Cima Corgo around Pinhão to a negative score of −50 on the high land around the margin of the demarcated region.

Vine training: A maximum of 100 points is awarded to traditional low-trained vines, with a negative score of −500 for high-trained *vinha ramada*. This effectively rules out the use of vines planted for decorative purposes.

Grape varieties: There are between eighty and ninety different grape varieties growing in the Douro, fifty red and nearly fifty white. Grapes are classified into five categories: very good, good, regular, mediocre and bad. Points are attributed from 150 for grapes that are very good to −150 for vines that are considered bad.

Slope: 'Bacchus amat colles,' wrote Virgil, and in the Douro, the best vineyards are those on the steeper slopes. 100 negative points are awarded to vineyards growing on flat land, with a positive score of 105 given to vines growing on slopes in excess of 35°.

Aspect: Depending on the vineyard location in the valley, −30 points are allocated to north-facing vineyards in the cooler Baixo Corgo, with a positive score of 100 for south-facing vineyards in the river valleys around Pinhão.

Density of planting: 50 minus points for densely planted vines (more than 6,900 per hectare). 50 plus points for vines spaced more widely (less than 5,700 per hectare). The Douro's soils are low in nutrients, and dense vineyards are therefore thought to be inappropriate.

Soil and its degree of stoniness: Stony soils are awarded a maximum of 80 points, with no points at all for vineyards with few stones.

Age of vines: As vines age, they make better wines. Vineyards with vines over twenty-five years old win 60 points. Vines that are four or five years old win no points at all.

Shelter: 60 points for sheltered vineyards, no points for vineyards that are unprotected.

After much number-crunching, vineyards with more than 1,200 points are awarded an A grade, with the ranks descending 200 points at a time to grade F vineyards that have won less than 400.

On this basis, the Casa do Douro distributes the *benefício* or benefit to individual growers. The total amount of Port that may be made from the harvest is calculated according to the market conditions and the stocks lying in Oporto. Official permits are then given for each vineyard, detailing the amount of grape that may be fortified to make Port. The amount varies according to the vintage, but as a rule of thumb, A and B grade properties may make up to 550/800 litres of Port per 1,000 vines, down to 400 litres per 1,000 vines for vineyards given an E rating. Any surplus grapes are turned into table wine. F grade vineyards are rarely allowed to make Port at all (see page 103).

This quality control system has served the region well since it was put into action in 1947, but a number of producers think it is time for a change. The most vociferous of these is Miguel Champalimaud, who owns Quinta do Cotto in the Baixo Corgo (see page 90), but other shippers like Cockburn and Ferreira who have invested in vineyards in the Douro Superior also believe that the system should be modified.

The Douro has changed more over the last twenty years than at any time since phylloxera wiped out whole swathes of vines at the end of the nineteenth century. The first and most noticeable change is the river itself. During the 1960s and early

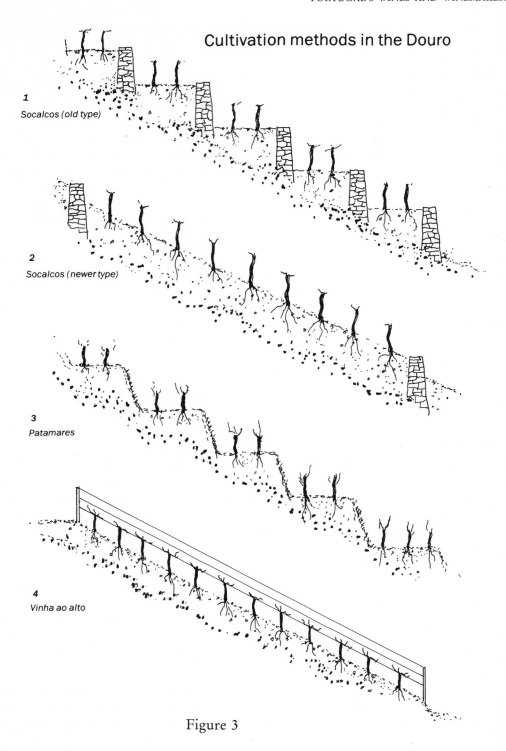

Cultivation methods in the Douro

1
Socalcos (old type)

2
Socalcos (newer type)

3
Patamares

4
Vinha ao alto

Figure 3

1970s the Douro was progressively dammed in five separate places between Oporto and the frontier. The river, once a trickle in summer but a devastating torrent in winter, is now a series of placid lakes which completely cover the narrow valley floor. Some growers believe that the dams have altered the microclimate by increasing the humidity. While there may have been a few localized changes, it is safe to say that the damming of the Douro has not had a detrimental effect on the quality of Port wine in the 1980s.

Methods of cultivation have also changed radically in recent years, transforming the Douro landscape. Labour shortages brought on by mass emigration in the 1960s, along with steadily escalating costs, prompted some growers to look carefully at their vineyards. The traditional terraces or *socalcos* built in the nineteenth century, when labour was cheap and plentiful, became expensive to maintain and were almost impossible to mechanize (Figure 3.1). Likewise, the inclined terraces built earlier this century with lower retaining walls (Figure 3.2) had become expensive to construct and difficult to cultivate. Alternative methods of cultivation had to be found.

Around 1970 the first bulldozers arrived in the Douro, and with them a new form of terracing gouged from the hillside called *patamares* (Figure 3.3). Instead of high retaining walls, the terraces were built with natural ramps bound together by weeds which flourish in the winter months but die off in the summer. With wider spacing between rows of vines and a series of carefully planned tracks leading up the hillside, small tractors can circulate through the vineyard.

Although widely adopted, *patamares* have run into problems. Some have suffered from soil erosion and evaporation, while growers have complained about the lower density of vines (3,500 per hectare compared with 6,000 on the old inclined *socalcos*). Port shippers Ferreira and Ramos Pinto pioneered a simple alternative: *vinha ao alto* (Figure 3.4), vines planted in vertical lines running up and down the natural slope. Tracks crisscross the vineyard, giving access to machines such as the giant cannons that are now used for spraying the vines against disease over the summer months. Like a maths master with a problem, João Nicolau de Almeida of Ramos Pinto illustrates the time that this saves: with a machine to spray the vines, one man can do in ten hours what used to take fifteen men fifteen days! With *vinha ao alto* he can also plant 5,000 vines per hectare, though access and erosion can be a problem with an inclination in excess of 30°, so vertical planting is really appropriate only on more gentle slopes.

There has been more activity in the Douro in the 1980s than at any time since the inhospitable virgin slopes were first colonized by farmers back in the eighteenth century. Whole hillsides, many abandoned after phylloxera, have been carved up and replanted. Much of the activity has been instigated by the World Bank, which set up a programme to aid farmers in 1982. The scheme was originally thought up as a means of helping smallholders in Trás-os-Montes, one of the poorest parts of Europe (see page 189), but it was quickly seized on by growers in the Douro, who were attracted to the low-interest loans on offer. A total of 2,500 hectares of vines have been authorized, restricted to 10 hectares per grower owning A/B grade vineyards. There are further conditions imposed on how and where the new vineyards can be planted. Maximum and minimum altitudes are specified, together with the type of cultivation, depending on the inclination of the slope of the vineyard on the hillside.

The World Bank Scheme also specifies grape varieties. Most growers in the Douro valley, as in the rest of Portugal, have little or no knowledge of the grape varieties growing in their vineyards. All the older plots are planted with a hodge-podge of vines: red growing next to white, Touriga Nacional growing next to something completely unidentifiable. But research into different varieties has come on a long way in the Douro since ADVID (the Associacão para o Desenvolvimento da Viticultura Duriense) was founded in 1982. It counts on the support of eight major shippers and works in close contact with the University of Vila Real. From the eighty-eight different grape varieties that are authorized in the Douro, research among shippers and growers has identified a top five which are now being planted in parcels rather than mixed together. Touriga Nacional, Touriga Francesa, Tinta Barroca, Tinta Roriz and Tinto Cão are now favoured by growers making high-quality Port, each contributing something different but complementary to the final blend. Touriga Nacional provides a good, solid, tannic base, Tinta Roriz brings accidity, Tinto Cão aromatic fruit, Tinta Barroca flesh and Touriga Francesa produces alcoholic wines with a scented character. A full exposé of these and all the main grapes used in making red and white Port can be found in Chapter 3 which covers Portuguese grapes in detail.

The vintage usually begins in the Douro in late September and lasts for around three weeks. The technical side of the wine-making is covered separately on pages 52–57, the romance of the harvest is not. The silence in the valley is broken by gangs or *rogas* of chattering peasant folk who descend on the Douro from outlying villages for the duration of the vintage. Some *rogas* have served the same *quinta* for decades, passing their knowledge and enthusiasm from one generation to another. As the pickers traverse the terraces, gabbled conversations can be heard above the hum of the wine-making equipment, which is silent for the rest of the year. Roads, normally empty, are jammed with farmers delivering truckloads of grapes and the air is filled with the heady aroma of sweet, fermenting must. The end of the harvest is a time for celebration, with *quintas* holding a party for the vineyard workers. Traditionally, a senior member of the workforce presents the *patrão* or owner with an elaborately decorated vine branch called the *ramo*. With much shouting of '*Viva o Patrão*' (long live the owner – something that no one thought would be heard again after the 1974 revolution) and a feast of food and drink, the vintage is over for another year.

The bulk of the new wine is shipped downstream only in the spring following the harvest. At one time flat-bottomed boats called *barcos rabelos* negotiated the rapids to take the wine downstream, but now nearly all the wine leaves the region by road.

Here begins a tale of two cities: Oporto, the city that lent its name to Port, and the town of Vila Nova da Gaia. The two face each other on either side of the river, linked by a two-tier iron road bridge built in 1886. From the upper deck the view of the two cities provides an intriguing counterpoint. On the Oporto side, narrow, grey houses five or six storeys high rise up the hillside towards the cathedral, while on the opposite bank a series of long, low buildings, their roofs blackened by mould, jostle for a position close to the river. This is the *entreposto* or entrepôt of Gaia, where most Port is blended, matured and bottled. Large signs – Warre, Croft, Cockburn, Sandeman – protrude from the rooftops inviting people to visit some famous names of Port. Inside the *armazéns* or lodges, long, cool cellars like cathedral naves are stacked with well-worn 'pipes' or casks. The humidity, usually around 85 per cent, is perfect for ageing Port.

Until 1987, all Port destined for overseas markets had by law to be shipped through the *entreposto*. The rule has now been relaxed to allow Port to be shipped either from Gaia or from the Douro demarcated region. The minimum stock which a Port producer must maintain to be allowed to ship has been reduced, giving single *quintas* the opportunity to export their own wine without having to sell it on to one of the major shippers.

One rule, however, remains firmly on the statute books. The *lei dos dois terços*, or law of two-thirds, restricts any individual Port shipper from selling more than a third of his stock in any one year. In theory this means that Port houses have a three-year stock rotation, though in practice, of course, some Port is sold younger (after about eighteen months in the case of a white Port or basic ruby), while premium wines like aged tawnies mature for considerably longer. However, the *lei dos dois terços* places a heavy burden on some Port shippers. When times have been hard, as they were in the 1960s, a number have found it difficult to finance their stock.

Where the Casa do Douro currently represents growers in the Douro, the body controlling the shippers in Vila Nova da Gaia is the Instituto do Vinho do Porto or IVP. The IVP is a government-run authority whose chairman is a political appointee. Its inspectors have the power to enter any lodge in Gaia to check stocks. Shippers therefore have to keep detailed records to prove to the IVP that quantities of wine coming from the Douro tie up with outgoing shipments. The IVP is also empowered to analyse and taste every shipment of Port before issuing a certificate of origin and the *selo de garantia* which is stuck to the neck of every bottle of Port leaving Oporto. In practice it passes most of the samples that are submitted, including some wines that are clearly substandard. In recent years the IVP has not acted as the guarantor of quality that it purports to be.

The market for Port has changed dramatically over the past thirty years. The

Englishman's wine that used to be drunk up and down the realm, from London clubs to street-corner pubs, became the Frenchman's wine when imports began to exceed those of the United Kingdom in 1963. France now takes nearly 40 per cent of all exports, followed by Belgium, Luxembourg and Holland with over 20 per cent of the market. In the 1980s the United Kingdom fell back to third place in terms of export volume and stands fourth in the world league, taking Portugal's own consumption into account.

But more than 300 years after the first Englishman set up in business in the Douro, the British market is still highly coveted by Port shippers. For although other countries may have overtaken Britain in terms of volume, it is the largest market for high-quality old tawny, late bottled vintage and vintage Port. The Douro, it seems, has a very special relationship with the British, particularly those making Port.

The Wines

Port used to be so simple to understand. Three basic styles – ruby, tawny and vintage – reached merchants' shelves. Then, with the decline in popularity of ruby in the 1960s, the marketeers invented all sorts of new styles and new names, leading to a proliferation of different types of Port.

The legislation on Port labelling is deliberately vague. The Port Wine Institute (IVP) permits seven different loosely defined categories of Port as well as any number of 'special designations'. Words like *reserva* (reserve), *superior* and *velhissimo* (very old) are regularly found on bottles of Port and have become almost meaningless.

Moves are at last being made to simplify the situation. The Exporters' Association (AEVP), in conjunction with the IVP, are talking about a return to a more closely defined system of labelling. But with so many conflicting interests among Port shippers, it will be some time before the much-needed clarification comes about. In the meantime, Port drinkers are forced to cope with numerous confusing, not to say misleading, names.

Ruby

There is something so simple and honest about a good glass of ruby Port. Surely there can't be much wrong with a wine that has been aged in bulk for two or three years and then bottled young, while it still has a deep ruby colour and a strong, fiery personality. Yet the term 'ruby' has acquired a somewhat down-market image. It used to be the Port that the British drank in 'Rover's Return' street-corner pubs, let out with fizzy lemonade to make a long drink. But the 'Port and lemon' market faded in the 1960s and poor old ruby was left on the shelf, tarred with the association of a once-popular tradition that everyone wanted to forget.

But ruby is still the basic Port for many shippers and it is usually their cheapest. Young wines from more than one year are aged in all sorts of vessels (wood, cement and occasionally stainless steel) before being blended together to make the sort of deep-coloured, lively, peppery wine that warms the soul by the fireside on a winter evening. Some wines suffer from being pasteurized to stabilize them before bottling and therefore smell and taste stewed, but good ruby, with its uncomplicated mulberry fruit aromas and flavours, can be an excellent drink.

When searching for a good ruby it is important not to be misled by qualifying adjectives like 'full rich' or 'fine old' on the labels of some brands. What matters ultimately is the intensity of fruit in the glass. Smith Woodhouse and Cockburn make good, inexpensive, unassuming ruby wines.

Tawny

Just to add to the confusion, the word 'tawny' covers very different styles of Port. In theory, tawny implies a wine which has been aged in wood for longer than a ruby until it loses colour and the wine takes on an amber-orange hue. But much of the tawny Port that reaches the shelves today is no older than the average ruby and is consequently on sale, side by side, at the same price. The difference between them is that whereas ruby is made from a blend of big, deep-coloured wines, tawny is often produced from lighter wines grown in the poorer Baixo Corgo vineyards, where grapes rarely ripen to give much depth or intensity of fruit. Carefully controlled autovinification (see page 66) also helps to make paler-coloured wines, and finally the colour may be adjusted further by adding a percentage of white Port so that the wine ends up a washed-out pink rather than an amber-brown. Many bulk tawnies are left up-river for longer than other wines for the heat to speed up the maturation. The resulting wines often display a slight brown tinge on the rim but tend to lack the freshness and primary fruit character associated with a young Port.

Tawny wines have filled much of the gap in the bulk market left behind by the demise of 'Port and lemon'. The French drink inexpensive, light, tawny-style wines as an aperitif, and this has become the bread-and-butter market for many of the larger shippers. But reliance on cut-price 'beret, baguette and Porto' is a risky business in the long term, and some shippers are seeing the merit in moving away from bulk tawny to so-called 'premium' styles.

Aged Tawny

Forget the words 'fine old' on cheap bottles of tawny Port, most of which are neither. 'True' tawnies are aged for longer and therefore cost more. Most are worth the extra. A Port that has matured in cask for six or more years begins to take on a smooth, creamy character as the big, spicy tannins and deep colouring matter begin to fall away. In order to be guaranteed a good tawny, it is wise to look for a wine with an indication of age. Indeed, there are now very few 'true' tawny wines that do not indicate their age on the label as ten, twenty, thirty or even forty years old. These are approximations, as tawny Ports rarely come from a single year. Instead they are made up from a number of different years and the date on the label is therefore an average or, more commonly, a blend tasted and approved by the IVP as conforming to the character expected from a wine that is, say, twenty years old. The legislation does not demand a closer definition.

Most tawnies are made from wines of the very highest quality, wines set aside from undeclared years that might otherwise have ended up in vintage lots. They mature in cask in the cool of the lodges at Gaia until the shipper considers that they are ready to blend and bottle. Labels on these wines state that the wine has matured in wood and give the date of bottling.

This is important, as aged tawny is bottled ready to drink and can deteriorate if it spends too long hanging around. The best time to enjoy the complexity of tawny is therefore as soon as possible after the wine has been bottled. Once the bottle has been opened, the wine oxidizes quite rapidly, losing its delicacy of fruit if it is left on ullage for much over a week. The Port shippers themselves often drink a good aged tawny in preference to any other. The almond and walnut character of a well-aged tawny suits the climate and temperament of the Douro better than the hefty, spicy character of a vintage, which is better adapted to northern climes. Indeed, a glass of tawny served cool from the refrigerator is positively refreshing in the heat of the day.

Aged tawnies will never be cheap, because of the stocks that are needed to back up a label and ensure a consistent style. For this reason, few shippers actively promote aged tawnies for fear of having to fall back on younger wines. But despite the price, 'true' tawny is worth tracking down. The following wines are to be recommended.

Tawny without indication of age: Usually less than 'ten years old' and therefore only just beginning to take on tawny character. Beware of cheap imitations. 'His Eminence's Choice' from Delaforce is a reliable brand.

Ten Years Old: Soft and creamy in style, just beginning to take on the fruit-cake-like subtlety of tawny. Burmester, Dow, Poças Junior and Ramos Pinto all make good ten-year-old wines.

Twenty Years Old: This is where tawny Port reaches its apogee, combining freshness and delicacy with the nuts and figs taste that develops with age. The smaller houses seem to have the stocks to handle this style well: Niepoort, Kopke and Burmester as well as Barros, Fonseca and Ramos Pinto make excellent twenty-year-old tawnies.

Thirty Years Old and Over Forty Years Old: Many wines with labels dated thirty and over forty years old tend to be past their peak, beginning to dry out and losing that exceptional freshness and balance found in a twenty-year-old tawny. Some major shippers, with insufficient stocks of their own, are forced to buy in wines from Douro farmers. These have frequently been aged in poorly maintained casks in the heat of the Douro, and the wines therefore take on a rather baked, oxidized character. But there are exceptions: Graham, Fonseca and Burmester have fine thirty-year-old and over forty-year-old wines.

Vintage

Vintage Port accounts for a tiny fraction of all Port sales (around 1 per cent) and yet it is the wine that receives the most attention and hype. British shippers, in particular, have built vintage Port into a flagship for all to see, declared in an atmosphere of speculation when both the quality and the market are judged to be fit. Port buffs enjoy poring over the merits of different years, while hopeful parents lay down vintages in order that their offspring may have something good to drink.

But all the hype (and expense) in laying down vintage Port belies the fact that it is among the simplest of wines to make. Wines from a single year or vintage are blended and bottled after spending two years in wood. Thereafter, the wine is sold and the consumer takes over nurturing the wine for fifteen, twenty, thirty or more years until the wine is ready to drink. It really is that simple. What sets vintage Port apart from its peers and puts it on a pedestal above the rest is the quality of the grapes from which the wine is made. Only grapes grown in the best-situated Cima Corgo vineyards, picked super-ripe following an outstanding summer, are destined to be made into vintage Port. Even then, nothing is certain until at least a year after the harvest when shippers have had time to reflect. If, after repeated tasting, the wine-maker feels that he has sufficient quantities of high-quality wine to merit the declaration of a vintage, he sends samples to the IVP accompanied by details of just how much wine he intends to release. Only when the shipper has received approval (something of a formality) will he be able to plump for a vintage declaration.

This is a decision which is not reached lightly. Unless the harvest has been a complete disaster, wine of vintage potential is made at the best *quintas* in most years. Quantity may, however, be lacking or the market may simply not be ready to support another vintage. The shipper has to take all these factors into account if the wine is to maintain its prestige once it reaches the open market. All the major houses work closely with one another before they decide to declare.

As hard as the speculators try, there is no law of averages about the regularity of vintage declarations. But, purely as a rule of thumb, on past record three years have been generally declared in a decade. The speculation tends to mount when there are long gaps.

Though by the very nature of the beast there is no excuse for poor vintage Port, there is considerable variation between the great and the good (and occasionally the bad and the ugly as well). Wines from individual shippers and different vintage declarations have their own characteristics; characteristics which put some at the head of the league table while others come well below par. But superlatives are much more common when it comes to describing vintage Port, so the following guide to different years separates the good from – well, the not quite so good.

Asterisks are awarded up to a maximum of five:
***** **an outstanding vintage**
**** **very good, some outstanding wines**
*** **good, all-round vintage**
** **average year; wines sound but generally unexciting**
* **indifferent**

Potential is rated in brackets

1987: Only a few shippers declared. So far the wines look well balanced, with plenty of intense, sweet fruit. Niepoort, Ferreira and Martinez declared rich, sold wines that are worth keeping. **(*)

1985: After a near-perfect summer, wonderfully healthy, ripe grapes were ready to harvest by the middle of September. Bruce Guimaraens, wine-maker at Fonseca, remarked that it was clear from the pungent aroma of the fermenting must that 1985 would be a high-quality year. Nearly all the shippers declared, making 1985 the first universal vintage since 1983. Six years on, the hallmark of the vintage is the power and concentration of the fruit backed up by broad, ripe tannin. A few wines show the heat of the summer and smell slightly roasted, but most are superb. The best of the 1985s need to be kept until the turn of the century and should continue to evolve for another thirty or forty years thereafter. Recommended wines: Cockburn, Fonseca, Graham, Martinez, Taylor. ****(*)

1983: Big, firm-flavoured wines were made in 1983 by the sixteen shippers who chose to declare. Initially they are much less easy to taste than the plump 1985s but most 1983s certainly have the backbone and intensity of fruit to last. It will be fascinating to see which of the two years develops to be the best. Most 1983s need to be kept until the turn of the century, perhaps longer, to allow for the rather austere tannins to soften. Thinking in terms of superlatives, Cockburn's 1983 is probably one of the very best Ports of the 1980s, with Calem, Dow, Fonseca, Gould Campbell, Niepoort, Smith Woodhouse and Warre running not so very far behind. ****(*)

1982: Some shippers chose to declare 1982 in preference to 1983. Most clearly made a mistake. The wines are much softer, lighter and earlier maturing, lacking the depth and structure of either 1985 or 1983. The best will be useful wines to drink while still waiting for the 1983s to come round, but these need keeping until 1994. Calem, Quinta do Côtto, Martinez, Niepoort and Offley Boa Vista will all be good to drink in the medium-term. ✳✳

1980: Of all recent vintages, 1980 is the most undervalued. Prices remain low and, although few of the wines have the structure of the classic 1983s and 1985s, many look as though they will develop well. Most wines tasted in 1991 are close to being ready to drink, with one or two already soft and approachable. Open berry-fruit aromas and flavours are the hallmarks of these attractive wines. Gould Campbell, Graham, Niepoort, Rabello Valente, Smith Woodhouse, Taylor and Warre all made wines that should stand up well through the nineties and into the first decade of the twenty-first century. ✳✳✳(✳)

1978: Two major shippers, Noval and Ferreira, preferred 1978 to 1977. Their wines are sound but not stunning. ✳✳

1976: A few shippers declared under their second labels in 1976. Of these, Fonseca-Guimaraens is by far the most outstanding with many years still to run. It regularly beats most 1975s in comparative tastings including Fonseca.

1977: A cool summer followed by a September heatwave had the grapes in perfect condition by the time it came to the harvest. Twenty-two shippers declared wines which have frequently been compared to 1963 in stature. Certainly the wines have wonderful intensity and depth, with broad, ripe tannins needing time to soften. Most 1977s won't be ready to drink until the end of the 1990s, but should last the first half of the next century. Dow, Fonseca, Graham and Taylor made wines that are turning out to be classics. ✳✳✳✳(✳)

1975: A hot debate still surrounds the wisdom of the 1975 declaration. It was the height of the revolution and was christened the *Verão Quente* (hot summer) both because of the political tempers that were flying out of control at the time and the temperature in July and August. The shippers badly needed a vintage at the time and all the major names declared. But the wines failed to live up to early promise and most are now soft, sweet and entirely ready to drink. One or two are already falling apart. Cálem, Dow and Graham are among the best for drinking now. Quinta do Noval's Nacional is exploding with fruit. ✳✳

1972: The few shippers that declared 1972 (Dow, Offley and Fonseca-Guimaraens) had their wines blighted early on by the alcohol scandal which broke soon after the vintage had been declared. German authorities carrying out routine carbon-dating tests found that the Junta Nacional do Vinho (JNV) had supplied shippers with synthetic alcohol made from coal in Yugoslavia instead of *aguardente* distilled from wine. Though harmless, it did nothing for the reputation of Port at the time. *

1970: The 1970s have come of age, and the best are only just ready to drink (one or two would even benefit from five more years in bottle). Early tastings tended to play down the wines, and they are only now beginning to be judged in their true light: firm though balanced wines with all the grip and staying power of a classic year. Delaforce, Fonseca, Niepoort, Noval and Taylor are all in the classic mould – big, chunky wines with thirty years' life ahead. 1970 was the last generally declared vintage to be shipped in bulk. Subsequent years have all been bottled in Gaia. ****

1967: Four shippers declared 1967 in preference to 1966, with Cockburn and Martinez both following their own idiosyncratic hunch that this was a better year. The wines are lighter and certainly not a match for the long-distance wines that were made in the preceding year. **

1966: History has been unkind to 1966, in the wake of the legendary 1963s. But although the standard across the board is not as high as the 1963 vintage, 1966 produced one or two wines which certainly rate among the all-time greats. The wines are rich, with a wonderful 'bitter chocolate' concentration. Dow and Fonseca and Noval's Nacional are simply stunning and equal, in my mind, the best of the 1963s. ****

1963: Legend has it that 1963 is one of the very best post-war years, and tastings continue to bear this out. The wines are powerful, with layer upon layer of ripe berry fruit backed up by massive, gripping tannins that have taken time to soften. One or two wines are only just ready to drink more than twenty-five years on, and anyone born in 1963 probably has a Port to drink for life. Cockburn, Fonseca, Taylor and Warre have all come up trumps with world-beaters in 1963. Though one or two subsequent years like 1977 and 1985 may come close, so far 1963 is one to beat for the sheer consistency of its mighty wines. Quinta do Noval's 1963 Nacional is one of the best ports ever made. *****

OTHER POST-WAR YEARS
1960: Good wines, some beginning to tire; drink soon. ***

1958: On the whole light wines, many now starting to dry up. **

1955: A classic year declared by all the major shippers. These concentrated wines have developed well and are now rich with deep plain chocolate intensity. Graham, Niepoort and Taylor made outstanding wines for long-term keeping, though most are perfect now. *****

1950: Good though light wines, now rarely seen. Most should have been drunk. ⁕⁕

1948: Big, solid wines with great concentration, made after a hot summer. Most are long-distance Ports with plenty of life ahead, but a few wine-makers had problems controlling fermentation temperatures. The 1948s are now difficult to find. ⁕⁕⁕⁕⁕

1947: High-quality Ports, many still full, rich and drinking well. ⁕⁕⁕⁕

1945: A classic declared by all the major shippers of the time and the first really great year since the twin 1934s and 1935s. Wines like the Graham '45 are still standing up well; rich, deep and still surprisingly 'green' after nearly forty years in bottle. Taylor is also stunning. ⁕⁕⁕⁕⁕

GREAT PRE-WAR VINTAGES

1935: An enormously successful vintage hard on the heels of 1934. Cockburn, Croft and Sandeman still give a good impression of youth with plenty of minty intensity remaining. ⁕⁕⁕⁕⁕

1934: Perhaps not quite up to the standard of 1935, though Fonseca and Noval are still remarkable; rich but elegant in their old age. ⁕⁕⁕⁕

1931: A fantastic year, not generally declared. At the time, the world was in the depths of depression and in no mind to buy vintage Port. Quinta do Noval (tasted in 1989) has an outstandingly deep colour and a long, powerful yet elegant flavour. Niepoort, though similarly concentrated, has a touch of roasted coffee-bean about it. ⁕⁕⁕⁕⁕

1927: A great year universally declared. Fonseca and Taylor (tasted in 1988) are quite magnificent, with the scented, plain chocolate and liquorice aromas and flavours that are characteristic of great vintage Port. Noval and Niepoort are still massive wines. ⁕⁕⁕⁕⁕

Colheita

Colheita means 'harvest' and (by extension) 'vintage' in Portuguese, yet *colheita* wines are very different from what we understand by the word 'vintage' when it appears on a bottle of Port. *Colheitas* are best understood as tawny ports from a single year, bottled with the date of the harvest on the label. The law is, as usual, fairly vague, but *colheita* wines are aged in wood for at least seven years (most are aged for considerably longer) until they take on all the nuances of an old tawny wine. It is not uncommon to find *colheita* Ports from early this century on sale in Portuguese shops, though wines from post-war years tend to be more reliable. All should carry the date of bottling, and it is worth remembering that few go on for ever. Small specialist firms like Burmester, Kopke and Niepoort have preserved the tradition in making very high-quality *colheita* wines. Cálem also have good *colheitas* going back to the 1940s, and Noval bottle some excellent dated tawnies under the name of House Reserve.

Late Bottled Vintage or LBV

A number of companies claim to have invented or, more precisely, revived the tradition of LBV wines, but whoever did it (and Noval, Taylor and Offley all claim the prize) they certainly spawned a style of Port which has been adopted by most shippers in the 1970s and 1980s.

LBV means what it says: a wine from a single vintage, bottled between the fourth and sixth year after the harvest. The problem is that two different styles of LBV wines have evolved. First there are the traditional wines, bottled without any filtration or treatment so that, like a vintage Port, they need to be decanted before serving. These wines tend to be made in good but undeclared years and are ready to drink earlier; four to six years after they have been bottled, though the wine will continue to develop.

But then there's a second style of LBV: wines which have been filtered and cold stabilized before bottling to prevent the formation of sediment. Though that in itself is no bad thing (decanting has always been a nuisance for restaurateurs), heavy-handed filtration removes much of the character from the wine. Most filtered LBVs are therefore a poor substitute for the massive minty style of a traditional LBV. Some, clearly making use of the word 'vintage' and a date on the label, are really no better than a standard ruby. There are now moves afoot to remove 'vintage' from the label and restrict shippers to the term LB together with the date of the harvest. I feel that this would be a positive step to take.

There's rarely anything on the label to distinguish between 'traditional' unfiltered LBVs and other wines that have been treated. Smith Woodhouse and Niepoort both make excellent wines in the traditional style and these are good, inexpensive alternatives to vintage Port. Cockburn, Dow and Graham produce rich, concentrated wines which have been filtered before bottling.

Vintage Character

This is the greatest misnomer. Vintage character Ports are not wines from a single year and few, if any, share the character of vintage wines. Though it is difficult to draw an admission from any of the shippers, vintage character was created, primarily for the British market, to revive the flagging fortunes of ruby, taking away the 'Port and lemon' image and replacing it with one associated with quality and tradition. Again the legislation is deliberately vague but, in theory, vintage character wines are 'premium rubies' aged for five or so years in wood before bottling. Many, however, are made from wines of indifferent character, aged for too long and then filtered and treated before bottling so that they taste washed out and characterless. A good, simple ruby without any of the marketing cachet is often a better alternative. It is time that the IVP, along with the Exporters' Association, took it upon themselves to outlaw this misleading category of wine, though with so many vested interests, especially among the powerful British and multi-national shippers, I find it difficult to see change coming quickly.

Single-*Quinta* Port

The wine-making *château* evolved in France in the eighteenth century. The single wine-making *quinta* is developing in Portugal in much the same way 350 years later.

Although both Quinta do Noval and Offley Boa Vista are well established single-*quinta* wines, Port made exclusively from the wine of an individual property is a fairly new phenomenon. Taylors brought out Quinta de Vargellas in 1958, and over the 1970s and 80s a number of other shippers have followed suit. Most are vintage wines: wines from a single year, aged in wood for two or three years and bottled without filtration so that they throw a sediment. They should be decanted like a vintage Port before serving.

But there are a number of significant differences which distinguish single-*quinta* vintages from declared vintage Ports. First of all, shippers' single-*quinta* Ports tend to be made only in good years which are not destined for declaration. In years which are declared, many of these wines will be the lots that make up the backbone of the vintage blend and are not therefore available for release as wines in their own right. Second, many single-*quinta* Ports are kept back by shippers and sold only when the wine is considered to be ready to drink, perhaps eight or ten years after the harvest.

Single *quintas* or individual vineyards in the Douro were given a fillip in 1986 by a change of legislation. Before that, all Port destined for export had to pass through the *entreposto* at Vila Nova da Gaia, and as this was effectively in the hands of the large shippers, individual producers were prevented from exporting their wines. The relaxation of this protective law opened the way for a number of small vineyard owners who, in the past, had been restricted to selling their wines to large firms. A number of single-vineyard wines like Miguel Champalimaud's Quinta do Cotto, the Vinagre family's Quinta da Romaneira and the Bergqvists' Quinta de la Rosa have since achieved limited success.

The large shippers with their established marketing networks have had much more instant success in launching their own single-*quinta* wines. Some, however, have mixed views about the long-term merits of the idea. While most support the concept, a few are firmly against this break with tradition and fear the fragmentation of Port production. But with so many houses launching wines from *quintas* that were previously hidden from public view, it seems as though another new category of Port has become firmly established. It remains to be seen whether these highly individual wines attract the same level of attention as the classed growth properties in Bordeaux. If they do, the following wines will rank highly in any classification: Quinta do Bomfim (Dow), Quinta da Cavadinha (Warre), Quinta da Eira Velha (Cockburn),

Quinta do Panascal (Fonseca) and Quinta de Vargellas (Taylor).

Finally, it is worth remembering that by no means all single-*quinta* Ports are vintage wines. Both Ferreira and Ramos Pinto make single-*quinta* tawnies. Quinta da Ervamoira and Quinta do Bom Retiro are, respectively, ten- and twenty-year-old tawnies from Ramos Pinto, while Quinta do Porto is a single-vineyard ten-year-old made by Ferreira.

For more information on vineyards shipping their own wine, see the section on wine-makers on page 81.

Crusted or Crusting Port

Crusting Port is so called because of the crust or deposit that it throws in bottle. In spite of the rather 'crusty' establishment name, it is a fairly recent creation thought up by British shippers to appeal to the enthusiast for vintage Port, though the coveted word does not appear on the label. This is because crusting Ports are not wines from a single year or vintage but blends from a number of years, bottled young with little or no filtration. The wines continue to develop in the bottle, throwing a sediment or crust in much the same way as a vintage Port so that the wine needs to be decanted before it is served.

Rather like traditional LBVs, many crusted or crusting Ports offer an excellent alternative to vintage, providing the Port buff with a full-bodied, dark, concentrated wine at a fraction of the price. So far this style has not been abused. Dow make an excellent example, packed with penetrating fruit.

Garrafeira

The word *garrafeira*, meaning 'private cellar' or 'reserve', is more commonly associated with Portuguese table wines than with Port. Just one shipper, the Dutch family firm of Niepoort, continues to support a very worthwhile tradition making *garrafeira* ports. These are wines from a single year aged for a short time in wood, followed by a longer period spent in five- or ten-litre glass demijohns colloquially referred to as *bon-bons*. After twenty, thirty or even forty years or more in glass, the wine is decanted off its sediment and rebottled in conventional 75cl bottles. An example is Niepoort's 1967 Port which was 'bottled' (i.e. put into glass demijohns) in 1972 and decanted in 1981. The wine combines depth of fruit with a smooth, silky texture and rarefied flavours akin to milk chocolate.

White Port

'The first duty of port is to be red' said Ernest Cockburn. The history of port is littered with rather pompous sayings, but this one rings with more than a note of truth.

White Port is made in much the same way as red except that the grapes are white and skin maceration during fermentation is much shorter or (in many instances) does not take place at all. *Aguardente* is added to arrest the fermentation, producing a pale yellow-gold wine, usually medium-sweet with a fat, neutral, grapey character. Although a glass of white Port can taste good in the Douro when served chilled with a twist of lemon and a dish of salted almonds, most wines are fairly insipid. It is wood ageing that lends character to white Port, turning it gold in colour and giving the wine an incisive, dry, nutty tang. But few wines ever see the inside of a cask nowadays, and most commercial brands are left in cement or stainless steel and then bottled after eighteen months or two years. These wines have little to recommend them; clean they may be, but they are lacking in character, with a mild, sometimes slightly peppery flavour.

Most white Ports contain a certain amount of residual sugar, even those labelled 'dry' or 'extra dry'. Intensely sweet wines, made for the Portuguese market, are labelled *lagrima* meaning 'tears' because of their viscosity and unctuousness. Another category, *leve seco* or 'light dry', has recently found favour among shippers seeking to boost their exports. These are wines with an alcohol content of around 16.5 or 17° compared to the traditional 20°. *Manzanilla* or *fino* sherry is a much more exciting alternative.

Barros, Noval and Taylor all make good, traditional white Ports with a slightly almond-like character from being aged in oak.

Moscatel

Moscatel, one of over thirty different grapes used for making white Port, is occasionally used on its own to make a fortified white wine. There are significant amounts of moscatel growing in vineyards around Favaios near Alijó. The local co-operative makes a rich, grapey Moscatel de Favaios, most of which is sold in local bars and shops. Niepoort produce a sweet white Port from Moscatel which is amber in colour from prolonged ageing in cask.

The Wine-makers

Port is made by the shippers themselves, most of whom own vineyards in the Douro, as well as by farmers and co-operatives. Most small farmers, especially those in the Baixo Corgo, deliver their grapes to one of twenty-two co-operatives that have been set up in the region since 1950. Although you rarely see their names on a label, co-ops make about 40 per cent of all Port. Most of it is sold on to shippers for their inexpensive brands.

Andresen

This small shipping group bottles wines under the names of Mackenzie, A. P. Santos and Vinhos do Alto Corgo.

Barros Almeida

This, one of the larger but less well-known shippers, is a relative newcomer on the scene. It was set up in its present form in 1919 and now includes the older firms of Hutcheson, Feist, Feuerheerd, Vieira da Sousa, Santos Junior, the Douro Wine Shippers' Association and Kopke. Only Kopke retains a measure of independence; the others have become brands.

The Barros Almeida empire was built up by Manuel Barros, who started out as an office boy at Almeida & Co. This is now run by the third generation of the Barros family.

Barros Almeida have two properties in the Douro: Quinta Dona Matilde, by the dam just above Régua, and Quinta de São Luiz, upstream on the south bank of the Douro on the way to Pinhão. This is their chief vinification centre, making around half the company's wines. The remainder is bought in, mainly from the high São João de Pesqueira and Nagozelo districts.

The bulk of Barros wines are young rubies and tawnies destined for the French and Portuguese market, but their real strength lies in stocks of aged tawny and *colheita* wines. They set aside high-quality wines for *colheitas* in most years, bottling to order after ten, twenty or even fifty years. Their 1937 *colheita* wine is still rich and concentrated but has nutty, spicy elegance from ageing in wood. Barros declare frequent vintages and the wines tend to be light and early maturing.

Borges & Irmão

Borges & Irmão are active throughout the Portuguese wine trade and now sell over a million cases a year, mostly table wine. The company was founded by two Borges brothers who, around the turn of the century, set themselves up trading in wine, tobacco, matches and textiles. They also founded a bank, making Borges & Irmão one of the best-known names in Portugal. But the story doesn't end there. In 1975, a year after the 25 April revolution, all Portuguese banks were nationalized and with them went subsidiary companies. In the confused political situation since then, Borges & Irmão has had to face up to an uncertain future as successive governments talk about ways of returning Portugal's moribund state sector to private ownership. At the time of writing, the directors of the company have no idea what will happen.

Borges own three major properties in the Douro. Quinta de Junco, in the Pinhão valley, is used for their vintage blends, with wines from Soalheira and Roncão being used to make ten- and twenty-year-old tawnies. Vintage wines like the 1979 Quinta de Junco are light and early maturing, while Borges tawnies are unreliable. The wines are sold mainly on the Portuguese market.

Burmester

Finding Burmester is like finding a well-kept secret. Hidden up an alley in the heart of the Vila Nova da Gaia *entreposto*, Burmester's small, immaculately kept lodge is the source of some remarkably high-quality wines.

The Burmesters came to Portugal from Germany in 1730 and the company is now run by the Gilbert family, who are direct descendants. They have no vineyards of their own, but instead buy in their best wines from small farmers in the Douro. This, they say, gives them more flexibility.

Although Burmester declare vintage Ports, their most exciting wines are old tawnies and *colheitas*. Being a small firm, they are able to maintain a consistent quality more easily than large companies saddled with well-known brands. Burmester's ten-year-old is delicate but rich, while their twenty-year-old tastes fresh but dry and nutty. Gilbert's and Souham's are subsidiary Burmester brands.

Butler, Nephew

Founded in 1789, this well-established shipper has been consigned to relative obscurity first by Gonzalez Byass and now by Vasconcelos, who bought both firms in 1983.

Cálem

Joaquim Manuel Cálem is one of the best-known figures in the Port trade, partly because the red Ferrari he drives is a talking point in Oporto society. Joaquim Manuel and his daughter Maria da Assunção are descendants of the Cálems who established the firm in 1859. They continue to run the business, along with other interests, with considerable dexterity, and have recently recruited Jeremy Bull, formerly of Taylor's, to handle the wine-making.

Cálem's wines come from eight well-placed *quintas* around the Pinhão and Torto valleys in the heart of the Douro. The best known of these is Quinta da Foz, stacked up the hillside above where the River Pinhão joins the Douro. Foz (meaning river mouth) provides the backbone for Cálem's high-quality, concentrated vintage blends, and for more than twenty years has also made an excellent single-*quinta* wine. Ten-, twenty-, thirty- and forty-year-old tawnies are of a high standard, but Cálem's best-known wine is a young tawny called Velhotes or Old Friends, which has established itself as the brand leader on the home market.

Churchill Graham

Johnny Graham left Cockburn's in 1981 and bravely set up his own firm (the first new Port house for more than fifty years), naming it after his wife, Caroline Churchill, and himself. He ran into difficulties early on after the Symingtons, who had bought Johnny's old family firm of W. & J. Graham in 1970, threatened legal action if he did not remove the 'Graham' name from the label. With the British-sounding name of Churchill, a lodge rented from Taylor's and a shoestring budget, Johnny Graham quickly gained a reputation for quality wines. Now, with a new lodge high above the river, Churchill Graham has become an established part of the

Port scene.

The firm has no vineyards of its own, but buys in wine from six *quintas* belonging to the Borges de Sousa family. The best known of these is Quinta da Agua Alta, adjoining Offley's Quinta da Boa Vista, which was launched as a single-*quinta* wine in 1983. Wines from other *quintas*, mainly in the Pinhão and Roncão valleys, are blended into a range of different Ports which include a good seven-year-old dry white, vintage character and crusted wines. Churchill Graham declared its first vintage in 1982, and since then they have made a rich, powerful 1985. They are planning to launch a ten-year-old tawny as soon as they have built up sufficient stocks. A word of warning: some of Churchill's earlier wines suffer from high levels of volatile acidity which tends to mar the fruit.

Cockburn Smithies

Over the past thirty years, Cockburn's has emerged from the relative obscurity of being a bulk shipper to being the brand leader on the British market. Clever television advertising, playing on the pronunciation of the name of the firm, has shot Cockburn's into the limelight at a time when many other Port shippers have been resting on their laurels.

Much of the credit for this change of direction must go to Harvey's (and subsequently Allied Lyons), who bought Cockburn's in 1962. Contrary to the policies of some of the multi-nationals who were buying up shippers at that time, Allied maintained the direct involvement of the Smithies and the Cobbs, both of whom had been running the firm for successive generations. John Smithies, a descendant of Henry Smithies who became a partner in 1854, retired in 1970, while Peter Cobb, whose family joined Cockburn's in 1863, still manages the firm.

Part of Cockburn's success must be attributed to its wide range of high-quality wines, from good ruby to some stunning vintages in recent years. Gordon Guimaraens, the tall, lean brother of portly Bruce, wine-maker at Fonseca, looks after the production at Cockburn's three wineries, spread across the Douro at Fozcoa, Tua and Lamego. The company also has three substantial *quintas* in the Cima Corgo and has pioneered the move east with a 250-hectare vineyard project at Vilariça, close to the Spanish border on the high plateau north of the Douro. There Miguel Corte Real is leading a research project into different grape varieties, their compatibility with various rootstocks and clonal selection. They have already identified over 150 different clones of Touriga Nacional.

Cockburn's largest brand is still their Fine Old Ruby, though over recent years a good vintage character style of wine, Special Reserve, has been catching up. During the 1970s and early 1980s the company had a rather eccentric view about vintage declarations, missing out the 1977s and 80s which were generally declared by other shippers. When Cockburn's at last decided to declare the 1983 they came back with a vengeance and produced a stunning wine which is sure to go down as one of the greatest wines of the decade. A single-*quinta* wine, from the Newman family's Quinta da Eira Velha, has recently joined the ranks of Cockburn.

Port shippers Martinez Gassiot (see below) were bought by Cockburn in 1961 and are now also part of Allied Lyons.

Croft

Wines from one of the oldest and greatest names in Port have so often been disappointing in recent years. The firm was founded in 1678 and became part of Gilbey's in 1911. Gilbey's were subsequently bought up by IDV (International Distillers and Vintners), and Croft is now run as a sub-division of Grand Metropolitan.

All this direction from above has obviously not been good for Croft, who seem to have lost their way when it comes to making quality wines. The firm owns a splendid property in the Douro, Quinta da Roeda, which provides the backbone for their vintage blends, though nothing spectacular has been declared in recent years. Croft Distinction, on the other hand, is a reliable tawny with an age of about eight years.

Delaforce

Delaforce was a family-owned company until 1968 when, unable to finance the two-thirds stock ratio during those bleak years, they sold out to IDV who also own Croft. The firm still has a strong family input from brothers David and Richard Delaforce, the fifth generation of this Huguenot family to have worked in Oporto.

Delaforce have a long-term agreement with the owners of Quinta da Corte, a beautifully sited terraced vineyard in the Torto valley. This was launched as a single-*quinta* wine, starting in 1978, and also provides the backbone for their vintage wines. Sadly, recent vintages seem to have suffered in much the same way as Croft, tending to be lighter, short-distance wines in comparison with those from other shippers. You have to go back to 1970 Delaforce to find a big, concentrated wine in the classic mould. His Eminence's Choice is a good aged tawny with about eight years in cask.

Dow

Dow is the well-established brand for wines produced by the firm of Silva & Cosens, and is called after James Dow, who entered the firm as a partner in 1877. But in the twentieth century the firm has been much more closely associated with the fortunes of the Symingtons, who first took a share of Dow in 1912.

The Symington family, who also own Warre, Graham, Smith Woodhouse, Quarles Harris and Gould Campbell, are careful to maintain the identity of Dow as an independent shipper with its own style of wine. Silva & Cosens bought Quinta do Bomfim at Pinhão in 1890 and, over the years, wines from the property have formed the backbone of Dow's vintage Ports in declared years. Dow's wines are a personal favourite of mine; they are made in a dry, often austere style which seems to add an extra dimension to their depth and intensity of fruit. Both 1977 and 1966 vintages are excellent examples of the massive yet tight concentration that is very much the hallmark of Dow.

Other wines from Dow are similarly big, firm and dry. Their crusted Ports share the breadth of some shippers' declared vintages while other wines like their LBV and vintage character are rich and packed with fruit. Quinta do Bomfim, which serves as the central winery for the Symington group, has now been launched as a single-*quinta* Port, starting off with the 1978 vintage.

Ferreira

Foi você que pediu (was it you who asked for) *Porto Ferreira*? That is the simple but effective advertising slogan that has made Ferreira the market leader in Portugal, with over 20 per cent of all Port sales. Until 1987 the firm was owned by descendants of Dona Antónia Adelaide Ferreira, *grande dame* of the Douro in the latter half of the nineteenth century. Ferreira, or Ferreirinha as the company has affectionately been called ever since, now belongs to Mateus Rosé producers Sogrape, though one or two members of the original family have retained their involvement with the firm.

Ferreira own three superb properties in the Douro. Quinta do Seixo and Quinta do Porto face each other across the river, not much more than a stone's throw from Pinhão, while the third, Quinta da Leda, is situated high up in the Douro Superior close to the Spanish border. All Ferreira's properties have been the subject of considerable research and investment in the 1980s. They pioneered the *vinha ao alto* or vertical system of planting, and transformed the view from Pinhão with a shiny stainless steel winery perched high above the confluence of the Douro and the Torto. This has become their principal wine-making centre. Ferreira also buy in wines from a number of other properties belonging to the family, among them Valado, Porrais and Meão. Until recently they had the use of Quinta do Vesúvio, one of the largest and most stately properties in the Douro, but now the portrait of Dona Antónia stares down on the Symingtons, who were the highest bidders when the property was put up for sale in 1989.

Ferreira is well known for aged tawny. Quinta do Porto is a reliable ten-year-old made from grapes grown on the estate and trodden in *lagares*. Twenty-year-old Duque de Bragança is blended from the wines of a number of properties, notably Quinta do Roriz, belonging to the van Zellers, cousins of the owners of Noval. The wine combines the richness of sun-dried fruit with an almond and walnut character brought on by extended age in cask. Duque de Bragança is consistently seen as a benchmark among tawnies.

With this reputation for aged tawnies, Ferreira's vintages are frequently underrated. Wines from the 1970s and 1980s are well structured, with staying power and sweet, spicy depth. But slogans sell volume, and best-sellers like 'superior' tawny and Dona Antonia's 'Personal Reserve' have much less to offer.

Ferreira are also important producers of Douro table wine with one of Portugal's best red wines, Barca Velha. This is covered in the next chapter.

Fonseca Guimaraens

The Guimaraens family began making Port in 1822, and Bruce Guimaraens, together with his son David who has recently entered the firm, are the fourth and fifth generations to work at Fonseca. Since 1948 the company has been owned by Taylor, but over this period the two houses have succeeded in maintaining separate identities and different styles of Port.

This is largely due to the ebullient Bruce Guimaraens, vice-president and wine-maker at Fonseca, who is devoted to the Douro and makes some of the finest of all Ports. Fonseca's best-known wine is Bin No. 27, a ripe-flavoured premium ruby-style wine with plenty of honest fruit. But the firm reigns supreme with some excellent aged tawnies and vintages which often rank above all others in blind tastings. Fonseca's vintage Ports are remarkable in that they combine both power and finesse. 1985, 1977, 1966, and 1927 are classic rapier-like wines, the hallmark of Fonseca. Wines from lesser years sold under the Guimaraens label are similarly well made but tend to lack the depth and concentration of Fonseca. Nevertheless, the 1978, 1976, and 1967 are excellent value.

Fonseca own two properties, Quinta do Cruzeiro and Quinta do Santo António, both well located in the Val de Mendiz above Pinhão. Wines from the two vineyards, amounting to just over 20 hectares, together account for about 80 per cent of Fonseca's vintage blend. A third property, Quinta do Panascal on the south side of the Douro, was acquired by Fonseca in a run-down condition in 1978. When replanting is finished it should count among the best Douro *quintas*, adding another 27 hectares of vines to the firm's vineyard portfolio.

Feuerheerd

Founded in 1815 by a German, Feuerheerd has been relegated to an obscure brand belonging to Barros Almeida. The firm used to own Quinta de la Rosa, but this has remained with the Bergqvists, descendants of the Feuerheerd family, who have recently launched their own single-*quinta* wine (see below).

Gonzalez Byass

Sherry giant Gonzalez Byass sold its Port interests to Vasconcelos in 1983. The brand has been little used in recent years, but Ports from the 1960s and 1970s occasionally turn up at auction. The 1963 is an excellent wine and often underpriced.

Gould Campbell

This is one of six companies belonging to the Symington group, collectively the largest single Port shippers. Gould Campbell is a relative unknown and is often thought of as a *sous-marque* of the more famous Symington brands. The name is used mainly for big, beefy vintage Ports which are often excellent value. For example, the 1983 Gould Campbell is a tight, austere wine with more depth than many of its better-known peers.

W. & J. Graham

Graham is one of the great names of Port. The firm began as a textile business and entered the wine trade rather by chance, after accepting a few pipes of Port in lieu of a bad debt. Until 1970 the firm was family-owned but, like so many Port firms, Graham's fell on hard times and the business was sold to the Symingtons.

Peter Symington, wine-maker and blender for the Symington group, is at pains to point out the differences between wines from Graham and those from other companies owned by the family. Graham tends to make a sweeter, more succulent style of wine than either Dow or Warre. This is best illustrated by their vintage Ports, which are consistently rich with ripe fruit backed up by a rod of tannin. 1985, 1963 and 1945 Graham are wines in the classic mould, balancing intensely sweet fruit and beguilingly firm, powerful tannin. Graham's LBVs are similarly fat, sweet and full of fruit, though lacking the depth of unfiltered wines like Smith Woodhouse.

Traditionally, most of the wine for Graham's vintage Port originated from Quinta dos Malvedos at Tua. This was hived off from the company and bought by the Symingtons only in 1981, by which time the 130-hectare property was making a few pipes of Port. Other wines are therefore bought in from nearby *quintas* and vineyards in the Torto valley. Confusingly, Graham's Malvedos, their excellent second-tier vintage Port, is not a single-*quinta* wine but a brand blended from a number of vineyards.

Gran Cruz

Almost an unknown in English-speaking markets, Porto Cruz is the largest single brand in France, putting the firm among the top ten houses with exports of some 700,000 cases a year. The company holds few stocks of its own. Instead it simply buys, blends and bottles wines made by other shippers, a practice that has proved to be extremely profitable for its Portuguese owners.

Cruz Ports are mostly the light, young, tawny-style wines favoured by the French, who drink them like a red vermouth as an aperitif.

Richard Hooper & Son

Hooper is an old name in the Port trade recently revived by Royal Oporto, who bought the company in 1951. Most of the wines are in the same league as those of

Royal Oporto, and are often badly flawed as a result of careless wine-making.

Hunt Roope
Ferreira bought Hunt Roope in 1956 from the Newman family, who kept Quinta da Eira Velha. For a time the name Hunt Roope virtually disappeared, but it has recently been revived. Quinta do Caedo, the property that has supplied Hunt Roope for over a century, has recently been acquired to ensure its continued presence in vintage blends. All the wines are bottled under the brand name of Tuke Holdsworth.

Hutcheson
This old-established firm was bought by the Barros family in 1927 and is now little more than a brand within the Barros group (see above). Few of the wines are of more than limited interest.

Quinta do Infantado
Situated on the right bank of the Douro, close to Ferreira's Quinta do Porto and Offley's Quinta da Boa Vista, there can be no doubt that Infantado is capable of making good Port. So far, though, I have found the wines disappointing.

Quinta do Infantado was one of the first privately owned properties in the Douro to make and market its own wines. The Roseira family, who bought the vineyard at the end of the nineteenth century, launched their own single-*quinta* wine in 1979. At the time legislation prohibited them from exporting the wine unless it was shipped directly from the *entreposto* in Gaia, so until the rules were changed in 1986, permitting individual estates to ship directly from the Douro, Quinta do Infantado was limited to the home market.

Now the Roseira family are exporting a wide range of Ports, from ruby through aged tawny to LBV and vintage. Although most of the wines are sound, many have roasted aromas and taste hard and ungenerous.

Kopke
Nicolau Kopke first came to Portugal in 1638, founding what is now the oldest Port house still in existence. It was bought by the Barros Almeida group (see above) in 1953 but is still run as a separate entity. Kopke's best wines come from the beautifully sited Quinta de São Luiz, on the south side of the Douro between Régua and Pinhão. Their aged tawny and *colheita* wines can be excellent. Recent vintages, with their backbone from São Luiz, are also good.

Martinez Gassiot
Martinez belongs to the category of old-established Port firms which keep a low profile both in Portugal and on export markets. The company was extremely successful in the last century, shipping Port in bulk for customers who bottled the

wine under their own label. Throughout much of the twentieth century, Martinez was competing with Cockburn's, another successful bulk shipper. Ironically the two fell under the same ownership after Harvey's, already the principal shareholder in Martinez, bought Cockburn's in 1962. Both companies are now run as a joint venture by Allied Lyons, with Gordon Guimaraens (the brother of Fonseca's Bruce) as wine-maker.

Unlike Cockburn's, Martinez has rarely been allowed to stand on its own two feet and has been retained for 'own label' sales. A small amount of Port is, however, bottled under the Martinez label and the wines can be stunning. Aged tawnies like the twenty-year-old Directors and vintages like the 1985 stand up among the best. With little or no image in the market place, Martinez Ports tend to offer good value for money and are worth seeking out.

Messias

This family-owned company entered the Port business in the 1930s and now runs it in tandem with table wine production in Bairrada (see page 135). Messias have a substantial vineyard holding in the Douro with two *quintas*. Quinta do Rei and Quinta do Cachão, amounting to more than 120 hectares of vines. Their wines tend to be unreliable, and Quinta do Cachão is often better as a table wine than it is as Port.

Montez Champalimaud

Is Miguel Champalimaud a *bête noir* among Port shippers or just a 'stalking horse'? Either way, he certainly has something against the status quo and has been waging a lone crusade to change things. Champalimaud takes a particular dislike to the present vineyard classification system, which rates Cima Corgo properties much more highly than the Baixo Corgo *quintas* west of Régua. The system, he believes, is manipulated by the big Port shippers.

He may have a point. Quinta do Côtto, belonging to Champalimaud, is 5 kilometres downstream from Régua. Vineyards surrounding the rambling seventeenth-century house produce some good Port. 1982 is the only vintage that he has released, but in comparative tastings it holds up well against the competition. Some of his table wines (see page 106) are even better, among the best in Portugal. If Champalimaud would stop ranting, more people might sit up and take him seriously.

Morgan Bros.

Morgan was bought by Croft in 1952 and is now mainly an own-label supplier to customers in the United Kingdom. Occasional vintages and aged tawnies are well made and of good quality.

Niepoort

Niepoort is a discovery. For five generations this Dutch-owned family firm has been hoarding wines in cramped cellars near the waterfront at Gaia. With stocks of fine Port dating back to the early part of the century, Niepoort is probably the most under-appreciated of all Port producers.

The firm was founded in 1842 and is now run by a father-and-son team, Rolf and Dirk van der Niepoort. They both share a commitment to quality, adopting a 'small is beautiful' philosophy. Until recently Niepoort possessed no vineyards of its own. Instead it relied on a number of small farmers in the Pinhão valley. In 1988 and 1989 Niepoort bought two properties, Quinta de Napoles and Quinta do Carril, overlooking the River Tedo, giving them 50 hectares of A grade vines. Dirk, who worked for six months in the Napa valley, is in charge of replanting the vineyards and making the wines.

Niepoort are best known for their tawnies, but from simple, spicy ruby to vintage Ports exploding with fruit and tannin, Niepoort ship small quantities of excellent wines that match and occasionally better many of the big names. Niepoort's 1970, 1955 and 1927 count among the best wines of those vintages; concentrated wines with the power and depth to develop further in bottle. Their *colheitas* and ten- and twenty-year-old tawnies are complex wines of similarly high quality, and traditional, unfiltered LBVs made in lesser years are better than many shippers' declared vintages. Niepoort also have a stock of *garrafeira* Ports, which age in wood and then in glass demijohns before being 'decanted' into bottles (see page 80).

The main markets for Niepoort's wines are Holland, Belgium, Germany and Denmark. They are rarely seen in English-speaking countries, where they deserve to be better known.

Quinta do Noval

Noval is the name both of a vineyard and of a shipper exporting wine. It was founded in 1813 and was known until 1973 as António José da Silva. The company has a chequered past, with family disagreements reflected in the quality of some of the wines. After a catastrophic fire in 1981 which destroyed 350,000 litres of stock along with all the company's records, Noval is very much back on an even keel. It is now run by a brother-and-sister team, Cristiano and Teresa van Zeller, who took on the company in 1982 when they were both in their early twenties.

Taking advantage of the change in legislation in 1986, Noval has moved out of Gaia. A new lodge, referred to unkindly by some as the 'great white elephant', has been constructed at the foot of the *quinta* above Pinhão. Noval experimented with ageing wines in the heat of the Douro, and Cristiano asserts that it makes no difference to the wine whatsoever.

Thirty per cent of the production originates from Noval's own vineyards, the remainder being bought in from properties scattered all over the Douro. Vintage

Ports are made from grapes grown on Noval's showpiece property stacked up above Pinhão. The wine is made in a traditional manner, trodden in deep stone *lagares*. Noval's reputation suffered from weak declarations in 1978 and 1982, though the 1985 vintage demonstrates that the wine-making is back on form. LB is a reliable premium ruby wine accounting for most of the firm's exports, while aged tawnies and *colheitas* labelled House Reserve are often excellent.

But Noval's most prestigious wine is the Nacional, made in exceptional years from the grapes of 5,000 ungrafted vines. The vines, mainly Touriga Nacional, Tinta Francisca, Tinto Cão and Sousão, lie on either side of the drive to the house. Their average age is around thirty years, so it is a mistake to refer to them, as many people do, as 'pre-phylloxera'. The fact that they are not grafted on to American rootstock makes them less vigorous than the surrounding vines and this, along with their age, combines to yield tiny quantities of fruit. The wines, as a result, are the most concentrated of all vintage Ports, with a deep, opaque colour when young and an almost overpowering concentration of liquorice and bitter chocolate fruit. The 1931 Nacional is legendary for being the most expensive bottle of Port ever sold. The 1963, 1966 and 1970 Nacional are among the best vintage Ports that I have had the good fortune to taste: massive wines, intensely ripe with flavours of allspice shrouded by tannin. Noval's Nacional is available only on a strict allocation basis, and bottles rarely come to be auctioned.

Offley Forrester

Offley is a firm with a complicated past. It was founded in 1737 and is historically associated with Baron Joseph James Forrester, sage of the Douro for thirty years until he was drowned in the rapids at Cachão da Valeira in 1862. One hundred years later Offley was bought by Sandeman, who then sold half the shares to Martini & Rossi in 1965. They picked up the remainder of the company in 1983 after Sandeman was sold to Seagram.

Offley's best Ports originate from Quinta da Boa Vista, 100 hectares of vines on the north bank of the Douro downstream from Pinhão. Until 1987 all Offley's declared vintages were single-*quinta* wines, dense and full of fruit but lacking the depth to place them in the top league. 1983 and 1985 Boa Vista are both good middle-distance wines, packed with peppery fruit. Ten- and twenty-year-old tawnies sold under the Baron de Forrester label are usually made to a high standard, though the Duke of Oporto brand, which constitutes most of Offley's sales, is frequently disappointing. It is sold mainly in Italy and Portugal. According to Jorge Guimarães, Offley's affable export manager, the United Kingdom has proved to be a difficult market.

Osborne

Osborne's instantly recognizable black bull logo, strategically placed along roadsides in Spain, is rarely seen in Portugal, for the company is more closely tied to sherry and brandy than it is to Port. But although Osborne has no vineyards of its own, it does now own a lodge in Gaia, which the company recently bought from Quinta do Noval. The company is actively seeking to diversify and build up a range of Port, though with little or no reputation in the Port trade they face an uphill task.

Poças Junior

The Poças family are relative newcomers to the Port business, having set up in business in 1918. They have succeeded in remaining independent and have recently invested in a brand new lodge, built above the established *entreposto* in Vila Nova da Gaia.

Of their 200,000 cases production, most is young tawny and ruby destined for French and Belgian markets. But Poças also make small quantities of high-quality aged tawny Port which they mature in the Douro without any detriment to the wine. Vintage Ports, first launched in 1960, are medium-bodied for mid-term drinking.

Poças have three vineyards of their own: Quinta da Santa Barbara and Quinta das Quartas, both near Régua, and Quinta de Vale de Cavalos, upstream in the Douro Superior. Together they account for around 15 per cent of the company's total production. The remainder is bought in from small farmers and co-operatives. Their wines are bottled under four different labels. Besides Poças Junior there are also the subsidiary brands of Pousada, Lopes and Seguro.

Quarles Harris

Founded in 1680, Quarles Harris is one of the oldest of all the Port houses. It was taken over by Warre (see below) in the eighteenth century and consequently now makes up part of the second tier of Symington Ports, along with Gould Campbell and Smith Woodhouse. The name may be obscure and is often incorrectly pronounced (it rhymes with 'squalls'), but the wines are well made and often well priced. Recent vintages have been excellent. Quarles Harris 1980 and 1983 are mainstream wines that will be ready to drink five or so years before the wines from the top tier of Symington Ports.

Adriano Ramos Pinto

Throughout the 1980s, Ramos Pinto has been at the forefront of research and development. Twin brothers Ricardo and João Nicolau d'Almeida exude enthusiasm for all the work that they have carried out on Ramos Pinto's five Douro *quintas*. But a visit to the firm's brightly painted, ornate lodge on the waterfront at Gaia belies all the development that has taken place. Stepping in through the door is like stepping back in time – all tiles and polished mahogany, with barely a computer in sight.

The success of Ramos Pinto dates back to the latter part of the last century, when the firm was set up to supply the lucrative Brazilian market. At the time the company instituted some pretty aggressive marketing, with a flourish of fairly *risqué* posters showing an orgy of scantily clad women celebrating with Ramos Pinto's wine. The lodge remains a museum to the firm's success.

But Ramos Pinto are being forced to change. In 1990 the forty-two family members sold the controlling share in the company to Champagne Louis Roederer, who, together with the Oporto-based sugar firm Rar, now control the purse-strings. The firm is looking to market its wines more actively on overseas markets to be able to put all the research that has taken place to good use.

Ramos Pinto is better known for its wood Ports than for vintages, which tend to be light and fairly forward. Ten- and twenty-year-old single-vineyard tawnies from Quinta da Ervamoira and Quinta do Bom Retiro combine maturity with fresh, delicate flavours. Quinta da Urtiga produces a full-flavoured vintage character wine. With replanting taking place in all Ramos Pinto's vineyards, they plan to produce all their own wines by the mid-1990s.

Real Companhia Velha

Any number of different labels are stuck on to the bottles of wine made by this unwieldy agglomeration of companies. Royal Oporto is probably the best known, but the wines are also bottled under the names of Real Vinicola, Silva Reis, Souza Guedes, Pitters, Richard Hooper and Companhia Geral de Agricultura do Alto Douro or Real Companhia Velha for short. There is also a long list of own-label wines to contend with, but no single well-known brand.

The firm has grown quickly this century, becoming for a time the largest single Port shipper before being pushed into second place by the Symingtons. The fortunes of the company centre on one man, Manuel de Silva Reis, who, starting off as an office boy in the firm of Souza Guedes, took over the company on the death of the owner in 1956. By the early 1970s Silva Reis had purchased twelve wine-producing companies, among them the monopoly firm set up by the Marquês de Pombal to control the industry in the eighteenth century. Then came a setback. Following on from the 1974 revolution, the company was occupied by the work force and nationalized by the government. In an effort to keep afloat, much of Real Companhia Velha's stock was sold off to other Port producers. Manuel de Silva Reis has never forgiven the other shippers for buying it. The company was returned to private hands in 1978 stripped of its most important asset: stocks of Port. It has since lurched from one financial crisis to another, selling wine on the principle of price rather than quality.

In 1990 a substantial share of the company changed hands twice. First of all, 40 per cent of the firm was bought by Cofipsa, a subsidiary of the Italian financier Carlo de Benedetti. But before the deal could be signed it fell apart and one of Port's quasi-official controlling bodies, the Casa do Douro, bought the shares. This insider dealing sent a wave of revolt through the establishment, many shippers believing that the acquisition of shares in a major Port firm by an organization purporting to represent 30,000 growers in the Douro was a major conflict of interest. Nevertheless, central government consented to the deal and, at the time of writing, other shippers can do no more than protest.

The Silva Reis family are the largest single landowners in the Douro, with no less than eight *quintas* adding up to over 2,000 hectares. But big does not mean beautiful, and while a number of vineyards undoubtedly have the potential to make first-class Port, many of the *quintas* are run down. Recent vintages are light and early maturing, often flawed by volatile acidity. Tawnies are more reliable but rarely exciting. Real Companhia Velha are also important table wine producers in the north of Portugal (see pages 110 and 150).

Robertson

With a name sounding as British as Robertson, it comes as a surprise to find that most of the firm's Port production is exported to the Netherlands. On English-speaking markets, their best-known wines are bottled under the name of Rebello Valente. This is a shipper taken over by Robertson in 1881, and the name has since been used exclusively for vintage Port. The wines vary. 1985 and 1963 are both good Rebello Valente vintages while some years in between have light and forward in their development. Robertson itself has been controlled by Sandeman since 1953.

Quinta da Romaneira

The best way to arrive at Romaneira is by boat. Although only 5 kilometres upstream from Pinhão, it is a splendidly isolated property with a long, dusty track for access. The *quinta* has been owned by the Vinagre family since the middle of the nineteenth century and, in spite of their unfortunate name, the Vinagres have built up a reputation for making good wines both in the Douro and in the Minho, where the family also make one of the region's best Vinhos Verdes (see page 123).

For a time the wine from Romaneira was a constituent of Taylor's vintage Port, but, after the change in legislation which took place in 1986, Antonio Vinagre took a courageous step and decided to go it alone, making, bottling and marketing his own single-*quinta* wine. Four years on he seems to have no regrets, and is now making a full range of wines from an intensely rich, fruity ruby to delicate *colheitas*. Vintages are simple and a little rustic in style, but there is no doubt that the property has great potential.

Quinta de la Rosa

The Bergqvists are risk-takers. Tim and his daughter Sophia have a business background which they are putting to good use, making and marketing their own single-*quinta* wine. It is the fulfilment of a family dream. For three decades the wines from this A grade *quinta*, in the heart of the Douro close to Pinhão, were made by Robertson, now a part of Sandeman, who bought and bottled the wines under their own label. According to Tim Bergqvist, wine-making standards had been allowed to slip and the family judged that the property was not maximizing its potential. In 1988 they decided that the time was right to sever their long-term contract with Robertson Brothers in order that they could begin making wine on their own.

After much family discussion, they arrived at a novel way of selling their wines. Taking a leaf out from the book of the Bordeaux *en primeur* market, they invited people to invest £1,000 in the property, for which they would receive five cases of Port from La Rosa over the following five years. Over 150 people have so far subscribed.

On tasting older vintages from La Rosa, it seems as though the speculators may have a worthwhile investment. Certainly Ports from the early 1960s are very much mainstream wines, firm and well focused with the capacity to age. Subsequent vintages have been feeble by comparison, partly due to the *movimosto* system (see page 55) that Robertsons installed when they were in charge of making the wine. This has now been removed from the *lagares* and, with help from the Symingtons, the winery, one of the most traditional in the Douro, is now being modernized.

The Bergqvists have been talking about broadening their range of wines to include a single-*quinta* tawny in addition to vintage Port.

Rozes

Founded in France in the last century, Rozes continues to feed the French market with inexpensive, young, tawny-style Port. After a number of changes of ownership in the 1970s, Rozes was bought wholly by Louis Vuitton Moët-Hennessey in 1987. The company has been supplied with Port at various times by Ferreira, Cockburn and Taylor, but now has its own stocks in Vila Nova da Gaia.

Sandeman

The Sandeman don, one of the most instantly recognizable of all logos, lost its way rather in the 1980s. The firm was family-owned and run from its foundation by Scotsman George Sandeman until 1980, when it was purchased by the Canadian drinks multi-national Seagram. The beginning of the end, according to the current chairman, David Sandeman, came when the family were forced to go public in 1952. The family quickly lost control and became easy prey for a takeover. Rumasa, chief predator in the sherry trade of the 1970s, were after Sandeman and so, forestalling an unfriendly bid for shares, the family sold to Seagram for what now seems to be the bargain price of £17 million.

During the 1980s the company has wandered directionless, building up quantity rather than quality. Their wines have lost something in the process as Seagram have built Sandeman into the largest single Port brand. Vintages seem to have lost some of their depth and dimension, while I am told that Founder's Reserve, one of the largest Port brands in America, is a pale relic of its former self.

But 1990, the bicentenary of Sandeman, could prove to be something of a milestone in the company's history. In a complete reversal of policy, the company has made a commitment to quality rather than quantity. George Sandeman, the chairman's son, has been appointed managing director of the firm, bringing back the direct involvement of the family. A number of low-grade vineyards were put up for sale, leaving the firm with Quinta do Vau, a spectacular riverside vineyard which they bought in 1988. For the first time in the company's history Sandeman has a large A grade vineyard which will form the backbone of future vintage blends.

With Eduardo Seixas in charge of the blending, and the family once again at the helm, Sandeman seems to have regained the direction that it needs to put it back in the top league of Port producers.

C. da Silva
This small Dutch-controlled shipper bottles Ports under three labels: Dalva, Presidential and da Silva. Most of their wine is inexpensive young tawny destined for France and West Germany, although occasional vintage Ports can be good.

Silva & Cosens
The name Silva & Cosens is usually seen only in small print. It is the holding company for the famous Dow brand belonging to the Symingtons (see above).

Smith Woodhouse
Peter Symington is a reserved, soft-spoken individual who is rarely given the credit he deserves. He quietly wears six hats as wine-maker for the Symington group, tasting and blending some of the finest Ports.

Smith Woodhouse is very much an exercise in blending. The firm came to the Symingtons with Graham, which they bought in 1970, and has no vineyards of its own. Keeping an independent house style going is therefore a difficult task, but it is something that Peter Symington manages with particular aplomb.

The fact is that Smith Woodhouse Ports are good, often extremely good, but are rarely fully appreciated. In the 1980s Smith Woodhouse vintage Ports have been among the best, midway between Dow and Graham in style, combining sweetness and strength. The 1983 is a case in point, combining cassis and bitter chocolate. It is one of my own favourites.

LBVs are also very fine, bottled without filtration after four years in cask. Even Smith Woodhouse ruby, bottled under a number of private labels, is impressive for its honest-to-goodness sappy young fruit. The wines are often good value, with vintage Ports often 20 per cent cheaper than the top-flight names.

Taylor, Fladgate & Yeatman

Taylor's has built up a reputation as a 'first growth' among Port shippers, with wines consistently selling at a premium price. The firm was the first to own property in the Douro after Bartholomew Bearsley, son of an Englishman who traded wine for cod, bought a vineyard at Salgueiral near Régua in 1744. It remains in Taylor's ownership today and is the main vinification centre for the bulk of the company's Port. It has recently been recognized with the launch of First Estate – Lugar das Lages, a wholesome, spicy young premium ruby.

But Taylor's best-known property is Quinta de Vargellas, which the firm bought in 1893. In a remote position, high up the Douro, it even has its own railway station. Alastair Robertson and his wife Gilly have furnished the place rather like an English country house, right down to copies of *Country Life* on the hall table and pictures depicting the Battle of Waterloo in the loo! They rather pride themselves on this 'last outpost of the Empire'.

There is a much more serious side to Vargellas, for it is in the stone *lagares* in the *adega* below the house that some of the finest Ports are made. The 41 hectares of vines at Vargellas, together with a further 37 hectares at Quinta da Terra Feita near Pinhão, make one of the best of all vintage Ports. In great vintages like 1927, 1948, 1963 and 1977, Taylor's wines are hugely concentrated with explosive tannins. There are few wines that rise to the challenge in comparative tastings.

Other wines win Taylor's a high reputation. Quinta de Vargellas is a long-lived single-*quinta* wine made in lesser vintages, and mature tawnies are soft and scented. Chip Dry, launched in 1934, was the first dry white Port on the market. It remains one of the best.

Taylor's is part of a larger venture with Fonseca, which together sell around 300,000 cases of wine a year. The principal shareholder in both companies is Alastair Robertson, who reluctantly took over the firm from his aunt, Beryl Yeatman, in 1966. At the time the Port trade was in the doldrums and he had to be persuaded to give it a go. Twenty-five years on and Taylor's has grown from a small, old-fashioned concern to one of the most successful of all players in the Douro.

Vasconcelos

Signs on the waterfront at Gaia pointing to Porto Vasconcelos point to a piece of history. The firm's entire stock was bought by Sandeman in 1989. Vasconcelos itself purchased the Port interests of Gonzalez Byass, and with it, the name of Butler, Nephew in 1983.

Warre

Warre (pronounced 'war') is where the Symingtons' empire-building began. Andrew James Symington arrived in Oporto, aged nineteen, in 1882. He began working for the textile firm of John Graham, but was soon attracted to the Port trade and in 1905 acquired shares in the firm of Warre & Co. 'A.J.' then bought the firm of Quarles Harris before taking all the shares in Warre. The Warre family themselves owned Silva & Cosens and Symington invited them to do a share swop, thereby gaining control of a third of Dow's. Symington's three sons entered the business in the 1920s, setting up a succession which is now in its fourth generation. Gould Campbell became part of the Symington group in the early 1960s, and this was joined by W. J. Graham & Co. and Smith Woodhouse in 1970, putting a total of six Port houses under family control. With the acquisition of a 40 per cent share in the Madeira Wine Company in 1989, the Symingtons have become one of the wine world's most powerful dynasties.

Warre has always been on the top tier of the Symington-owned Port houses and its wines reflect this. The style of the wine is in between that of Graham and Dow, perhaps without the tannic rod that penetrates the wines of Smith Woodhouse. Since 1980 grapes from Quinta da Cavadinha have made up the backbone of Warre vintages, and this small vineyard has recently been equipped with some of the most up-to-date wine-making equipment in the Douro. Other Warre wines worth seeking out are the single-*quinta* vintages from Cavadinha as well as Warres Nimrod, a mature tawny. Warre also sells large quantities of wine to France under the brand name of Cintra.

Wiese & Krohn

Two Norwegians (from a country not usually associated with Port) founded Wiese & Krohn in 1865. The firm passed into the hands of the Carneiro family in the 1920s and the third generation continues to run the business as a private concern.

Wiese & Krohn have developed a good reputation for *colheitas* and aged tawnies. The firm's frequent vintage declarations, on the other hand, are often overlooked. This is a shame, because the Carneiros make consistently elegant wines, lighter than the mainstream perhaps but worth seeking out. Krohn is unusual in that much of the wine-making is done by women. Maria José Aguiar and Iolanda Carneiro buy in and blend wines from small growers. In 1989 Krohn also bought a small vineyard, Quinta do Retiro Novo, in the Torto valley.

Most Wiese & Krohn wine is sold in Portugal, France and Holland.

Visiting the Douro

The Douro means different things to different people. Portuguese author Miguel Torga wrote about it in melodramatic mood as a 'tragedy' running deep through the heart of Portugal, while a farmer living and working in the region once described it to me as 'a forgotten wonder of the world'. Looking at some of the pyramids of terraces built by hand in one of the most inhospitable parts of Europe, few people visiting the region could disagree.

Much the best way to enjoy the grandeur of the Douro is to take a train. The roads up-river are poor and dangerous. Given the narrow valley, the roads tend to criss-cross the Douro and there are few opportunities to view the best vineyards in the heart of the region. Trains leave Oporto's São Bento station for Pocinho, the end of the line, every two hours. The station is worth a visit in itself. The cavernous concourse is covered in tiles illustrating Portuguese history and the evolution of the train. The capture of Ceuta by João I is a dramatic way to start off a journey. The ride up the Douro takes about three hours and rarely keeps to the timetable. Be sure to buy a first-class ticket. Second-class carriages are grimy and uncomfortable and it is often difficult to find a seat.

On leaving the suburbs of Oporto you travel through Vinho Verde country. There are plenty of vines and tall-growing cabbages but no views of the river until about an hour of the journey has elapsed, when the line rejoins the Douro below Baião. From here, all the way to the end of the line, it snakes alongside the river. It is easy to spot where the Port vineyards begin. Grey granite gives way to silvery schist and vines take over the hillside. The first stop inside the demarcated region is Régua. For some *inter-cidade* or inter-city trains this is the end of the line, but the town itself is uninteresting and it is worth going on upstream at least as far as Pinhão. This is the heart of the Cima Corgo, and vineyards belonging to all the major Port shippers surround the town.

It is hard to imagine that in such a spectacular location there could be somewhere as unattractive as Pinhão. It owes its existence to the railway, and is made up of one street with a few down-at-heel cafés and shops. A Port shipper once described the place to me as 'a one-horse town where the horse has left'. Apart from the station, which is again covered with *azulejos* (tiles) depicting vineyard scenes, there is nothing at all to see.

It is much better to venture on to the end of the line. Between Pinhão and Pocinho, a further 40 kilometres upstream, the train passes within view of some of the most famous Port vineyards. Croft's Quinta da Roeda, Quinta do Roriz which produces wines for Ferreira, Graham's Quinta dos Malvedos, and Cockburn's Tua are all within sight of the train. At Cachão de Valeira, a few kilometres from Tua, a massive outcrop of granite seems to squeeze the valley into a narrow gorge. This marks the place where, before the Douro was dammed, there used to be a flight of treacherous rapids. The legendary Baron Forrester (see Offley Forrester above) was drowned here when his boat foundered in 1861. The water no longer crashes over the rocks, but it is still a sinister place with lofty, grey mountains towering over the jet-black river. A few Port shippers still pay their respects as they pass.

Upstream are two of the grandest of all vineyard properties: Taylor's Quinta de Vargellas and the Symingtons' Quinta do Vesúvio, both of which have their own private railway stations. Beyond this the vineyards peter out until at Pocinho, no more than a collection of dusty houses and rusting steam engines in Douro Superior, there are more olive groves to be seen than vines.

The round trip from Oporto to Pocinho takes an entire day and can be exhausting, particularly in the heat. Accommodation is scanty in the Douro but there are small *residencias* at both Régua and Pinhão to break the journey. Should you choose to travel up the Douro by car, there is a small *pousada*, the Pousada Barão de Forrester, at Alijó, 16 kilometres from Pinhão. This is also one of the best places to eat. Food in the Douro tends to be rustic, but the *pousada* serves good *cabrito* (kid), *cozidos* (stews) and delicious egg and almond sweets. They also have a good selection of Port to sample, though some of the bottles may have been sitting on the shelf for too long.

Much the best place to sample Port is in Vila Nova da Gaia. The road along the waterfront, the Avenida Ramos Pinto, is linked with *barcos rabelos*, mothballed after years of shipping Port down the Douro. They now set sail in June each year for a good-humoured race between the two road bridges across the Douro. Multilingual signs by the quay direct passing visitors to one of the lodges. All but the smallest houses conduct regular tours, finishing with a tasting and an opportunity to buy wine. Ferreira also organize a boat trip in the summer months.

Oporto, on the opposite side of the river, is Portugal's second city, and bears a close resemblance to a city in the north of England. Like Manchester it is grey, always seems to rain and is a centre of the textile industry. The British have a large colony in Oporto, centred on their own club, the Oporto Cricket and Lawn Tennis Club on the Rua Campo Alegre. But the Factory House on the Rua Infante Dom Henrique, formerly the Rua Nova das Ingleses (New Street of the English), is the oldest British institution. The Factory was founded in the eighteenth century, inspired by colonial *feitorias* set up by the Portuguese in Africa and India. The solid Georgian building looks curiously out of place among the jumble of buildings by Oporto's river front. It was designed by an Englishman and has been the fulcrum of the British Port trade since 1790. The Factory House is still very much a British institution, with membership open only to British-owned Port shippers, who use the place for official engagements and to meet at the strictly men-only Wednesday lunch. At times when there is no function arranged, the Factory House or Feitoria Inglesa is open to visitors. Behind the grey façade is an elegant interior with English furniture and china. There are two identical dining-rooms placed end to end, both of which are used by shippers and guests. You eat in the first then leave, taking your napkin, to sit at the same place in the adjoining room where the tradition is to guess the vintage Port free from the detracting smell of food.

Close by, the Salão Arabe or Arab Hall of the Oporto Stock Exchange is worth visiting for its ostentatious internal decoration, inspired by the Alhambra in Granada. It is completely out of key with the staid, grey character of the financial district.

Oporto is well served by hotels and restaurants. The Hotel Infante de Sagres in the city centre is five-star by any standards. Built in the 1930s, it has a lavish Edwardian interior and an elegant dining-room – the Restaurante Dona Filipa. The dowager of Oporto's hotels is the Grande Hotel do Porto. It is much less expensive than the Infante and is in need of a face-lift, but it retains its somewhat faded genteel charm. There are also modern hotels belonging to the Sheraton and Meridian chains, but these are located outside the city centre.

The inhabitants of Oporto are often called *tripeiros* (tripe-eaters) after the city's staple dish – *Tripas à moda do Porto*. This dates from the time when Oporto was under siege from French troops during the Peninsular War and the citizens, running short of food, resorted to offal and tripe. The tradition stuck, and rich, spicy tripe dishes are to be found on restaurant menus all over town. The Portucale, Escondidinho and Tripeiro are all good places to try *tripas* or Oporto's other staple, the trusty *bacalhau* (salt cod), which can be seen hanging in old-fashioned grocers' stores. At Foz do Douro, a wealthy suburb at the mouth of the river, the Dom Manoel and Greens are both good places to go for more international cooking. Nearby is the Praia dos Ingleses – the English Beach!

5

The Douro:
The Future for Table Wine

At the end of August each year, an eagerly awaited *anúncio* appears in the Douro press. It is a wordy advertisement; not the sort of thing that would grab your attention unless you grew grapes in the Douro valley, but it tells farmers just how much must will be 'authorized' to make into Port during the forthcoming vintage.

Depending on the year, something over half the Douro's total production is not fortified but is fermented right out to make table wine. In 1991, for example, 110,000 pipes of must were authorized for fortification by the ruling Instituto do Vinho do Porto (IVP), accounting for around 40 per cent of the year's total production. The proportion of Port rises only in crisis years like 1988, when grapes are in short supply.

Under the complicated vineyard classification system outlined in the previous chapter, individual properties are graded from A to F according to the number of points they score. Vineyards in the Baixo Corgo downstream from Régua and those up on the hills close to the Douro's 650-metre boundary are considered to be less suitable for making Port than vineyards in the heart of the region. Outlying *quintas* therefore receive lower grades (C or below) and, under the *benefício* or 'benefit' licences doled out annually by the Casa do Douro, they are not permitted to fortify as much of their must to make Port. The remainder must be fermented dry to make red or white table wine.

These more temperate vineyard sites on the margins of the Douro demarcation make better table wine than those along the river valleys around Pinhão. Super-ripe grapes grown in the stifling summer heat of the Cima Corgo are ideal for making deep, dark, tannic Port but tend to produce tough, ink-black table wines. On the other hand, grapes ripening in the cooler, wetter parts of the region tend to make light, early maturing Ports but softer table wines with higher levels of acidity and more finesse.

Table wines are not new to the Douro. Until the early part of the eighteenth century, most of the wine exported from the region was fermented dry without the addition of spirit. Legend reports that it was the poor quality of the table wine that drove eighteenth-century merchants to lace it with a few litres of brandy to stabilize it prior to shipment. It became accepted practice to add *aguardente* or brandy during the fermentation only towards the end of the eighteenth century. But the practice was controversial and the traditional, dry Douro wines retained their advocates. Baron James Forrester, the great Douro eclectic who did so much for the region in the mid nineteenth century, advocated a return to Port made without the use of brandy. Forrester's words went unheeded and, ever since, light wines have been largely neglected in favour of Port.

It is somewhat surprising to find that many of today's shippers, fine-tuning the most delicious tawny and vintage Port, display a curious lack of understanding about the wine world outside their own. At stately lunches in the Port lodges in Gaia and at the Factory House in Oporto, the wine served with the meal is often a let-down. All the serious talk is reserved for the Port.

Even if something of Dr Johnson's 'Claret is liquor for boys, Port for men' attitude still persists, Douro table wines are slowly receiving more attention. The region was demarcated for table wine in 1979, over two centuries after it was delimited for Port, and a few wine-makers now see possibilities in making something good out of all the surplus grapes that have traditionally been turned into rough and ready hooch for vineyard workers. The 1990 vintage may have spurred one or two shippers on. Because of the rejection of a large consignment of brandy earlier that summer by the IVP, there was insufficient to meet the needs of the growers and shippers. As a result, must that would normally have been fortified was instead left to ferment into table wine.

But the slow revival of Douro table wine began back in 1950, when the technical director at Ferreira, Fernando Nicolau de Almeida, returned from a visit to France with the idea of making a table wine. At first no one took him very seriously but, forty years on, with Ferreira's Barca Velha (see below) well established as one of the finest red wines in Portugal and commanding prices on a par with vintage Port, others are starting to sit up and take notice. Both Quinta do Noval and the Symingtons are currently experimenting with table wines.

The Wines

In the early eighteenth century, when the English refused to trade with the French, Douro reds were known derisively as 'black-strap': big, dark, austere red wines with none of the finesse of Claret or Burgundy. Nearly 300 years on, little seems to have changed. The wines are still criticized for being dry and over-austere, often tasting rather burnt or baked. The problem is not just the wine-making but also the raw material. Most Douro vineyards are geared to making Port and are planted with a rout of different grape varieties often muddled up together. Over fifty different red grape varieties are legally allowed for Douro wine, with many more illegal grape varieties planted besides. Most are the same as those used for making Port. Some give colour, some backbone, others flavour and acidity; between them they share all the different qualities needed to make dark, rich Port. But with most vineyards planted in a muddle, little or no research has taken place to find out which might be the most suitable for making table wine. The Denominacão de Origen Controlada legislation therefore simply enshrines the status quo.

When it comes to making table wine, the wine-maker's priorities are wholly different from those of a Port producer. Fermentation takes place over a longer period, so that the extraction of colour and tannin, which has to be carried out rapidly in Port vinification, is of much less significance. Grapes that lend much needed colour and backbone to Port often make hard, ink-black, mouth-numbing wines when all the sugar has fermented out.

But there are at least two Douro grapes that are eminently suited for making table wine as well as Port. Touriga Nacional and Tinto Roriz are among the so-called 'top five' approved for the new vineyard planting currently taking place in the Douro with support from the World Bank. Both have already proved themselves elsewhere. Roriz is grown all over Spain, where it is variously called Tempranillo, Cencibel and Tinto Fino, as well as in the Alentejo province of southern Portugal where it masquerades increasingly successfully under the name of Aragonez. Touriga Nacional is one of the recommended grapes in the Dão region, on the granite soils immediately to the south. Here, as in the Douro, it has the capability to make generously flavoured, chunky red wines if carefully handled. In the Douro the elegance of Roriz combined with the depth of Touriga could prove to be a happy marriage for table wine.

Most of the vineyards in the Baixo Corgo and on the high land around Vila Real, Alijó, Murça, Vila Flor and Armamar on the edge of the region belong to small farmers. Few have the resources to make their own wine, and most therefore deliver their grapes to one of twenty-two co-operatives within the demarcated region. Just as in the rest of Portugal, co-operative wine-making tends to be primitive, and while some are fairly well equipped for making Port, few have the necessary temperature control equipment or the expertise to make good table wines.

The recent advance in Douro wine-making has therefore taken place in private hands, with firms like Ferreira and their parent company Sogrape taking time and trouble over their wine-making. With temperature-controlled fermentation in stainless steel and regular *remontage* or pumping over instead of autovinification (see page 55), appealing red table wines combining ripe fruit with the pepper and spice of young Port can be made.

Likewise white wines, too many of which currently suffer from runaway fermentation temperatures, also have potential. Over forty different grape varieties are legally permitted, many of which are not particularly suitable for white Port let alone table wine. But, with careful handling, grapes like Malvasia Fina, Viosinho and Gouveio are capable of making fresh-tasting white wines, even in the heat of the Douro.

The Wine-makers

Quinta da Cismeira, São João de Pesqueira

Brussels has found its way to the Douro. A Belgian named Marc Velge bought an old *adega* high above the Douro at Quinta da Cismeira in 1988. With European Community help, the winery was equipped with the latest stainless steel technology. As yet, the *quinta* has no vineyards of its own but buys in grapes from growers who would otherwise sell their produce to the local co-operative. As co-ops are notoriously slow to pay their members, Cismeira has tractors queuing at the winery door during the harvest. Unlike the Douro co-ops, Cismeira's wine-makers are attempting to ferment different grapes separately. Tinta Roriz, Touriga Nacional and Touriga Francesa are the main varieties used to make two reds sold under the somewhat obscure 'Scarpa' brand name. But the wines show the enormous potential that exists in the region. Their youngest red, released a year after the vintage, is packed with ripe, Port-like fruit while the Reserva has a smoky, savoury character from ageing in new Portuguese oak. Although Cismeira's wines are still a little rough and ready around the edges, they bode well for the future of table wine in the Douro.

Cockburn Smithies

Cockburn's are known internationally for Port, but in Portugal they are also highly regarded for a brand of Douro table wine called Tuella. The wine is named after Cockburn's *quinta* and wine-making centre at Tua, though Tuella is made on the opposite side of the river at Vila Nova da Fozcoa, with grapes from high vineyards around the town. Production began in 1972, but quantities are small and the wine is not seen outside Portugal. The white Tuella is made mainly from Malvasia Fina along with small amounts of Códega and Rabigato. It is cleanly made with crisp, sherbet-like fruit. The red is a dense, solid wine with a deep colour and a full finish.

Quinta do Côtto, Cidadelhe

Miguel Champalimaud is a vociferous critic of the status quo in the Douro, believing firmly that the Baixo Corgo is the best part of the Douro for Port. But he does have to abide by the rules, and only a portion of the crop from his C-D rated vineyard near Mesão Frio can be fortified. He is forced to turn the rest into table wine which, since his first vintage in 1980, has quickly become one of the most highly regarded in the Douro. The wine to look out for is the Grande Escolha; a full, spicy red made only in the best years (often those which coincide with a Port vintage). Touriga Nacional and Tinta Roriz grapes are destemmed, crushed and pumped into autovinification tanks, where the juice ferments at between 26 and 28°C. The wine then spends eighteen months in new Portuguese oak, taking on a powerful toasted vanilla and tobacco character. The wine deserves acclaim.

Ferreira

When Fernando Nicolau de Almeida, the chief blender at Port producers A. A. Ferreira, visited a *château* in Bordeaux during the vintage in 1950, he was surprised to find that they made wine in vats. At the time, all grapes in the Douro were being trodden by foot and fermented in open stone *lagares*. Having learned that the French made good table wine by fermenting it slowly and pumping the juice over at regular intervals to extract the right amount of colour and tannin, he returned to Quinta do Vale do Meão, high in the Douro Superior, to put their ideas into practice.

At first he had to make do with the primitive technology available. There was no electricity in 1950 (a hydro-electric station has now been built just a few kilometres away), making temperature control in the raging heat of the Douro impossible. 'We made good wine by mistake,' declared Nicolau de Almeida.

Barca Velha was launched in 1952. Blocks of ice were brought 120 kilometres up-river from Oporto, covered in sawdust to prevent them melting. A rudimentary system of temperature control was rigged up by passing the fermenting must over the ice to keep it cool. Over the years, as technology has improved in the Douro, Barca Velha has become less hit and miss and more of an exercise in fine wine-making. It is widely agreed that Fernando Nicolau de Almeida, who continues to supervise the wine-making, has created a legend in his own time.

The wine is still made at Quinta do Vale do Meão, one of the most easterly of all the great vineyards in the Douro. Grapes with higher levels of acidity from far-flung hill vineyards are fermented together with high-quality Port grapes from the valleys. Tinta Roriz forms the backbone of the blend (about 60 per cent), together with small quantities of Touriga Francesa and Tinta Barroca. The grapes are destemmed, crushed and fermented in stainless steel vats at around 25°C. Regular but carefully monitored pumping over ensures that the extraction of colour and tannin is controlled according to the vintage. After the malo-lactic fermentation, the wine is transferred to Vila Nova da Gaia where it matures for a year and a half in casks made from new Portuguese oak.

Barca Velha, rather like vintage Port, is declared only in exceptional years. Wine that is considered not to be up to scratch is sold under a second label: Ferreirinha

Reserva Especial. The wines are released on to the market only when they are considered to be ready to drink, and in the opinion of José Maria Soares Franco, the young oenologist who is now in charge of the wine-making at Ferreira, Barca Velha needs about eight years to develop. The best vintages continue to evolve for two or three decades.

In the preparation of this book, I have been fortunate enough to taste a number of recent vintages of Barca Velha and Reserva Especial, along with one sample that, at the time of writing, had not been declared.

1985 (not then declared): Opaque ruby-black colour, rich, concentrated berry fruit aroma, still tight and closed; ripe, warm, naturally sweet taste with a backbone of firm tannin rising to a big finish. Perhaps the finest Portuguese red wine I have tasted: almost certain to be sold as Barca Velha.

Reserva Especial 1984: Deep crimson-purple colour; tight plain chocolate aromas; firm, quite lean, with higher acidity than the 1985, plenty of fruit followed on by a rather hard finish that needs time to soften.

Barca Velha 1983: Deep 'black' colour; dried figs and coffee beans on the nose; initially soft with ripe, oaky tannins building up to firm finish. Well balanced by acidity, though not one of the best Barca Velhas to be declared.

Barca Velha 1982: Dense crimson-black colour; massive but tight, withdrawn fruit on the nose, underlying plain chocolate intensity sometimes found in the best vintage Port; rich, intense chocolate fruit backed up by firm, spicy tannins and a long, ripe finish. Ready to drink but retaining the puppy fat to last.

Barca Velha 1981: Deep colour showing little sign of age; spicy new oak and ripe berry fruit bouquet; wonderful concentration of rich, dried fruit and peppery tannin. Solid, ripe finish.

Reserva Especial 1980: Again dark, just showing signs of tawny on rim; ripe minty bouquet, 'sweet' ripe fruit backed up by firm tannin, not quite as long as the Barca Velha but still a well-made wine that should continue to develop with age.

Barca Velha 1978: Remarkably deep and youthful in colour for its age; stalky, coffee-bean aromas combining with well-ripened fruit; rich, minty character hinting at the New World, vanilla oak combined with ripe tannin lingers on the finish. Mature: rich but supple.

Previous declared Barca Velha vintages that can still be found occasionally in Portugal are 1966, 1965, and 1964. Reserva Especial was produced in 1977 and 1975.

It is difficult to sum up the style and appeal of Barca Velha, other than to say that it has come to be regarded as Portugal's 'first growth'. The wine has a strong affinity with Iberia's other legendary red wine, Vega Sicilia, which is made 250 kilometres upstream where the Douro becomes the Duero. The two wines share the same austere style and occasionally the same high-toned, almost volatile character that is actually a part of their charm. They also fetch the same high prices and, just as anyone contemplating buying a bottle of Vega Sicilia would be well advised to try a bottle of their second wine, Valbuena, first, so anyone looking to try Barca Velha would do well finding a bottle of Reserva Especial, which often retails for less than half the price.

Ferreira make two other table wines. Esteva, named after the sticky gum cistus bush (*Cistus lusitanicus*) which fills the Douro air with its heady aroma in spring, is made from grapes grown in high vineyards of the Torto and Pinhão valleys. The Touriga Francesa grape accounts for half the blend, the remainder being made up by Roriz and Barroca. Fermentation takes place in a modern stainless steel winery at Quinta do Seixo, perched on a hill above the confluence of the Torto and the Douro. The fermenting juice is separated from the skins at an early stage, making Esteva relatively light and fruity without the excessive tannin that plagues many Douro reds. A small proportion of the wine ages in Portuguese oak before bottling. It is ready to drink two or three years after the harvest.

Monopólio, a dry white made for the Portuguese market, is made from grapes grown on the Ferreira family's Quinta do Valado near Régua and in the high vineyards around Lamego. Traditional vinification produces a fat white wine lacking the freshness and acidity to which we have become accustomed with the more widespread use of temperature-controlled fermentation.

In 1987 Ferreira was bought by Sogrape, who also have table wine interests in the Douro (see below). Production, however, is kept entirely separate, and the only noticeable change in direction at Ferreira to date is the wider distribution of their wines. It gives more people the opportunity to try some of the finest red wines in Portugal.

Quinta da Pacheca

Father and son Eduardo and José Serpa Pimentel own one of the few flat vineyards in the Douro. It is planted on low-lying land across the river from Régua, by a meander in the River Douro. Traditional Douro grape varieties are planted alongside plots of Riesling, Gewürztraminer, Sauvignon and Cabernet Sauvignon. Of these Cabernet is the most successful, adding a dollop of blackcurrant to Pacheca's wines. The reds are made in traditional stone *lagares* and sometimes suffer from excess volatile acidity. Whites are fermented at low temperatures in stainless steel, and the Vinho das Madrucas, made from traditional varieties, is better, to my mind, than the varietal Riesling, Gewürztraminer and Sauvignon, which nevertheless sell for a high price in Portugal.

Real Companhia Vinícola do Norte do Portugal

Real Vinícola are the table wine arm of Port producers Royal Oporto (see page 94). The Silva Reis family, who control the agglomeration, are the largest landowners in the Douro, with ten *quintas* spread out between Pinhão and São João de Pesqueira. Most of the Douro table wine comes from the 480 hectares of C-F rated vineyard on the high plateau near Alijó. A huge winery at Casal da Granja is used to make Port and table wine which is bottled under the Casal da Granja and Evel labels. Rather like Royal Oporto's Ports, the wines (both red and white) are often flawed by careless wine-making.

Sandeman's Quinta do Confradeiro

Quinta do Confradeiro at Celeirós belonged to Sandeman until 1990, when it was sold to a local farmer. Sandeman, however, continue to buy grapes from this D grade vineyard and a proportion of the crop is turned into table wine. A blend of Touriga Nacional, Touriga Francesa, Tinto Cão and Tinta Roriz produces a firm, meaty red wine which is supple from being aged in French oak. At the moment it is available only in small quantities on the Portuguese market.

Quinta da Santa Julia, Loureiro

Eduardo Seixas does a clever double act. He is both chief taster and blender at Sandeman as well as a pioneer producer of Douro table wine. With considerable ingenuity, Seixas makes both red and white wine from 70 hectares of vines high above Régua in the Baixo Corgo. He began making table wine in the mid 1980s, using the most rudimentary technology. A couple of steel tanks used for transporting Port were adapted as fermentation vats, cooled by garden sprinklers. Seixas has since built himself a new winery, although red wines are still fermented in *lagares*. The fresh-tasting white Quinta da Santa Julia, made from Malvasia Rei, Códega and Viosinho, is better than the red, which is somewhat austere.

Quinta do Valprado, Lamego

Caves do Raposeira, the Seagram-owned makers of Portugal's leading sparkling wine (see page 205), have planted a small amount of Chardonnay in the hills above Lamego. A small amount is used to produce a still wine, Quinta do Valprado, which tastes honeyed and buttery and similar in style to a well-made Mâcon Villages. It is currently one of only two Portuguese Chardonnays (the other is made on the Setúbal Peninsula by João Pires), and its rarity therefore commands an excessively high price.

Caves Vale do Rodo, Régua

Of the twenty-two co-operative wineries operating in the Douro, few make anything of quality. One of the exceptions is the co-op at Régua-Caves Vale do Rodo. Every year the winery produces around 50,000 hectolitres of Port and a further 30,000 hectolitres of table wine from grapes brought in by almost 1,000 small farmers in the Baixo Corgo. Most of the Port is sold to large shippers for blending into their bread-and-butter rubies and tawnies, but much of the table wine is bottled under the co-operative's own label. Much of the best wine from Caves Vale do Rodo is a red with the curious name Cabeça do Burro ('head of the donkey'). It is made from a blend of local grapes: Touriga Francesa, Malvasia Preta, Tinta Amarela, Tinta Roriz, Tinta Barroca and Tinta Carvalha, bottled after spending a time ageing in wood. The wine is round with a warm, ripe smoky flavour; the opposite of austere Douro 'black-strap'.

Sogrape Vila Real

The Guedes family control the largest single wine-making firm in Portugal – Sogrape. It began with the creation of Mateus Rosé (see page 201), but in recent years the company has diversified into Port, beer and banking as well as widening its range of table wines.

The Sogrape winery at Vila Real was originally built to make Mateus but, with much of the production moving to the Bairrada, the plant has been thoroughly updated to make the most of the surplus of quality grapes growing in high-altitude vineyards on the northern edge of the Douro demarcation.

Sogrape began by reviving the Planalto brand: a crisp, cold-fermented white wine made from Viosinho, Malvasia Fina and Gouveio grapes growing on the plains above the Douro. The wine was an overnight success and quickly became a favourite among the British community living in Oporto, most of whom enjoy the wine's squeaky-clean style.

Other Douro wines have followed since. Vila Regia, the Roman name for the city of Vila Real, is a fresh, fragrant dry white with slightly less alcohol than Planalto, and a well-made red with all the wild berry aromas and flavours of Port grapes Touriga Nacional, Touriga Francesa, Tinta Barrocca, Tinta Roriz and Bastardo. A red Reserva aged for a year in new Portuguese oak has more depth and intensity of fruit with a warm, rousing finish.

But Sogrape's best wine to my mind is their white Douro Reserva. Juice from Malvasia Fina, Viosinho and Gouveio grapes is fermented at 18-20°C in 550-litre casks made from new French and Portuguese oak. The wine is fat but balanced by good acidity with peach and apricot flavours and a buttery depth from having spent six months ageing in cask. Sogrape Reserva is a wonderful example of some of the great potential that there is for table wine in the Douro.

Visiting the Douro

Anyone wishing to visit the Douro should read pages 99–102. With the exception of Sogrape, there are no producers of Douro table wines geared up to receiving passing visitors

6

Vinho Verde Country

Vines flourish in the damp maritime climate of north-west Portugal. They clamber over shady pergolas, climb trees, scale walls and even scramble over the sagging roofs of small houses. Wherever you look there seems to be a riot of greenery.

This is Vinho Verde country; the largest demarcated wine region in Portugal, making fresh, crackling 'green wine'. Rain-bearing winds blowing off the sea support intensive cultivation, and the countryside between the Rivers Minho and Douro has always been favoured by groups of marauding settlers, marking out its independence from the rest of the Iberian peninsula. When the Moors invaded, the wine-loving Christians fought back, driving them southwards out of the long, narrow strip of country that is now Portugal.

Portugal's birthplace, together with Spanish Galicia just to the north, has become one of the most densely populated parts of rural Iberia. Twenty per cent of the country's inhabitants live within the Vinho Verde demarcation, which covers just over 9 per cent of mainland Portugal. Over the years, the pattern of independent land has become increasingly fragmented as succeeding generations have staked their claim to a piece of their inheritance. This has made much of the north-west of Portugal unworkable. Tiny holdings, the majority less than half a hectare in size, can really support only subsistence farming. Most are reduced to owning a cow or a goat, some tall, spindly cabbages, a plot of maize and a few straggling vines. According to the Oporto-based Commissão de Viticultura, which is charged with the unenviable task of regulating the Vinho Verde region, 80,000 individual growers are farming 25,000 hectares of piecemeal vineyard.

In order to make the best use of this cramped environment, vines have been trained to grow high above the ground, leaving space for grazing and the cultivation

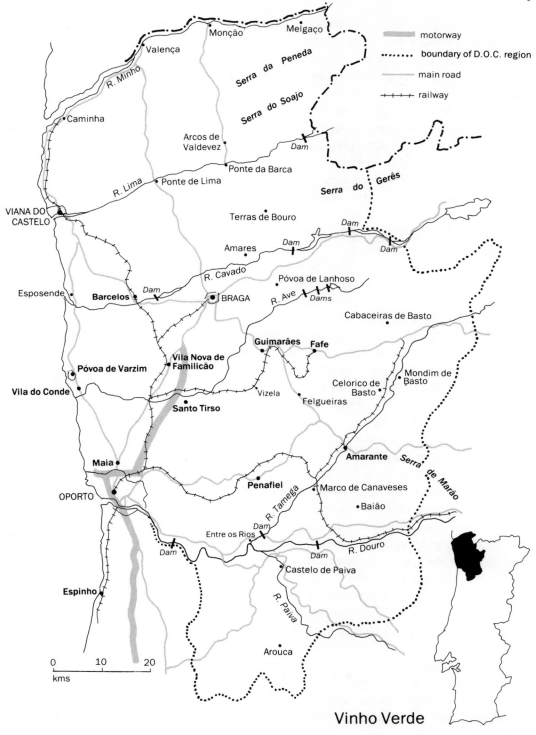

motorway
boundary of D.O.C. region
main road
railway

Monção
Melgaço
Valença
Serra da Peneda
R. Minho
Serra do Soajo
Caminha
Arcos de Valdevez
Dam
Ponte da Barca
R. Lima
Ponte de Lima
Serra do Gerês
VIANA DO CASTELO
Terras de Bouro
Dam
Amares
Dam
Dam
R. Cavado
Póvoa de Lanhoso
Esposende
Barcelos
Dam
BRAGA
R. Ave
Dams
Cabaceiras de Basto
Guimarães
Fafe
Póvoa de Varzim
Vila Nova de Familicão
Mondim de Basto
Vila do Conde
Vizela
Celorico de Basto
Felgueiras
Santo Tirso
Maia
Amarante
Serra de Marão
OPORTO
Penafiel
Marco de Canaveses
R. Tamega
Baião
R. Douro
Entre os Rios
Dam
Dam
Dam
Castelo de Paiva
Espinho
R. Paiva
0 10 20
kms
Arouca

Vinho Verde

of other crops underneath. In the past, vines were trained to climb the trunks of tall trees, usually chestnuts or poplars. This impractical form of cultivation is called *enforcado* (hanging), because of the way that fruit-bearing tendrils are festooned through the branches and sometimes hung along a long line of trees bordering a plot growing other crops.

The *arejão* or *arejada* (meaning aired or ventilated) in Figure 4.1 is really an extension of the *enforcado* system. Wires are stretched between trees or tall pillars to form a screen of vines sometimes up to six metres high. Over the last century both *enforcado* and *arejão* viticulture have declined in importance, though on the roadsides in more secluded parts of the north-west you still occasionally see farm-workers climbing precarious-looking ladders to prune back unruly tree-trained vines.

Most *enforcado* has been replaced by the *ramada* or *latada* cultivation illustrated in Figure 4.2. Stout granite posts up to three metres in height support a network of trellising covered by vines. Planted over paths, driveways and round the edges of fields, the *ramada* system has an ornamental look about it, but for much of this century, legislation prevented growers from planting grapes in any other way. In an attempt to increase the production of maize, a law was imposed decreeing that vines could only be planted for 'decorative' purposes. This left smallholders coaxing as much as they could from a few supposedly 'decorative' vines.

Apart from obvious space-saving, high-trained vines have a number of other advantages in north-west Portugal's damp climate. With an annual rainfall exceeding 2,000mm in places (over double that of Manchester), rot is endemic in the warm summer months. Raising the crop of grapes above the ground reduces the risk of damage from rot and occasional late spring frosts by allowing the air to circulate freely in the vineyard canopy.

But these practical advantages are outweighed by problems. Since the latter part of the last century, the grafted vines planted in the wake of phylloxera have been unable to grow with the same vigour as those planted on their own rootstock. Varieties have therefore been selected for their vitality and yield rather than for the quality of the grapes they produce. Inevitably, high-yielding hybrids have crept into Vinho Verde vineyards, where most growers seem to be more attentive to quantity rather than the quality of their crop. These vigorous plants bearing large amounts of fruit tend to produce grapes that are high in acidity and low in the natural sugars that fermentation converts into alcohol. Added to this, the blanket of leaves over the pergola is often so thick that the grapes are shaded from the sun and never really have a chance to ripen.

Most of the larger growers are aware of these defects. So, taking advantage of a relaxation in the rules that followed the 1974 revolution, the few farmers owning small private estates have abandoned pergolas around the edge of fields in favour of more extensive vineyards planted with lower-growing vines. The *cruzeta* system

Vinho Verde trellising

3 to 6m

1   *Arejão*

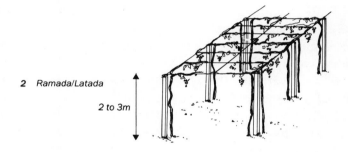

2   *Ramada/Latada*

2 to 3m

1.5 to 2m

3   *Cruzeta*

Figure 4

(Figure 4.3) was developed in the 1970s to replace labour-intensive *vinha ramada*. Four vines are planted around the base of a wooden or concrete pole two metres in height. A crossbar (hence the name *cruzeta*) supports two lateral wires along which the vine's fruit-bearing arms are trained to give the plant order and shape.

Though *cruzetas* are certainly an improvement over traditional pergolas and allow a degree of mechanization, they have not been popular among growers, who find them expensive to maintain. The most enterprising farmers have therefore moved on to a more simple system based on the French cordon. The *barra* or *bardo* as it has been christened has a single wire supported by upright poles a metre or a metre and a half high. It has the dual advantage of giving grapes more uniform exposure to the sun and allowing tractors to work in between the rows. This is almost essential when it comes to spraying the vines against mildew and rot. When it kept on raining through July 1988, rot ran rampant through Vinho Verde vineyards, reducing the crop that year by as much as 80 per cent.

Vineyards in the south of Vinho Verde country are being swallowed up by building. The Ave valley between Braga, Famalicão and Guimarães, Portugal's first capital, is the centre of a burgeoning textile industry, while shoes are made in small sweat-shops around Felgueiras, Vizela and Penafiel. All the way along the main roads driving north out of Oporto, ribbons of small, modern factories are springing up almost uncontrollably among the eucalyptus and vines. This is causing problems for farmers, for although pay is still relatively low (hence all the labour-intensive, low-technology factories), agricultural wages are considerably less than in industry. Many of the women who at one time relied on seasonal employment in the vineyards have now been lured into manufacturing by a mirror of the industrial revolution that changed so much of British agriculture in the last century. As a result, the production of Vinho Verde will inevitably be driven north and east, away from the heavily populated countryside around Oporto.

Vinho Verde country divides into six officially recognized sub-regions: Monção, Lima, Braga, Basto, Penafiel and Amarante. Physical conditions are fairly similar throughout. From the flat coastal belt, the land rises to the mountain ranges that separate the Minho and Douro provinces from Trás-os-Montes ('behind the mountains') inland. Soils all over the region are poor, often shallow, based on hard underlying granite. Rainfall is abundant everywhere, ranging from around 1,500mm in the south-east to nearly 3,000mm on the windward slopes of the mountains to the north.

With rainfall so plentiful, the irrigation of vineyards (prohibited in theory by both European Community and local legislation) should never be necessary. But water is often needed during the summer for other crops, and the law does not stop growers from diverting some of it in the direction of their vines to increase yields. These are naturally high and, with a little help from irrigation, yields often top 80 hectolitres per hectare. With so many individual smallholders, it is almost impossible for the regulatory Commissão de Viticultura to ensure that everyone stays in line.

The Wines

It comes as something of a shock to find that about two-thirds of all Vinho Verde is not the widely exported white but a rasping, slightly fizzy, dry red. Though the flavour is something of an anathema to most foreign wine drinkers, red Vinho Verde is knocked back in large quantities in country bars and cafés all over the north of Portugal. Much of the red wine drunk locally is made from vigorous hybrid varieties which grow easily on the high-culture systems used by small farmers. Grapes like Isabella and Jacquet may have poetic-sounding names but they make miserably thin, astringent wines that the locals call *vinho morangueiro* because of its supposed strawberry-like flavour.

On the other hand, *Vitis vinifera* varieties like Vinhão, Azal and Espadeiro produce some good, deeply coloured, sappy, rasping reds. Again, these are something of an acquired taste and few go very far outside the region other than to Portuguese emigrants working overseas, but they deserve a fan club all the same. The low levels of alcohol (usually 9 or 10 per cent), slight spritz and abrasive peppery flavours make red Vinho Verde one of the most refreshing wines to drink with rich, oily food.

The production of white Vinho Verde falls into two camps. First of all there are the traditional wines, made from an omnium-gatherum of different grapes in the back parlour of houses and roadside *tascas* all over the region. Pressing and fermentation still occasionally take place in open stone troughs or *lagares*, after which the wine is run off into casks. At this point the secondary malo-lactic fermentation begins, converting the large amounts of harsh malic acid into softer lactic acid. Carbon dioxide is given off in the process and some of this is retained in the wine, giving it a slight natural sparkle. This was how Vinho Verde began; a sort of rough, often cloudy, scrumpy wine which can still be drunk in village bars and cafés in some of the more remote parts of the region.

With the advent of the co-operative movement, which reached Vinho Verde country in the 1950s, more modern vinification methods have come to be used. Most farmers now deliver at least a portion of their crop either to a local co-op or to one of the larger private wineries where they are pressed mechanically (often in continuous presses), and the must is fermented either in lined concrete vats or in temperature-controlled stainless steel tanks. After the alcoholic fermentation has finished, wines are dosed with sulphur dioxide to prevent the malo-lactic from taking place. When it comes to bottling in the late winter or early spring after the harvest, the wine will be given its spritz with an injection of CO_2.

The Portuguese tend to drink white Vinho Verde bone dry, in the year after the vintage while the wine is still fresh and crackling in the glass. But all too often, the Vinho Verde that is prepared for overseas markets is sweetened and then stabilized to prevent it re-fermenting with a heavy-handed dose of sulphur dioxide. By spending too long on warm, well-lit supermarket shelves, Vinhos Verdes consumed abroad are often far removed from the clean, crisp, young, 'green', sparkling wines that are drunk in Portugal. Most Vinhos Verdes don't have a vintage date on the label, so perhaps it is time someone started with 'sell-by' dates on bottles to ensure fresher-tasting wines.

Vinho Verde's six sub-regions are distinguished from one another by the different grapes that go into making the wines. Monção, on the Spanish border in the north, produces one of the best but least typical of all the dry white Vinhos Verdes from the Alvarinho grape. This small, thick-skinned variety makes a wine with fragrant, flowery aromas and flavours akin to biting into a crisp Cox's apple. Alcohol levels of up to 13° set Alvarinho wines apart from other Vinhos Verdes, and because yields are low and production is small the wines tend to be correspondingly expensive. They find their way into all the best restaurants in Lisbon and Oporto, but you won't find many being drunk by locals in the region.

South of Monção, the Lima valley and the adjoining coastal part of the Braga sub-region is now making some equally good wines from Loureiro grapes. This is a more productive variety than Alvarinho, but provided that yields are kept under control, it makes light, aromatic dry whites with around 9 or 10° of alcohol. They occasionally bear a certain similarity to German *trocken* or *halb-trocken* Riesling. Often Loureiro is blended with two other grapes, Trajadura and Paderñā, both of which tend to fill out the wines, sometimes to the detriment of aroma.

In the vineyards of the Basto, Penafiel and the 'urban' zone south of Braga, Azal, Rabigato, and Batoca join Trajadura, Paderñā and occasionally Loureiro. These areas produce the bulk of Vinho Verde sold in the shops under well-known brand or supermarket own-labels. Blends of so many high-yielding grape varieties combine with often indifferent wine-making to produce neutral-tasting wines, high in acidity and low in alcohol.

Wines with more character are being made around Amarante, where another grape, Avesso, tends to ripen to produce fuller flavours, particularly in the warmer, drier vineyards on the banks of the River Douro.

Wines from these six zones are now able to add the name of the sub-region on the label. Few do, although some producers making wines from Alvarinho and Loureiro now choose to add the name of the predominant grape variety where it *is* Alvarinho or Loureiro. But most Vinho Verde is blended from a mish-mash of grapes grown all over the region.

The Wine-makers

Wine-making in Vinho Verde country is regulated by the Oporto-based Commissão, working in close contact with co-operative *adegas*. But there are also several large independent producers and an increasing number of single *quintas* or estates which are making their own highly individual wines.

Co-operatives

The post-war co-operative movement advanced by central government was designed to bring some sort of order to the hundreds of thousands of smallholders in the north of Portugal who were all previously doing their own thing. Vinho Verde country now has twenty-one widely scattered co-ops, from Monção in the north to Vale de Cambra in the south. The largest, at Felgueiras in the heart of the region, has a capacity for 4 million litres of wine.

  Few co-ops are able to pay much of an incentive for quality grapes, so they tend to make do with poor varieties which are often either unripe or rotten when they reach the winery. Most sell their wines in bulk to private merchant companies, who bottle usually rather tired, oxidized wines under their own brand names. A group of thirteen co-operatives have joined forces to establish their own fairly reliable Vercoope or Verdegar brands. The co-op at Ponte da Lima makes good red wines and a fragrant Loureiro which, to my mind, is the best of all the co-operative Vinhos Verdes.

Large Independent Producers

Most of Portugal's larger privately owned wine-making firms have interests in the Vinho Verde region. They are generally in a much stronger position than the co-operatives, as they can afford more up-to-date technology and are able to support their own brands. Many work closely with the growers, offering better prices for their grapes and rapid payment.

Quinta da Aveleda, Penafiel

Fantasy gardens with avenues, ponds and fountains surround the sixteenth-century *quinta* at Aveleda, near the scruffy town of Penafiel. Hidden behind the oak trees and giant camellias is one of Portugal's largest and most modern privately owned wineries. It belongs to the Guedes family, cousins of the Guedes who own Sogrape, and until they went their own way after a domestic dispute in 1979, Aveleda was a part of the Sogrape group (see below).

  Aveleda is a long way from the vine and cabbage patch league. The 60 hectares of vineyard surrounding the gardens provide Aveleda with just 10 per cent of its needs.

The rest, mainly Trajadura and Padernã, is bought from local farmers who are supplied with viticultural expertise to help them to grow better grapes.

Four different wines are made at Quinta da Aveleda. Casal Garcia is the best known and one of the best-selling brands of Vinho Verde. With 9 per cent alcohol and 11 grams per litre of sugar from the addition of concentrated must, it is a clean, medium dry export wine. Aveleda and Quinta da Aveleda are two separate wines made from better-quality grapes, most bought in from local farmers. The first is sweeter and geared to export markets, while the second is classic Vinho Verde – bone dry with crisp, appley acidity. Confusingly, Aveleda's best wine, made entirely from the property's own Loureiro and Trajadura grapes, is bottled under the name of Grinalda.

Quinta da Aveleda is geared up to receiving passing visitors, and it is well worth going to the property both to see the gardens and to taste the wines.

Honra de Azevedo, Barcelos (Sogrape)

After the Guedes family rupture which left Sogrape, Portugal's largest wine-maker, without a Vinho Verde, they bought the Honra de Azevedo estate near Barcelos and set about launching their own wine. Gazela is now the main brand made from grapes grown in the Cavado valley and fermented in stainless steel. 12 grams per litre of residual sugar are left in the wine by curtailing the fermentation with sulphur dioxide, and centrifuging and filtering the wine to remove active yeasts, leaving a fresh, grapey sweetness.

Chello is a dry version of Gazela, while Quinta de Azevedo is an excellent single estate wine from 30 hectares of Loureiro, Trajadura and Padernã grapes growing around the squat, crenellated granite house at the centre of the property. A small section of the vineyard has been set aside for experimentation with different clones.

Borges & Irmão, Oporto

It is something of a misnomer to call Borges & Irmão 'independent' private producers, as they were nationalized along with the banks during the revolution and, at the time of writing, had not returned to private hands. Borges have the largest share of the Vinho Verde export market, with both supermarket own-label wines and their own brand, Gatão, the biggest single brand in Portugal.

Some of the wine is bought in from co-operatives, the rest is made in a rather old-fashioned *adega* at Lixa in the hills above Amarante. With 17 grams per litre of residual sugar, Borges Vinhos Verdes are often marred by the heavy-handed use of sulphur dioxide.

Caves do Casalinho, Felgueiras

Granite outcrops on the Monte de São Bento, near the spa town of Vizela, are painted white by local growers to signify a good harvest. (No one relates what they did in the disastrous harvest of 1988.) On the opposite side of the valley, at Santo Adrião de Vizela, the Camelo and Faria families own 30 hectares of vines surrounding a nineteenth-century *solar* or mansion house named Casalinho. The families buy grapes and wine for the firm's two main brands, Três Marias and Casalinho. These are based on Avesso grown in the hills between Felgueiras and Baião. Casalinho wines therefore have a slightly fuller style than those Vinhos Verdes made from grapes grown nearer to the coast.

Casalinho make a traditional red Vinho Verde from grapes that are foot-trodden in granite, and a small quantity of white that gains its natural sparkle from undergoing malo-lactic in bottle, giving it an attractive yeasty, biscuit-like quality.

Single Quintas

One of the most encouraging developments in the Vinho Verde region in recent years has been the emergence of a number of single estates or *quintas* making their own wine from grapes grown on the property. In 1985 an association, APEVV (Associacão dos Produtores-Engarrafadores de Vinho Verde), was founded to promote the interests of individual growers making their own wine. Conditions for joining are fairly strict. All the grapes must come from the member's own vineyards and the wine must be made and bottled on the property. A number of single-*quinta* producers buying in grapes to make other wines have therefore been refused membership. APEVV started with eighteen members and has now risen to thirty-five individual producers. Most are working hard to make more distinctive wine, uprooting old vines and updating old-fashioned cellars. By no means all have succeeded, but those that have are coming up with some high-quality wines. Those listed here are making Vinho Verde as it should be – clean, fragrant and refreshing. An asterisk (∗) denotes that the owner is a member of APEVV.

∗ Paço d'Anha, Anha, Viana do Castelo
The small port of Viana first exported wines to Britain in the seventeenth century, exchanging them for the *bacalhau* (salt cod) that became Portugal's staple food. The Alpuim family have been making wine at Paço d'Anha just south of the town for nearly as many years. The vineyards were re-planted in 1973, mainly with Loureiro and Trajadura. They perform well in the cool, coastal climate, making a light style of wine with lemon and lime flavours.

Solar das Bouças, Amares
Albano Castro e Sousa built up the reputation of Solar das Bouças as one of the first single-*quinta* wines, and was a leading light in APEVV until he sold his property to the van Zeller family of Port shippers Quinta de Noval in 1989. Twenty-five hectares of vineyard close to the River Cavado, upstream from Barcelos, are planted mainly

with Loureiro. Only the earliest and most gentle pressings are used to make a wonderfully perfumed, dry Vinho Verde with a hint of freshly picked Muscat-like fruit.

❖ Palácio de Brejoeira, Moncão
It is hard to believe that Brejoeira started to sell wine only as recently as 1976, such is its fame (and price) on the Portuguese market. Maria Herminia Pães is the redoubtable owner who planted 17 hectares of Alvarinho vines around this rambling, classical eighteenth-century palace 4 kilometres from the Spanish border. The wine is made from free-run *lagrima* juice in a modern, purpose-built stainless steel winery and bottled young. Alvarinho yields less than other Vinho Verde grapes and produces wines with higher alcohol and more flavour. Brejoeira occasionally reaches a strength of 13° and has a peach and citrus fruit flavour. It is certainly one of Portugal's best white wines but is it really worth paying the price? Depending on where you find it, Brejoeira is between two and four times the price of other single-*quinta* Vinhos Verdes.

❖ Casa de Cabanelas, Bustelo, Penafiel
The current president of APEVV, Luis Gusmão Rodrigues, owns this fifteenth-century property not far from Quinta da Aveleda, just to the north of Penafiel. Azal, Loureiro, Trajadura and Padernã grapes produce a good aromatic, dry Vinho Verde.

Paço do Cardido, Ponte da Lima
High in the Alto Minho, Peter Bright, Australian wine-maker at João Pires, makes a balanced Vinho Verde mainly from Loureiro grapes. The exposure of the vineyard on the south-facing slopes of the Lima valley ensures a wine with more alcohol and fruit than most wines from this area.

❖ Casa de Compostela, Requião, Famalicão
Set in the industrial heartland between Famalicão and Guimarães, Compostela, with 36 hectares of vines, is one of the largest wine-making properties in this congested part of Portugal. Textile manufacturer Manuel Gonçalves makes 3,000 hectolitres a year of light, crisp Vinho Verde, predominantly from Padernã grapes. The modern *adega* is well equipped with stainless steel vats and temperature control.

❖ Quinta do Crasto, Travanca, Cinfães
This is one of the most southerly of all the Vinho Verde single estates, located south of the Douro with terraced vineyards overlooking the River Paiva, one of the most beautiful valleys in Portugal. Traditional wine-making produces a fairly sharp, acidic dry white wine from a blend of Avesso, Azal and Padernã.

Quinta da Franqueira, Franqueira, near Barcelos

There's an Englishman making Vinho Verde. Captain Brian Gallie, a former officer in the Royal Navy, bought Quinta da Franqueira as a ruin in 1966. He set about restoring the property, and his son Pires began planting 6 hectares of vines in 1980, taking over the property on his father's death. Having vinified his early wines in cask, with European Community help he recently built a winery and equipped it with an up-to-date pneumatic press. The wine, made from a blend of Loureiro and Trajadura, is delicate and well balanced with a steely, grapefruit-like acidity.

It is worth noting that the Gallies have opened their house, an old monastery, to paying guests or *turismo de habitacão*. They invite people for Earl Grey tea, chocolate cake and, just to remind you where you are – Vinho Verde.

✳ Quinta do Paço, Lago, Amares

Look out for the Terras da Corga label on the wine from Quinta do Paço in the Cavado valley north of Braga. Loureiro grapes, pressed and fermented in stainless steel, make Terras da Corga one of the most fragrant of all Vinhos Verdes. The Teles e Castro family who own the property make 1,500 hectolitres a year.

Quinta da Pena, Pousada

António Morgado Pires, a company lawyer, bought this run-down property near Braga in 1983 and set about restoring the eighteenth-century house and garden to its former glory. Over 100,000 contos (£400,000) have so far been spent on a new *adega*, well equipped with the latest stainless steel technology. The first harvest from the 21-hectare vineyard took place in 1990. Loureiro, Padernã and Trajadura combine to make a fragrant, lemony Vinho Verde with an alcohol content well above the average.

✳ Casa de Sezim, Nespeira, Guimarães

Former ambassador António Pinto de Mesquita makes a clean, steely dry Vinho Verde from Loureiro, Trajadura and Padernã grapes grown on pergolas. The property has been in the family since 1376 and there is evidence that wine was being made here as long ago as 1390, even though it came on to the market only as recently as 1984. The house, set in the hills south-east of Guimarães, is noted for its collection of rare wallpapers.

✳ Quinta do Tamariz, near Barcelos

António Vinagre is a quiet, soft-spoken man with an unfortunate name, given that he is making one of the best of the region's wines. Over the past ten years he has uprooted most of the mixed *ramada* on his 17-hectare property and replaced them with lower-trained vines. Quinta da Tamariz is now made almost entirely from Loureiro, cool-fermented to keep the distinctive scented aroma and flavour of the grape. An adjoining property, Quinta de Portela, produces a lesser wine from a traditional mix of Vinho Verde grapes.

❋ Paço Teixeiró, Teixeiró, near Mesão Frio

On the leeward slopes of the Serra do Marão, Paço Teixeiró is just a few kilometres from the edge of the demarcated region where Vinho Verde meets Port. The property belongs to the Montez Champalimaud family, who also own a Port *quinta* on the other side of the town of Mesão Frio which marks the border. Miguel Champalimaud, who looks after the wine-making, is a much less controversial character when it comes to Vinho Verde than he is when it comes to Port (see page 90).

The Avesso grape, growing on schistous rather than granite soil, makes a wine which has a slightly higher alcoholic strength (around 11°) than most Vinhos Verdes and a softer, less acidic dry flavour.

❋ Casa da Vila Nova (Tormes), Santa Cruz do Douro, Resende

Overlooking the River Douro, the sturdy, granite Casa da Vila Nova was the inspiration for one of Portugal's greatest nineteenth-century authors, Eça de Queiroz, who wrote *A Cidade e as Serras* (*The City and the Mountains*) there. Maria da Graça de Castro, the widow of Eça's great-grandson, now makes wine on the property and bottles it under the fictional name of Tormes. The terraced, 2-hectare vineyard is mostly planted with Avesso which, fermented in barrel, produces an old-fashioned, savoury style of wine. João Pires (see page 171) have recently taken on the property and plan to make some sweeping changes.

Visiting Vinho Verde Country

Much the best way to explore Vinho Verde country is to leave the congested main roads and travel back in time down the narrow lanes, which are often cobbled with cubes of local granite. Here you will find rattling ox-carts, loaded with grapes at harvest time, and little roadside bars or *tascas* selling their own, often home-made, Vinho Verde.

Everything about this part of Portugal seems to be green. The white sandy beaches north of Oporto, backed by green pines, have earned the name Costa Verde (green coast), although some of the resorts have grown in recent times, turning the skyline into a concrete grey. It is much more interesting to visit the towns inland: places like Barcelos, Braga and Guimarães, all of which are closely linked to the early history of Portugal and have remained important cities in their own right. Barcelos is worth visiting on a Thursday, when the town has the largest outdoor market in Portugal. Street traders from all over the north of the country converge on the enormous central square with everything including the kitchen sink.

Braga, some twenty kilometres away, is Portugal's chief episcopal centre, the seat of the archbishop and a place of pilgrimage for many thousands of devout Christians, who trail around the churches lighting candles for Our Lady. They are kept busy by the claim that Braga has more churches and saints per capita than Rome. Away from the bustle of the city centre, Bom Jesus do Monte is almost a religious theme park for pilgrims, who climb an elaborate set of interwoven baroque steps to reach a sanctuary, cafés, shops, a park and boating lake. The Hotel Elevador, overlooking the funicular lift, is a good place to stay, while Guimarães, Portugal's first capital, has an elegant *pousada* converted from an old convent.

A number of *quintas* or manor houses making their own wine also have accommodation. There are some particularly beautiful properties in the Lima valley, around the towns of Ponte de Lima, Ponte da Barca and Arcos de Valdevez. These are the best way of exploring the more rural north of the region or Alto Minho and the Peneda-Gerês National Park.

Cooking in Vinho Verde country is also 'green'. The spindly cabbages that grow under vines and along roadside verges are used to make a regional staple: *caldo verde* (green broth). This is an economical, potato-based soup enlivened with finely shredded cabbage leaves which can be picked off the tall-growing plants as and when they are required. A few slices of *chouriço* may also be added, releasing spicy oil into the broth. The locals often eat *caldo verde* as a meal in itself, but most restaurants have it as an almost obligatory starter.

Freshwater fish is good in this part of Portugal and goes well with a glass of Vinho Verde. There are salmon in the Minho and trout in the fast-flowing streams of Gerês. For those fancying a glass of red Vinho Verde, the local dish of *rajões a moda do Minho*, a rich, spicy pork stew, goes well with the austerity of the wine. Restaurante Victor at São João de Rei in the hills near Povoa de Lanhoso is a rustic establishment much favoured by local wine-makers. But much the best place to try all the regional dishes is Zé da Calcada (Joe on the Pavement) restaurant at Amarante. It is much more palatial than it sounds. You dine overlooking the River Tamega, and a few simple but well-furnished bedrooms are kept for those who feel that they can't travel any further.

7

Dão:

Portuguese Perestroika

Dão is the name of a river and of a wine. The river is a seasonal stream which cuts a narrow gorge through tough granite hills in the centre of Portugal. The wine comes from vineyards planted in clearings among the aromatic pine and eucalyptus forests that cover most of this part of the country.

The demarcated Dão wine region in fact takes in three river valleys hemmed in on nearly four sides by mountain ranges: the Serras of Buçaco, Caramulo and Estrela. Until 1989, the access to this isolated patch of country was along corkscrew roads that twist inland from the coast to the Spanish border. But now the building of a new, impressively dangerous, mountain-breaching road is sure to bring change to this beautiful but secluded part of Portugal.

Wine-making is changing as well. Since the 1950s, the production of Dão's red and white wines has been concentrated in the hands of the co-ops, who have been the only ones permitted to buy grapes to make into wine. The main reason for this was an attempt by central government to impose some sort of order on the many thousands of tiny farmers all growing their own few vines. In Dão alone, over 100,000 growers farm 20,000 hectares of vines. Simple mathematics puts the size of the average plot of vines at less than 0.2 of a hectare; not much more than a back garden. Often these miniature vineyards are broken up still further by outcrops of rough granite which occasionally stick out through the sparkling, sandy, quartzite soils. Straggly, bush-trained vines climb up the girdle of mountains that surround the Dão to a height of about 500 metres, although most of the wine production comes from lower-lying vineyards around the towns of Nelas, Mangualde and Penalva do Castelo. Viseu, the elegant regional capital, is the administrative centre and the headquarters for the Commissão Vitivinicola which controls Dão.

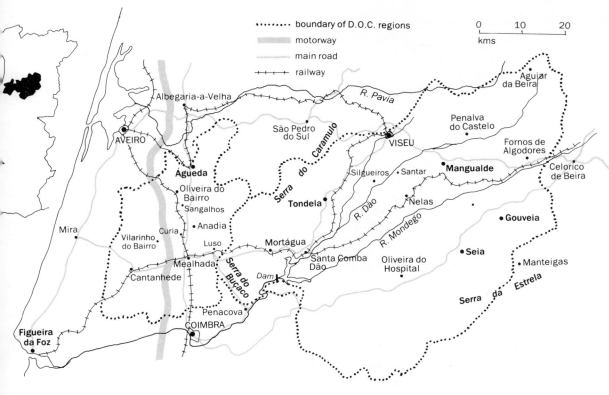

Dão and Bairrada

But Dão's monolithic system for making wine is starting to break up as a consequence of Western *perestroika*, imposed by Brussels. With Portugal's entry into the European Community, the legislative nonsense that gave Dão's co-operatives a stranglehold for over thirty years has been swept away. Overnight, private wine-makers have been given the right to buy grapes from any individual farmer, effectively putting them on equal terms with the co-ops.

At the moment Dão is suffering from the legacy of the past. Over 80 per cent of all the growers still send their grapes to the co-operatives to be made into wine. The co-ops in turn sell most of the wines on to around seventy individual merchants who age, blend and bottle the wine to sell under their own brand labels. Only a handful currently have cellars in the region, though this is beginning to change as the merchants themselves see a future in Dão wine-making now that they can buy in grapes from local growers.

Single *quintas* making and bottling wine from their own vines are also beginning to re-emerge. In post-war years the number of single estates had dwindled to just one property, the Conde de Santar estate, who continued to process their own grapes. A number of historic *quintas* are on the point of launching their own products, helped by enthusiastic merchant-wine-makers who see the potential that exists in the region.

Looking at these important developments as an outsider, one is tempted to exclaim: 'I have seen the future and it works.' This bit of *perestroika* in a region that has suffered from central control for so long is certain to bring about more individuality in Dão wines, as producers are freed from the shackles of sloppy, outdated co-operative wine-making. In turn, farmers have an incentive to grow better grapes.

The Wines

Over two-thirds of Dão wines are red, made from anything up to nine different officially authorized grapes. Touriga Nacional, one of the main Port grapes, has been accepted as the best for the Dão region, and this must now account for a minimum of 20 per cent of any blend. The main also-ran varieties making up the other 80 per cent are Bastardo, Jaen, Tinta Pinheira, Alfrocheiro Preto and another Port grape, Tinta Roriz, alias Spain's Tempranillo. Illegal hybrids, however, are a perennial problem in Dão's muddled vineyards.

Dão reds tend to be firm but are frequently hard and austere from being fermented for too long on the stalks, which gives the wines a harsh, tannic taste. Yet healthy grapes can give the wines attractive raspberry aromas and a blackcurrant-like depth of flavour. One of the difficulties is that few wines are bottled sufficiently early, and the fruity flavours of a young Dão are frequently allowed to fade with protracted ageing in old wooden casks or cement vats. The minimum age of a Dão red before it may be bottled is in fact enshrined in the conservative local law. Eighteen months ageing in bulk with six months in bottle is the minimum for most Dão wines, with at least two years in bulk and a further year in bottle for *garrafeiras*. A number of young, fruity red wines have been rejected in the past by the commission of Dão wine producers, who are empowered to taste samples of all Dão wines before they are put on sale.

White Dão wines also suffer from being aged for too long and can taste oxidized and oily by the time they are drunk. But younger, fresher wines made in temperature-controlled stainless steel are starting to appear, and these can taste clean and lemony. Encruzado, the best grape for making white Dão, is certainly capable of making more of these fragrant dry whites. But mostly it is thrown together with other varieties like Assario Branco, Cerceal and the strangely named Borrado das Moscas ('fly droppings'), called Bical in nearby Bairrada.

The general standard of both red and white Dão wines could be improved enormously with better wine-making in the co-operatives that control the region. But rich, ripe-flavoured reds from good wine-makers are starting to turn up, showing that Dão is capable of making some of Portugal's best wines.

The Wine-makers

Ten co-operatives make more than 80 per cent of all Dão wine, the largest of which are at Silgueiros, Tazem and Tondela. Three merchants, Sogrape, José Maria de Fonseca and UDACA, have kept cellars in the region, while others have bought in bulk and bottled outside Dão.

José Maria da Fonseca, Moimento do Dão

The solid, granite-built Adega de Alcafache at Moimento do Dão is an old railway building converted by Setúbal-based José Maria da Fonseca to age and bottle red and white Dão called Terras Altas (high lands). Like most other Dão wines, Terras Altas has been tied to the co-operatives but José Maria da Fonseca could soon break free and start to make wine on their own. In the past the red has been typically firm and spicy, but with Californian-trained Domingos Soares Franco in charge and a proportion of new oak now being used to age the richer *garrafeiras*, a softer style of wine is beginning to evolve. The white, which used to lack freshness and fruit, has (since 1989) been transformed by stainless steel and temperature control into a cleaner, more zesty wine.

José Maria da Fonseca are launching a wine from a single *quinta*: Casa da Insua, near Penalva do Castelo. This eighteenth-century family-owned property has been making impressively concentrated reds for years, using a proportion of Cabernet Sauvignon grapes. But until now, Cabernet production has been kept back for the household and the rest blended into Terras Altas. From the 1985 harvest it has been sold on its own, though local grape variety laws prohibit Insua from being sold as Dão wine. The white includes a small amount of Sémillon. (See page 168 for more information on José Maria da Fonseca.)

Messias, Mealhada

Messias, the second largest wine-maker in Bairrada, also bottle a good Dão. Wines from co-ops and small farmers around Sampaio, Mangualde and Penalva are aged in the firm's cellars at Mealhada and blended to produce a chunky red which retains plenty of firm fruit. With the relaxation of the laws in Dão, Messias, who also own vineyards in the Douro, are looking to set up their own winery in the region.

Conde de Santar, Santar

In recent years, Conde de Santar has been the only Dão estate to make its own wine. Nearly 200 acres of vines surround the long, low-eighteenth-century house that takes its name from this aristocratic little village in the heart of Dão. Sadly, wine-making standards have been allowed to slip but with the return of the owner's son, Pedro Vasconcellos, from a wine-making course at Montpellier University followed by a stint in Bordeaux, Santar's wines are sure to improve. At the moment, all the wine is bottled by the Port firm Cálem who have a distribution contract until 1994.

Caves São João, São João de Anadia

A merchant outside the Dão region bottles one of the very best Dão reds. Bairrada-based brothers Luis and Alberto Costa select wines carefully from established contacts all over Dão. The backbone of their wines in fact comes from one of the larger private estates, Casa Santos Lima at Silgueiros, who make high-quality wines which they sell in bulk. Caves São João reds labelled Porta dos Cavaleiros, after one of the city gates in Viseu, are solid but generous and ripe-tasting wines that age well. The 1983 Porta dos Cavaleiros Reserva is firm, full and concentrated. Like the 1970, which is still full of liquorice-like fruit, it should last for twenty years. (See page 136 for more information on Caves São João.)

Quinta do Serrado (Carvalho, Ribeiro & Ferreira), Penalva do Castelo

Fourteen hectares of vines surrounded by tall waving cypress trees are the result of a recent investment by Ribatejo-based wine merchants Carvalho, Ribeiro & Ferreira (see page 160). A fresh, fruit-salad-tasting white and a tough, plummy red will soon join the growing ranks of single-*quinta* Dão wines. The company has built its own small winery on site. With CRF now part of Costa Pina, itself a wholly owned subsidiary of the British drinks group Allied Lyons, progress is likely to speed up.

Sogrape – Vinicola do Vale do Dão

Bought by Sogrape (makers of Mateus Rosé) in 1957, Vinicola do Vale do Dão has taken a leading role in the reform of the region's wine-making. In 1981 they did their best to circumvent the law by establishing a contract with the co-operative *adega* at Vila Nova de Tazém. The company guaranteed to buy most of Tazém's production on the condition that Sogrape's technicians were put in charge of the wine-making. The agreement resulted in a marked improvement in Grão Vasco, the leading brand of red and white Dão.

Anticipating changes in Portugal's wine laws following accession to the EC, Sogrape spent 70,000 contos (£280,000) in 1988 buying Quinta dos Carvalhais, a run-down 100-hectare property in the heart of Dão between Mangualde and Nelas with 15 hectares of scrubby old vines.

So began a seven-year plan which is helping to revitalize Dão. Sogrape 'borrowed' two of Portugal's most experienced wine-makers, José Maria Soares Franco and Manuel Vieira, from sister company Ferreira (see pages 86 and 107) to help expand the vineyard and design a new winery. Hazelnut and pine trees have been uprooted and the shallow granite soils planted out with vines. One hectare has been set aside as an experimental vineyard where 12 main regional varieties together with a few foreign interlopers have been planted on eight different rootstocks. The remainder of the property is planted out in plots of Touriga Nacional, Tinta Pinheira,

Tinto Roriz, Jean and Alfrocheiro Preto for red wine and Encruzado, Cerceal and Assario favoured for whites.

But the vineyard at Quinta dos Carvalhais is rather less than half the story. Early in 1990, Sogrape received the go-ahead for a new winery costing 1.5 million contos (£6 million). Six months later (in what proved to be an early vintage) the plant was ready to receive the first grapes. The agreement with Tazem co-op was terminated and Sogrape established contracts with local farmers who now supply the company with around four million kilos of grapes a year.

The winery at Carvalhais has been built with both quality and quantity in mind. At the height of the vintage, six different production lines (three each for red and white) work simultaneously according to the vinification method and the style of the wine. In total, 178 temperature-controlled vats are monitored by a computer software package developed especially for the winery. Below the battery of bright stainless steel, air-conditioned cellars have been filled with new Portuguese oak casks.

Sogrape's wine-makers are aware that Dão has a reputation as a tough, tannic red. For this reason the winery runs by gravity feed to limit unnecessary extraction from pumping. Oak ageing is kept down to two months for white wines and eighteen months for the most venerable Reservas and Garrafeiras. Gone are the days when vibrant, sappy Dão fruit was whittled away by extended ageing in grubby cement vats.

Quinta dos Carvalhais has produced a quantum leap in the quality of Grão Vasco. The crisp, clean dry whites and ripe, peppery reds are a world away from the tired, thin flavours of co-operative-made wines.

Sogrape have also taken charge of the vineyard at nearby Quinta das Fidalgas belonging to descendants of the Portuguese royals. It is soon to be launched along with Quinta dos Carvalhais as a high-quality single estate Dão. (See page 201 for more information on Sogrape).

Sete Torres, São João de Lourosa
Against the odds, José Carlos Oliveira makes good red Dão in an old granite *adega* from grapes growing in vineyards south of Viseu. His wines, especially the Reservas, have a rustic but fleshy character reminiscent of traditional, pre-co-operative Dão.

UDACA, Viseu
This rather institutional name is short for União das Adegas Cooperativas do Dão. As the name suggests, it works with the co-operatives, blending, bottling and marketing some of their wines under the UDACA label. The organization is headed by Fernando Moreira, a lively, wiry old man who for the last forty years has been 'Mr Dão' and the dynamo behind some of the co-ops. From musty, old-fashioned premises in the centre of Visseu, UDACA has recently moved to an ultra-modern

stainless steel winery outside the town. Funded partly by the European Community, it should help to take the co-operatives out of the wine-handling dark ages. UDACA already bottles some of the best co-operative-made red Dão wines, which can taste vigorous and fruity if caught young.

Visiting Dão

Away from the new highway which cuts across the region, a network of narrow roads twists through the pines and vineyards between solid granite towns and villages. Viseu, itself built on an outcrop of granite, is the only place of any size. Around the grey Gothic and Baroque cathedral and the cramped old town, spacious parks, gardens and squares give Viseu a dignified air. Grão Vasco (apart from being the name of a wine) was the leading member of the school of painting which flourished here in the sixteenth century, whose works can be viewed in the museum adjoining the cathedral. The Hotel Grão Vasco in the centre of town is a good place to stay.

Near Viseu there are attractive wine-making villages set in rocky country. Santar and Penalva do Castelo are probably the most interesting. Around the edge of the Dão region are high mountains with attractive spa towns like Caramulo, São Pedro do Sul and Manteigas, all of which have summer hotels. The Palace Hotel at Buçaco, which makes its own excellent wines, is not far away and is a good base from which to visit both the Dão and the Bairrada wine regions. (See pages 138 and 195).

Food in Dão can be rustic, though some of the best is to be found in one of the most rustic of restaurants, the Martelo at Silgueiros near Viseu, which is worth a special visit. In the absence of a cellar for keeping wine, bottles are dug up cool out of the earth floor. Kid (*cabrito*) cooked over charcoal goes well with a bottle of red Dão, as does one of Portugal's most famous cheeses, the tangy Queijo da Serra. It has a demarcation all of its own extending from the Serra da Estrela. O Cortiço, behind the cathedral in Viseu, is another good place to eat the local food and sample bottles of Dão wine.

8

Bairrada:
Baga, Baga, Baga

Between the mountains and the coast south of Oporto is Bairrada, a strip of fertile maritime country on the Portuguese *litoral* (see map, page 127). *Barro* is the Portuguese word for clay, while *Bairro* means a settlement. Taken either way, astride the north-south highway which slices through the region, there is a maze of narrow lanes linking industrious little villages eking a living from the Bairrada's rich clay soils.

Like most of northern Portugal, Bairrada is an area of agricultural smallholdings. Clumps of tall pine and eucalyptus sway in the Atlantic breeze, sheltering small plots of cereals, beans and knotty old vines.

Although Bairrada was demarcated only fairly recently, it has been producing wine for centuries. In fact by the early 1700s Bairrada's dark, tannic red wines were being drunk in Britain, often in Port-like blends with wines from the Douro valley to the north. Then along came the Marquês de Pombal, Portugal's powerful eighteenth-century Prime Minister. At the same time as drawing boundaries around the Douro, making it one of the world's first delimited wine regions, he ordered that Bairrada's vineyards should be uprooted to protect the authenticity of Port. After suffering the great vineyard plagues of oidium and phylloxera, Bairrada only really re-emerged as an important wine region in the early years of this century. It missed out on the wave of demarcations in the early 1900s and, after years of campaigning from Bairrada's growers and wine-makers, finally gained official status in 1979.

Today's Bairrada stretches nearly 40 kilometres, from the outskirts of the lagoon city of Aveiro in the north down the pine-clad coast to Coimbra, Portugal's Oxbridge, in the south. In between, 20,000 hectares of vines are farmed by as many small growers, most of whom deliver their grapes to one of six co-operatives to be made into wine. But, unlike neighbouring Dão (see page 126), Bairrada has never been constrained by rules protecting co-ops, and over twenty merchants also have cellars in the region making and/or buying and blending Bairrada wines. More recently a number of single estates have started making their own wines, and these are where some of the most distinctive Bairradas are to be found.

The Wines

Over 80 per cent of Bairrada's wines are red; big, ripe, but often hard, tannic reds that need time in bottle to soften. The reason for this is the Baga grape (pronounced rather like an expletive), which by law must make up at least half of any Bairrada red and usually accounts for rather more. *Baga* means berry, which aptly describes these small, dark, thick-skinned grapes which give both colour and tannin to the wines. Matters are sometimes made worse by fermenting with the stalks, to produce reds that are so numbingly green and tannic when young that they take five years or more to soften up into something drinkable. But styles are changing and, in order to make Bairrada wines that are more appealing to drink young, some producers are experimenting with carbonic maceration and shorter skin contact to make softer, earlier-maturing wines. Over two-thirds of Bairrada's Baga vineyards are more than fifty years old, so few vineyards achieve the maximum permitted yield of 55 hectolitres to the hectare. Most produce considerably less, and as a result can make wines with a wonderful intensity of fruit underneath a mask of tannin. Modern vineyards are including more Castelão Frances as well as some Cabernet Sauvignon, to make firm but approachable reds.

White grapes account for around 10 per cent of the region's production. Most are used to make sparkling wines (see page 204), though there are a few still white wines, some of them deliciously fresh and aromatic. Maria Gomes (not a girl but a grape), with help from Bical, Arinto and Cerceal, can make crisp, grapey whites which are sometimes enhanced by macerating the fermenting must on the skins to give the wine more aroma. There is also some experimental Chardonnay in the region, successfully making small quantities of dry white wine.

The Wine-makers

Co-operatives make over 40 per cent of Bairrada's wine. Only a small quantity of this is ever sold under the co-op's own label, and most is bought by merchants both inside and outside the region who age, blend, bottle and sell wines. More than forty merchants are currently authorized to bottle Bairrada but only twenty have cellars in the region. From this long list, there are a handful who make their own wine as well, producing some of the best and most distinctive Bairradas.

Caves Aliança, Sangalhos

Founded in 1920, Caves Aliança is one of the most up-to-date of the larger merchants operating in Bairrada. By enlisting the help of local growers, Aliança now control much of their own production of Bairrada and are currently leading the way with vinification experiments to make softer, fruity reds and clean, fresh-tasting whites.

Wine-maker Dido Mendes trained in California and some of his international experience has rubbed off on the wines. He aims to make a red Bairrada that is drinkable in its second year or even earlier, judging by the 1988, which was good to drink after just ten months. Carbonic maceration with whole grapes works in much the same way as it does in Beaujolais, although the wines are still dark and firm with plenty of blackcurrant-like fruit. Less Baga and more Castelão Frances also helps.

Aliança's white wines are crisp and aromatic from skin maceration followed by a long, cool fermentation in stainless steel. The secondary malo-lactic fermentation is prevented, leaving the wines with a fresh, steely taste.

Caves Aliança also buy and blend wines from other parts of Portugal, including the neighbouring Dão and Vinho Verde. Their cellars at Sangalhos produce brandy and sparkling wines for the domestic market. (See Chapter 16.)

Messias, Mealhada

The Messias family have wine-making interests in the Douro, Dão, Vinho Verde country and in Bairrada, where they are the second largest producers. The company owns 160 hectares of vineyard in the region, growing mainly white grapes, and buys in Baga from small farmers to make their own red wines. Most of the white wine is used to make a good, clean *espumante*, but grapes growing at Quinta do Valdoeiro near Pampilhosa are kept back to make an aromatic dry white that is fresh and grapey from being fermented at cool temperatures in stainless steel.

Red wines, fermented in cement autovinification tanks, are supple and well rounded without the hard tannins that make so many Bairradas difficult to drink. Young wines made entirely from Baga have plenty of colour and a rich, fleshy character, while older *garrafeiras* are ripe and round, maintaining good depth of fruit. There is, however, a problem with inconsistent quality from Messias.

Luís Pato, óis do Bairro

Luís Pato began making his own wines only in 1980 but has quickly established himself as the Bairrada's most innovative wine-maker. He inherited 60 hectares of vineyard from his father, João, and took to wine-making full-time in 1984 after leaving a job in ceramics. Now, with vineyards scattered around the heart of Bairrada, he makes better wines as the years go by, forever experimenting with new techniques and ideas.

One of Pato's best wines to date is his 1985, the first year he destalked his crop of Baga before fermentation. He is currently experimenting with different types of oak, to get the right sort of tannin in place of the harsh and often bitter flavours that come from stalks.

Grapes from different vineyards are vinified separately. Those from the heavy clay soils typical in Bairrada make richer, fuller wines, while the more sandy vineyards make reds that are softer and lighter. Two wines, one labelled Luís Pato, the other Quinta do Ribeirinho, reflect this, the former being fuller and more generous in flavour. Another red, made with Cabernet Sauvignon and Baga, is ripe and minty after spending two months in new oak casks.

White wines are made from native grapes, including one called the Cercealinho, a cross between Cerceal and Vinho Verde's Alvarinho. Fermentation on the skins and early bottling makes a fragrant, floral white with overtones of a dry Muscat.

Luís Pato's sparkling wines include a deliciously fruity rosé and a white made entirely from the red Baga grape. There seems to be no end to Luís Pato's thirst for experiments.

Caves São João, São João de Anadia

Neat cobwebby cellars on either side of a narrow lane in the heart of the Bairrada are stacked with bottles of some of the best long-lasting reds in the region. Most of the wine is bought from co-operatives, although Caves São João have 16 hectares of their own vines at Quinta do Poço do Lobo ('well of the wolf') near Cantanhede. Two fastidious brothers, Alberto and Luís Costa, are responsible for the careful selection of wine that makes their Bairradas so good. Wines sold under the Frei João label, with a small picture of the monastery at Buçaco on the front, are ripe and long-living. The 1980 is well balanced but still tannic after ten years and should last for another ten or twenty. The Frei João Reservas, distinguished with a cork label, will last even longer. The 1966 is deep in colour with a big, spicy flavour.

A new wine, Quinta do Poço do Lobo, made from 3 hectares of their own Cabernet Sauvignon, has a firm, blackcurrant varietal character. The Costa brothers are also experimenting with ageing wines in new French oak and now have some stainless steel to make a small amount of fresh, dry white. Older whites fermented and aged in oak can taste rich and buttery. Caves São João's Dão wines (see page 130) bottled under the Porta dos Cavaleiros label are worth looking out for.

Sogrape, Anadia

Bairrada has long been the hidden source of Mateus Rosé, one of Portugal's best-known exports. Sogrape, the makers of Mateus, have a gleaming high-tech plant in the heart of the region at Anadia and they are now using this to make a red and white Bairrada named Terra Franca. To begin with, rather heavy-handed thermo-vinification (heating the unfermented must for an hour to 70°C to extract colour rather than tannin) showed up in the wines. However, recent Terra Franca reds made from a blend of Baga, Castelão Frances and Tinta Pinheira grapes have been more attractive, combining the deep berry-fruit character so typical of young Bairrada with soft approachable tannin. The Terra Franca *garrafeira* is more traditional with untamed but astringent Baga-fruit flavours.

Sogrape have recently acquired their own vineyards in Bairrada including Quinta de Pedralvites near Mealhada which produces a delicate dry white wine with an aroma of nuts and apples. It is made entirely from the Maria Gomes grape. The white Bairrada Reserva fermented and aged in new Portuguese oak combines fragrant fruit with a rich, Burgundian character. Finally, the latest addition to Sogrape's ever expanding range of wines is a classical Bairrada rosé called Nobilis. (For more information about this and the history of Sogrape see pages 201–2.)

Adega Co-operativa de Vilarinho de Bairro

In a country where co-operative *adegas* have been the byword for inefficiency and uninspired wine-making, Vilarinho de Bairro stands out from the crowd. Drawing on grapes from over 700 growers around the villages of Vilarinho, São Lourenco de Bairro, Paredes de Bairro and Amoreira de Gandara the co-operative produces deep, dense red wines that are demanded by merchants all over Portugal. Caves São João who are held in high regard for their traditional red Bairradas (see page 136) are one of the most significant buyers.

Other merchants buying and blending some good red wines from Bairrada include Caves Acácio on the coast at Miramar, Caves Primavera at Mealhada and Vinexport near Coimbra. Beware, however, of a certain amount of variation between different bottles of the same wine.

Visiting Bairrada

Many people pass through Bairrada without even realizing it. The Lisbon-Oporto motorway slices straight through the vineyards, and vines even spill over on to roadside embankments. On the old main road you certainly knew when you were in Bairrada from all the restaurants with big signs outside reading '*Ha leitão*'. *Leitão* is Bairrada's delicacy: suckling pig baked in brick ovens until it is crisp and peppery. The local firm-flavoured reds go well with *leitão*, cutting through the rich, oily flavour. The town of Mealhada and the Pedro dos Leitões restaurant are usually thronged with hungry travellers who make detours to go there.

Away from the main routes, Bairrada is a rural haven. A series of villages called 'something do Bairro' mark the centre of the vineyard region. At Sangalhos some of the larger wine producers welcome visitors, and the Estalagem Sangalhos in the pinewoods outside the town is a good place to stay. Two rather old-fashioned spa towns, Curia and Luso, have a number of hotels, while on the edge of the region, the national park of Buçaco has a splendid hotel installed in a former royal palace making its own excellent wine. More information on this can be found on page 195.

9

Oeste Country

The rolling countryside north of Lisbon is covered with vines. The Oeste (pronounced like a sort of drunken 'wesht') produces more wine than any other single region in Portugal, yet few people have ever heard of it. The reason is that this strip of land running from Lisbon's hinterland up Portugal's west (*oeste*) coast makes few wines of any quality.

Henry Vizetelly, writing in 1877, reports that the 'neutral-tasting red wines' from the Oeste were 'exported in large quantities to France for mixing with the pale and poorer growths of the northern wine-growing departments'. The rest was either drunk in Lisbon or distilled to make the grape spirit used to fortify Port. Some wine is still sold for the manufacture of Portugal's national brands of vermouth, but the remainder is simply drunk by thirsty locals. Most of the wine from these lush Atlantic vineyards goes into anonymous blends, sold in the plastic-covered five-litre *garrafões* that can be seen in roadside taverns or *tascas* all over Portugal or anywhere in the world that there is a Portuguese community.

This provides little incentive for farmers to produce good grapes. Most of the region's growers put quantity before quality in order to maximize returns from their tiny plots of land. As a result, vines have been planted for their yield and resistance to disease in the Oeste's humid Atlantic climate. Few growers seem to be concerned about the varieties growing in their vineyards and, in spite of incentives from the European Community to improve things, many are still riddled with high-yielding hybrid vines. Although, legally, wine made from hybrid grapes may no longer be sold in bottle in the European Community, the locals seem to have developed a taste for it and much continues to be drunk in the fields and at home.

There are as many as thirty-three different grapes officially permitted in the

Oeste but, because most farmers do not seem to know which varieties are growing in their vineyards, you really cannot be sure. With a tradition of making wine for distillation, there are more white grapes planted than red. The main white varieties are Vital, Jampal, Arinto, Fernão Pires and Rabo de Ovelha, all of which could make clean white wine if handled carefully. Among the reds are the Periquita or João de Santarém depending on what you want to call it, Trincadeira, and Tinta Miuda ('small red one'), which is supposed to be the same as the Graciano planted in small quantities in Rioja. But there are also the Carignan and the dreary *teinturiers* Alicante Bouschet and Grand Noir, vines which the French have suffered for long enough in their Midi vineyards and which they are busy replacing with *cépages ameliorateurs* that make better-tasting wine.

Viticultural practices in the Oeste are rudimentary. Vines are pruned and trained to grow large quantities of grapes, and yields from the region's over-vigorous, straggly, unkempt vines frequently exceed 100 hectolitres per hectare. Irrigation is, in theory, forbidden unless permission is granted in special circumstances by the IVV, but this does not stop some smallholders turning on the tap occasionally to water their vines.

When it comes to the harvest in mid-September, tractors towing trailers piled high with grapes groan along winding roads. Most are delivering to the local co-operatives which control the region's wine-making. They pay the growers on the basis of the weight of the grapes and their alcoholic strength. There are few, if any, price incentives for bringing quality varieties. Grapes from muddled vineyards therefore end up being dropped off in a heap and vinified together in huge vats.

Wine-making in the region is improving, although, as in the vineyards, practices are still fairly sloppy and rudimentary. Cement vats are part of the fabric of many Portuguese co-operatives, most of which were built to the same basic design. Although some stainless steel is now being installed in some of the larger, wealthier co-ops, it is almost impossible to take away the old concrete vats without rebuilding the winery altogether. Few co-ops have the apparatus to cool fermentations and wines, white and red, are often made at dangerously high temperatures. Most are then aged in cement as well, and are bottled tasting oxidized and devoid of fruit.

The Oeste illustrates the folly of Portugal's (and the European Community's) demarcation system. Of the twenty-eight new regions proposed by the government in 1989, six are in the Oeste. Óbidos in the north and Alenquer close to Lisbon in the south are perhaps the only two new IPRs (Indicacão de Proveniência Regulamentada) to show any real potential. The others, Encostas d'Aire, Alcobaça, Arruda and Torres Vedras, really only have co-operatives to their name. Although there are some climatic differences between the cooler, damper coastal zones and the parched hills inland, at the moment any differences in the quality and style of the wines are really governed by the level of co-operative wine-making skills.

But even against this rather depressing backdrop there are signs of improvement in the Oeste. First of all, the authorities are beginning to talk about grape varieties and a research establishment has been set up at Dois Portos in the heart of the region to look into the matter. Co-operatives, at one time concerned only with levels of potential alcohol, are beginning to give inducements to growers bringing in better grapes from which they can make varietal wines. With help from the European Community, some co-ops are modernizing and improving the standard of their wine-making. But the best prospect for the Oeste lies in the few single estates which are bravely sticking their necks out to make and market individual wines, and there is one co-op that has scored a hit in the UK with a good, inexpensive red wine.

The Wines from north to south:

Encostas d'Aire

This is the largest of the Oeste's new regions, covering the arid limestone hills of the Serra d'Aire around Leiria, Fatima and Pombal. White varieties 'recommended' in the IPR legislation are Fernão Pires, Arinto, Malvasia, Tamarez and Vital, with Alicante Branco, Boal, Borrado das Moscas, Diagalves and Rabo de Ovelha 'authorized' to pull up the rear. Crazy yields of up to 80 hectolitres per hectare are permitted. Red wines should be made from João de Santarém, Baga and Trincadeira Preta, with Grand Noir an 'authorized' variety presumably because there is so much of it. Most of the wine-making takes place in co-ops but, to date, there is no one worthy of note.

Alcobaça

The low hills around the abbey town of Alcobaça are sprouting with lush green vines. The climate is cooler and more Atlantic than on the barren slopes of the Aire mountains and is therefore favoured by growers seeking high yields. The IVV have their out-of-town headquarters here. Vital grapes yield large quantities of low-alcohol white suitable only for distillation. Reds tend to be thin from over-production, while the law states that they must age in bulk for at least fourteen months before bottling. But then the law is so often an ass!

Óbidos

In spite of the name, the walled showpiece town of Óbidos falls just outside the boundaries of the region. The nearby village of Gaeiras and two enormous co-ops at Bombarral and Cadaval are the principal wine-making centres. Rules on permitted grape varieties are a bit tighter than in Alcobaça, though yields of up to 90 hectolitres per hectare are allowed for white wines; 70 hectolitres for reds. João de Santarém, Bastardo, Tinta Miuda and Camarate are recommended for making red wines, with no more than 5 per cent of Carignan and/or Grand Noir allowed to enter a blend.

Production from the region amounts to over a million hectolitres, mostly low-alcohol white wine for *aguardente*. But two producers in the region show that there is some potential.

Alenquer

Alenquer is a quiet whitewashed country town stacked up the side of a narrow, meandering valley. It gives its name to the most promising and best co-ordinated of the Oeste's IPRs. Alenquer's chief strength is that its wine-making is not just in the hands of the co-ops. There are three co-operatives in the villages of Merceana, Olhavo and Labrugueira but there are also three single estates making their own wines.

Vineyards along the banks of the Alenquer and Ota rivers are planted predominantly with Camarate, João de Santarém and Tinta Miuda for reds and Arinto, Fernão Pires, Jampal and Vital for whites. One grower has also planted some Chardonnay. The red wines are the most interesting. Protection from cool, damp Atlantic breezes by the Serra da Montejunto ensures that the grapes ripen well, making full-flavoured, spicy wines, some of which develop with age. A small amount of Cabernet Sauvignon is growing in the region with some success.

For a time Alenquer's future as a wine-making district seemed to be permanently blighted by the decision to build Lisbon's much needed new airport over the existing airstrip at nearby Ota. An alternative site south of the Tagus has now been announced (see page 172).

Torres Vedras

Torres Vedras has had a conspicuous start to life as an IPR but for all the wrong reasons. When the Instituto da Vinha e do Vinho came out with a list of new denominations in 1989, the Torres Vedras region was designated 'Torres'. Portugal, possibly trying to pull a fast one on her ambivalent neighbours, caused enormous problems for Bodegas Torres, owned by the Torres family in Penedés, Spain. Because of a European Community rule which forbids a wine-maker from calling his wine or winery after a demarcated region, Torres Vedras threatened to steal the name of one of the world's best-known wine-makers. Miguel Torres managed to hang on to his name only after canvassing the support of Portugal's own leading wine-makers, few of whom have much time for the new legislation, and some high-level negotiations in Brussels and Lisbon. And the argument has all been over a co-operative making some pretty dreary wines.

The Torres Vedras region embraces productive vineyards between the Serra de Montejunto and the coast. Large amounts of acid dry whites are made, mainly from Vital and Jampal. Much mysteriously ended up as Vinho Verde after the disastrous 1988 harvest. Some of the rest was sold more honestly as *vinho leve* – 'light wine', with 9° of alcohol.

Red wines made from Mortagua, João de Santarém and Tinta Miuda with more than a drop of Alicante Bouschet are often thin and weedy. Even so, the law says that they must be matured for a minimum of eight months before bottling.

Arruda

This is the last piece in the Oeste's complicated jigsaw puzzle of IPR regions. It fits tightly into the hills between Bucelas, Alenquer and Torres Vedras, 8 kilometres from the Tagus at Vila Franca da Xira. The dozy little town of Arruda dos Vinhos has wine enshrined in its name. Every September the place wakes up as hundreds of tractors brush past lanky vines towing trailers brimful with grapes. The windmill-capped hills surrounding the town are some of the most intensively cultivated in Portugal, producing about 12 million litres of wine a year, the bulk of which is made by the local co-operative.

Red wine dominates. Camarate, João de Santarém and Tinta Miuda ripen well in the shelter of the hills and make deep-coloured wines that taste firm and sappy when young. Under the new rules, these grapes must add up to at least 80 per cent of a blend, with Alicante Bouschet and Grand Noir making up no more than 10 per cent of the rest. White wines rely on Fernão Pires, Jampal and Vital, while Arinto, highly thought of over the hill in Bucelas, is limited to 20 per cent of an Arruda blend. Yields are frighteningly high – 80 hectolitres for red wines and 90 for the whites.

The Wine-makers

Quinta da Abrigada, Abrigada (Alenquer)

Some of the best wines in the Oeste are made at this 400-hectare property at the foot of the Serra de Montejunto. The house dating from the fifteenth century is surrounded by 35 hectares of vines planted early this century by Francisco Pinheiro Gorjão Henriques whose descendants own the nearby lavatory factory and continue to make wine.

João Machado and Carlos Empis currently oversee the production of some good though traditional, leathery cask-aged reds made predominantly from João de Santarém grapes. Garrafeiras, aged in an increasing proportion of new oak, are often excellent and continue to develop in bottle. Abrigada's white wines made entirely from Arinto are less distinctive but recent vintages taste cleaner and fresher now that they are cool-fermented in stainless steel. A second red, labelled Terras do Rio, is light and insubstantial.

Adega Co-operativa de Arruda

From the outside, Arruda looks much like any other rural co-operative; a dreary, utilitarian building of the sort put up by the state all over Portugal in the 1950s and

1960s. But the wines are much more interesting. Since they were tracked down by Britain's Sainsbury's supermarket, the red Arruda has almost become a household name. A blend of local grapes, mainly João de Santarém and Tinta Miuda, makes a full, sappy, red wine tasting of ripe cherry fruit. It sees no wood and is bottled young to be on the supermarket shelves after two years. The white Arruda is much less good and shares the problem of many of the other white wines in the region – out-of-date methods of vinification.

Adega Co-operativa de Bombarral (Óbidos)
Over 90 per cent of the wine made at this up-country co-op with over 2,000 members is old-fashioned, acid, dry white made from locally grown Vital and Seminario grapes. Red wines made predominantly from João de Santarém can taste pleasantly fresh and fruity when drunk young.

Quinta de Folgorosa, Folgorosa near Dois Portos (Torres Vedras)
Ribatejo-based merchants Carvalho Ribeiro & Ferreira (see page 160) took a courageous, some would say foolhardy, decision when they decided to buy this delightful hill-top property in 1980. The district has a dreadful reputation making it difficult to launch a new wine on the domestic market.

Most of the 45-hectare property has been replanted with João de Santarém and Tinta Miuda for the reds and Vital, Arinto and Fernão Pires for white wines. With investment in a new winery and the appointment of José Nevado, a well-qualified wine-maker, Folgorosa's wines should be much better. The white is reasonably clean but characterless while the reds taste lean and astringent after spending two years ageing in oak vats before bottling. After suffering a shortage of capital CRF were bought by Costa Pina, a subsidiary of Allied Lyons. Folgorosa is likely to improve.

José Gomes, Gaeiras (Óbidos)
The scruffy little village of Gaeiras is within sight of pristine Óbidos but is well thought of locally for its wines. 'Oiro de Óbidos' from José Gomes is the best-known label, and the reds, made mainly from João de Santarém grapes, can taste good in a rustic sort of way. The white wine, like most from this region, are best avoided.

Quinta das Pancas, Pancas (Alenquer)
The Guimarães family inherited Pancas at a difficult time. When they moved in in 1973 there was only the most primitive of *adegas*, and no tractor to cultivate 45 hectares of muddled old vines. A year later came the 25 April revolution, prompting a period of political instability and high interest rates that have held back investment all over Portugal. This is the reason why Pancas, a splendid sixteenth-century *quinta* just outside Alenquer, looks rather run-down and out of sorts. But Joaquim

Guimarães has some big ideas. With grants from the European Community he has already replanted 20 hectares of vines, supplementing Arinto and Jampal with Chardonnay and João de Santarém and Camarate with Cabernet Sauvignon. The wine-making is still fairly basic, though Guimarães intends to rebuild the crumbling *adega* and remove the concrete vats. At the moment he makes three different wines. The white Vinho Maior is fermented in stainless steel at around 18°C and bottled young, six months after the harvest. It tastes clean and fresh though the Chardonnay, which accounts for around a third of the blend, gives little character to a rather neutral wine. The red Vinho Maior is a more successful 50/50 amalgam of berry-fruit Cabernet and João de Santarém, aged for eight months in oak bought from João Pires. The third Pancas wine, Vinho de Parrotes, made entirely from native grapes, is rather too light and insubstantial; an 11.5° wine more typical of the Oeste.

Quinta dos Platanos, Merceana (Alenquer)
Like Pancas, Quinta dos Platanos is an old-established estate which has belonged to descendants of the Dukes of Merceana for over 400 years. It was developed into a wine-making property in the last century and planted with Fernão Pires and Vital for making white wines and Camarate, João de Santarém and Tinta Miuda for reds. The red wines are the most interesting: big, firm and chewy with good underlying cherry fruit.

António Bernardino Paulo da Silva, Azenhas do Mar
Paulo da Silva, or Chitas for short, has managed to survive the demise of vineyards in Colares only by buying in and bottling wines from the Oeste. Two wines, Beira Mar and Casal de Azenha, are often confused with Colares but are in fact blends from growers inland. They are among the best wines made in the region; dark, four square but packed with ripe fruit. Some of the vintages on the labels are a little too far-fetched, though, especially on the 'older' *garrafeiras*. (See page 150 for information on Paulo da Silva's Colares wines.)

Adega Co-operativa de Torres Vedras
The Torres Vedras Co-operative is the largest in the country, with 1,800 member growers together responsible for a staggering output of nearly 50 million litres of wine. But in this case big is not beautiful. Founded in 1949, Torres Vedras belongs to the early days of the co-operative movement in Portugal and even now there is little to see in the way of up-to-date wine-making. Torres Vedras wines tend to lack fruit and taste old-fashioned. The young varietal reds are better than the whites, most of which continue to be fermented at high temperatures and consequently lack freshness.

Visiting the Oeste

The Oeste takes up a major part of Portugal's Estremadura, the humid coastal belt stretching from the Setúbal Peninsula through Lisbon as far as the city of Leiria. Being so close to the capital, the Oeste has always been densely populated and new houses are springing up all over the countryside. In the south, Lisbon's suburbs are slowly spilling over the hills, taking over the city's agricultural hinterland. But the gaunt convent at Mafra, the largest building in Portugal, dominates the windswept limestone plateau and is a landmark for miles around.

Further north the region is more rural and the roads become frustratingly twisty, particularly in September and October when they are crowded with an assortment of slow-moving vehicles delivering grapes to the local co-op. Óbidos is one of the best-preserved towns in Portugal, and the ramparts that completely encircle the old whitewashed houses provide a good vantage point to survey the surrounding landscape. Nearby, at Alcobaça and Batalha, are two beautiful monasteries built out of the local honey-coloured stone. At Alcobaça there is also a small wine museum belonging to the Instituto da Vinha e do Vinho, which has a display of old vineyard implements and wine-making equipment.

The coastline is wild and windy. Old fishing communities like Ericeira, Peniche and Nazaré have developed into small, neat resorts. All have good hotels, and beachside restaurants serve freshly caught fish, making up for the lack of culinary tradition in the Oeste. Inland at Óbidos there's a *pousada* and a number of privately owned *solares* or mansion houses offering *turismo de habitacão* accommodation. The Alcaide, on the main street, is a good place to eat and sample the local Gaeiras wines.

10

Lisbon's Vineyards: Disappearing Tricks

There was a time when vineyards penetrated deep into Lisbon's tightly drawn city boundaries and wines were made where washing now hangs in tall streets. Henry Vizetelly describes the vineyards in Lisbon's Termo: 'a succession of hills and dales' with 'ample sites for the cultivation of the vine'. Camarate, Sacavém and Olivais, important wine-producing villages in the nineteenth century, have grown into scruffy suburbs surrounding Lisbon airport.

Today, vineyards as far as 40 kilometres from the centre of the capital are threatened by rising land prices and rampant development as Lisbon joins other towns and cities in a quest for more space. Three regions, Colares, Bucelas and Carcavelos, officially demarcated early this century, are caught between the ever-expanding city, the river estuary and the coast (see map, page 165). The saddest part of it is that two of them, at least, are capable of making some of Portugal's most distinctive wines. Three significant recent developments may be just enough to save each of these historic vineyards.

Colares

You have to be an incurable wine romantic to appreciate what's left of Colares. All that remains of this once great wine region on Portugal's west coast are a few hectares of gnarled cliff-top vineyard buffeted by Atlantic westerlies. The vines that earned their fame by surviving Europe's nineteenth-century phylloxera crisis are having difficulty resisting the commercial pressures of the latter part of the twentieth century.

Finding the vineyards in Colares is a bit like playing a party game of 'hunt the thimble'. There are now only a handful of growers tending less than 100 hectares of straggly vines. The vines, though, are unique. The Ramisco is probably the only *Vitis vinifera* grape variety never to have been grafted. It is to be found planted only in a narrow strip of pale-coloured sand about 200 or 300 metres above the Atlantic, which you hear crashing on to the rocks below. These dune soils, three metres or more in depth, protected Colares from the root-munching phylloxera louse that ravaged European vineyards in the nineteenth century. Then, when the rest of Europe had to graft their vines on to phylloxera-resistant American rootstock, Colares continued to plant its own ungrafted Ramisco vines.

Ironically, the sandy soils that protected Colares are making it less and less viable to make wine there today. Every time a vineyard is replanted a trench has to be dug, excavating the sand to reach the underlying clay in which the roots of the young vine are anchored. This used to be done by hand. One man would dig the hole while another would wait at the top ready to throw a basket over the head of the digger to prevent him suffocating if the sides of the trench should suddenly cave in. Not surprisingly, there are few people prepared to go to these lengths to plant a vineyard today. This is why Colares is now left with a few hectares of old, twisted vines.

But ungrafted Ramisco vines will go on producing grapes for over 100 years compared with the mere thirty- or forty-year life-span of vines growing on American rootstock in other European vineyards. The plants are trained to creep along the ground, and may be pegged down and layered to give rise to what seem to be half a dozen or more independent plants all rooted on a single mother vine. On the other hand, one sturdy trunk may sprawl like a giant snake, supported at intervals by *pontões*, small bamboo props which prevent the bunches of grapes being scorched in summer by the burning sand. From a distance, the vineyards of Colares look rather like an abandoned kitchen garden, protected from relentless sea breezes by a chequerboard of woven bamboo windbreaks and a few stunted cane bushes and apple trees.

The growers are not unlike the vines. Small, bent old men toil in their tiny, fragmented vineyards in the same way as they have for centuries. With yields low by any standards – below 40 hectolitres per hectare – their sons have left the vineyards to find more profitable and less arduous work, like building the little seaside villas that are taking the place of vines all along this wild and beautiful coast.

It all sounds like a story of despair, but there is one recent development that might just be enough to save Colares from extinction. A local producer, Tavares & Rodrigues, has recently planted 12 hectares of Ramisco vines in a clearing in the pinewoods near Azenhas do Mar. The sandy soils were excavated with a mechanical digger and the vines have been planted, pruned and trained in an orderly manner to allow for the future use of machinery. With screens of bright blue plastic netting taking the place of the traditional bamboo wind breaks, it all looks quite futuristic for somewhere as conventional as Colares. At a cost in the early eighties of around £10,000 a hectare for the planting alone, it makes this small patch of vines one of the most costly anywhere in Portugal. If these unique seaside vineyards are to be saved, the wines will have to start paying dividends.

The Wines

Three different types of wine are permitted to use the name Colares: two styles of red and one white. The most highly prized Colares comes exclusively from the *chão de areia* – the sandy soils along the coast. Here, the small, dark Ramisco grape must make up at least 80 per cent of the blend, giving true Colares its deep colour and attractive raspberry and cherry fragrance and flavour. Wine from three other varieties, including the ubiquitous João de Santarém grape, may be added to fill out the blend. These austere, tannic wines need time to soften and lose their initial astringency. The best need at least ten years.

A second and much less good red wine comes from the *chão rijo* or hard ground away from the coast. These are heavier, sturdy wines made from a number of grapes more productive than the low-yielding Ramisco. Blending them with the *chão de areia* wines is technically forbidden. They are occasionally to be seen in bottle under a separate Colares label with the words Chão Rijo on it. More usually they are sold in bulk for blending.

A small amount of undistinguished, old-fashioned, oily white wine is also made, principally from ungrafted Malvasia grapes which crop up all over the region. There are better Portuguese white wines to choose to drink with the excellent local fish.

The Wine-makers

Adega Regional de Colares, Banzão

Since 1931 all growers have been obliged to deliver their grapes to the local Adega Regional to be made into wine if it is to be sold as Colares. These government-run cellars were established when the popularity of Colares was at its height in the 1930s, in a rather brazen attempt to protect standards. Wine-making has not changed much since then, which goes some way to explain the hard, unyielding style of the wine, as stalks and all ferment without temperature control in large oak vats. The wines are aged in old oak vats ranging from 4,000 to 14,000 litres in size, until they are either bottled or returned to the grower/merchant who delivered the grapes there in the first place.

With Portugal's entry into the European Community, Colares is being forced to change. The Adega Regional is to lose the control it has exercised for over forty years and looks set to become a co-operative where growers can take their grapes if they wish. Most of the small growers will continue to do so, but with less than 150 *associados* or members remaining out of the 500 growers who were members in the 1930s, the long, low, white-washed buildings of the Adega Regional are due to be adapted to a more profitable use. They already serve as a good auditorium for summer concerts.

Three merchants still operate in Colares, buying, maturing and bottling wines bought from the Adega Regional. Two in particular seem well placed to benefit from the relaxation of the rules. A third, the Oporto-based Real Companhia Vinicola, buys wine directly from the Adega Regional and does not own either vineyards or cellars in the region.

Real Companhia Vinicola, Vila Nova da Gaia

Port producers Royal Oporto buy their Colares direct from the Adega Regional. The wines are bottled young and therefore tend to be hard and astringent.

Wines from two other local merchants, Visconde de Salreu and Viúva Gomes, who have both recently ceased production, can still be found gathering dust on the shelves of the little local stores and *tascas*. A quantity of 1965, 1967 and 1969 Colares from Viúva Gomes has recently been found in a local cellar and released for sale. The wine has been well stored and is still in good condition. It is likely that other wines from these merchants have been less well kept and are not therefore worth buying.

António Bernardino Paulo da Silva (Chitas), Azenhas do Mar

One look at Paulo da Silva's tidy, old-fashioned office and you know he is the sort of proud, fastidious character that Colares needs if it is to survive. His family have owned Adegas Beira Mar ('cellars beside the sea') since the turn of the century, together with 4 hectares of vines at Magoito along the coast. Sadly, though, he has no family to succeed him in the business.

Paulo da Silva, helped by his wife, makes not only Colares but a range of good, fleshy red wines with locally grown grapes bought in from outside the Colares demarcation. The full-flavoured Casal de Azenha and the lighter, fragrant Beira Mar are worth seeking out, even if you sometimes have to exercise your imagination to believe the vintage dates on the label. His 1979 Colares Chitas has all the wild blackberry fruit aromas and the firm, cherry-fruit flavour of ripe, healthy Ramisco grapes, while the 1974, with the benefit of a few more years in bottle, has more depth but retains the characteristic firm, tannic backbone that helps these wines to last.

Tavares & Rodrigues, Azenhas do Mar

The two small, shabby, cliff-top buildings that house Tavares and Rodrigues belie the backing they have received from their owners, Ribatejo-based merchants Carvalho, Ribeiro & Ferreira. Tavares & Rodrigues have taken a lead in investing in new vineyards and now own the largest single plot of Ramisco. Their healthy young vines are capable of producing over half the total 20,000 litres of true Colares produced each year. Tavares & Rodrigues intend to build their own winery when the law allows. At present their wines, bottled under the name of Manuel José Colares, tend to be hard and mean, lacking the depth of flavour that develops in these wines with age.

Visiting Colares

For anyone staying in Lisbon or on the Estoril coast, Colares is an attractive place to visit, with nineteenth-century villas banked up on the Sintra foothills or set amid pinewoods that resemble the Landes in south-west France. There is a tram that starts by the Adega Regional at Banzão and goes to Praia das Maçãs (apple beach). It is a bracing walk along the coast to Azenhas do Mar and there are a number of good, simple restaurants at Almocageme, Praia das Maçãs and Colares. By the river at Banzão, there's even one called the Ramisco!

There are plenty of good hotels around Colares, being so close to Lisbon. In Sintra there is the Palácio dos Seteais, an eighteenth-century palace with a stately feel. Nearby, two elegant *quintas*, São Thiago and Capela, have been opened to paying guests, while close to the village of Colares itself there is an old villa which has been converted into a small *estalagem*.

Bucelas

Despite being less than 30 kilometres from the hub of Lisbon, Bucelas is still no more than an overgrown village shielded from the Tagus industrial belt by a range of barren hills. Bucelas nearly became better known for chickens than for wine. When, a few years ago, the number of wine producers had dwindled to one, it looked as if wine-making would end up being replaced by one of the largest factory farms in the Iberian peninsula. But both chickens and sugar are bringing Bucelas back to life, and two new wine-makers are currently reviving the traditions of this once fashionable dry white wine.

Bucelas is the wine thought to have been Shakespeare's Charneco in *Henry VI*

Part II, named after the nearby hillside village of Charneca. It became especially popular in the last century when Wellington's officers, having been stationed not far away at Torres Vedras, brought it back to Britain at the end of the Peninsular War. It was known in those days as Portuguese hock, something that would horrify the legislators in Brussels today.

This perpetuated the story that the principal grape in Bucelas, the Arinto, was somehow related to Germany's Riesling, having been brought to Portugal either by Teutonic Crusaders or by the Marquês de Pombal, depending on which version you wanted to believe. There is in fact no truth in either, though the Arinto does share with Riesling the capacity to make a crisp, fragrant white wine.

The Bucelas vineyards cover rolling limestone hills either side of the River Trancão, a small, stinking stream heavily polluted by the local poultry farms but hidden from view by thickets of bamboo. At the last count there were only 150 hectares of vines in Bucelas, producing an average of 2,500 hectolitres of wine a year. With 70 hectares of impressive new vineyard being planted on the hillside above Bucelas, production is bound to rise.

The Wines

Although a small amount of red is made in the region, the name Bucelas can be used to label only dry white wines made from four different grapes. The Arinto is the main variety which must legally account for 75 per cent of the blend, with the Esgana Cão ('dog strangler'), Cerceal and Rabo de Ovelha ('ewe's tail') grapes making up the rest. Both the Arinto and Esgana Cão manage to retain fiendishly high levels of acidity, even in the 40°C summer sun, and are capable of making lemon-fresh wines that develop well with age. Until very recently, old-fashioned wine-making has meant that neither grape has really had the chance to prove itself, as most Bucelas has tasted tired and woody from being kept for too long in old casks. The local law is the usual ass and has enshrined this by stipulating that the wine must spend at least ten months in vat before it can be bottled. Two producers are now trying bottling as early as possible and using modern methods to make cleaner, crisper wines.

The Wine-makers

Quinta do Avelar, Friexial

Grapes from the vineyards of Quinta de Avelar used to be sold to Caves Velhas until Nuno Barba bought the property with the profits from the family poultry farm. Since his first harvest in 1981, Sr Barba has used a modern, stainless steel winery to make a cleaner, cool-fermented white wine. A high percentage of Arinto gives the wine aroma while a small amount of Esgana Cão reinforces the acidity, producing a balanced wine that retains its freshness with age. Sr Barba describes the style of his wines as being between a traditional *vinho maduro* and a crisp, dry *vinho verde*. They are certainly at odds with the style of wine that has traditionally been associated with Bucelas. Nuno Barba's Quinta das Murgas, a red wine and therefore not entitled to the Bucelas DOC, has more in common with the thin, lean-tasting wines of the Oeste immediately to the north.

Quinta da Romeira, Bucelas
In a move that surprised everyone, a Portuguese subsidiary of Britain's sugar company, Tate & Lyle, recently bought 140 hectares of land between Bucelas and Alverca. A large swathe of barren hillside has been ploughed up and an immaculate 70-hectare vineyard is taking shape. The whole project is being overseen by Nuno Cancela de Abreu, who is widely respected for his work with the Douro research establishment ADVID. A well-equipped winery has been built on the site and the first wines will be available commercially in 1993.

Caves Velhas, Bucelas
For some years Caves Velhas (also known locally by its old name of Caves Camillo Alves) was the only producer of Bucelas. The company is controlled by the state-owned brewery which makes Sagres beer, which seems to have done little to update the wine-making at Caves Velhas since it was established in 1939. Caves Velhas have 70 hectares of vineyard of their own, and buy in grapes from another twenty-five small growers to satisfy their annual production.

Wine-making at Caves Velhas is primitive, and although their wines have all the aggressive natural acidity of the local grapes they tend to taste flat and woody. Their youngest wine is confusingly labelled as *velho*, meaning old, and uses the archaic spelling of the word, Bucellas. It spends eighteen months in vat before being bottled, while the *garrafeira* spends two years sitting about steadily losing its freshness and fruit. Still, there is a loyal following in Portugal for this unashamedly traditional type of wine and Caves Velhas would be foolish to change its style overnight.

Visiting Bucelas

'Bucellas, which boasts a shabby little praça or public square, bordered by a few trees, has straggled from the valley half-way up the adjacent hills.' Those were Henry Vizetelly's words on visiting the village in 1877. Little seems to have changed, for Bucelas is a laid-back, scruffy village that comes to life once a year every year at the time of the harvest, with its own colourful vintage festival. There are a number of good country restaurants, among them the Barrete Saloio in the *praça*.

Carcavelos

Of all Lisbon's vineyards, Carcavelos is the most under threat from the ever-spreading city. Vineyards with rural-sounding names like Quinta da Bela Vista and Quinta das Rosas have disappeared from the map under a carpet of concrete. There are now only two vineyards left, stranded in the suburbs, as villages all the way along the coast from Lisbon to the resorts of Estoril and Cascais have been joined up in a chaotic ribbon of flats and houses.

A cynic's view of Carcavelos is that it was invented by Portugal's all-powerful eighteenth-century Prime Minister, the Marquês de Pombal, only because he had to do something with the grapes from his country residence at nearby Oeiras. In order to profit from them, he even flouted his own regulations and insisted on them being blended with Port. In doing so, though, he established the reputation of a wine that became popular in Britain in the early part of the nineteenth century. Phylloxera and oidium in the latter part of the century dealt Carcavelos its first blow, but by the 1930s it was back, producing over 40,000 litres of wine a year.

The region was officially demarcated in 1908, but in the last thirty years Carcavelos has almost completely disappeared under blocks of ugly apartments. Only Pombal's palace and a few rather shambolic vineyards are left behind as relics.

The Wines

You have to taste a good Carcavelos to realize that the wine is worth saving from extinction. It is made from a blend of up to nine different red and white grapes – probably anything that happened to be growing in Pombal's vineyards – fermented dry and fortified with grape spirit up to between 18 or 20° of alcohol. A small amount of *vinho abafado*, grape must preserved with the addition of alcohol, is added after fermentation, giving the wine a sweet, raisiny taste. Five or more years ageing in large oak casks add a slight nutty flavour to the wine, almost in the style of a tawny Port. With production in the 1980s limited to a single property making less than 1,000 cases of rather inconsistent wine a year, it is difficult to find a good bottle to try.

The Wine-makers

Quinta do Barão, Carcavelos

The descendants of the Dukes of Riba d'Ave have hung on to Quinta do Barão, fighting off the property speculators, until their country estate has been encased on all sides by gawping blocks of flats. Until the end of the 1980s wine-maker Manuel Vieira has soldiered on making a traditional wine, trodden in *lagares* and fermented in oak vats. The resulting wines can be attractive, with a heady scent and a ripe, if rather cooked, raisiny flavour. But in 1991 the crop was not harvested and, at the time of writing, it seems as though one of the region's historic *quintas* could finally fall prey to the developers.

Quinta dos Pesos, Caparide

Manuel Bulhosa has an expensive hobby – he is single-handedly trying to revive the fortunes of Carcavelos. The former owner of Galp petroleum until it was nationalized after the 1974 revolution farms an immaculate property in the hills behind Estoril. Here, just inside the now rather meaningless official demarcation, Sr Bulhosa has planted a small but beautiful vineyard with a number of traditional and experimental grape varieties, including some Cabernet Sauvignon. His first harvest was in 1987 and the wine, made under the careful supervision of Australian wine-maker Peter Bright, is clean and fragrant, with an attractive almond-like aroma and flavour. The wine gains in complexity from being left to age for three years in casks of new Portuguese oak seasoned first with Periquita wine. An old farm building has been cleverly converted into a rather stylish *chai*, seemingly closer to the Médoc than it is to the Lisbon suburbs. But even Quinta dos Pesos is not immune from urban invasion: a new motorway linking Lisbon and Cascais has been built straight through the *quinta*.

Visiting Carcavelos

A spectacular but dangerous corniche road, locally called the *Marginal*, bypasses the old villages of Carcavelos and Oeiras. Despite being enveloped by the suburbs, both places retain some of their identity and charm. Oeiras is worth a diversion to see Pombal's pink eighteenth-century palace and gardens, and Carcavelos for its large and lively Thursday morning market. Two beaches at Carcavelos and Santo Amaro de Oeiras are separated by the fortress of São Julião de Barra, which used to guard the entrance to the Tagus and is now used to accommodate visiting heads of state. The Hotel Praia Mar at Carcavelos belongs to the small hotel chain that runs the Palace Hotel at Buçaco (see page 195).

II

Ribatejo:
Martelos and *Garrafeiras*

The broad valley of the River Tagus (Tejo) is Portugal's agricultural heartland. Fertile alluvial soils support prolific quantities of kitchen garden produce. Fat, irregularly shaped tomatoes, beans, maize, melons, apples and citrus fruit are grown to stock the colourful markets of the towns and cities around the Tagus estuary.

The Ribatejo is one of the wealthiest parts of rural Portugal. The river is roughly the dividing line between the poor agricultural smallholdings of the north of Portugal and the vast estates that cover the south. The intensive one-man farming that spills over the hills into the Ribatejo from the Oeste quickly gives way to extensive *latifúndios*, some of which cover hundreds of hectares of flat, low-lying plain.

Grapes grow prolifically here. The Ribatejo is second only to the Oeste in the amount of wine it turns out each year: 35,000 hectares of vines make up to 900,000 hectolitres in a productive vintage. Vines planted on the fertile flood plain of the Tagus are naturally irrigated most winters by the swollen, mud-grey river. As a result, yields are high. Juicy white grapes often yield in excess of 100 hectolitres of must per hectare. As in the Oeste, most of this is turned into insipid dry white by badly equipped co-operatives, who then sell it on in *granel* (bulk) to fill the 5-litre *garrafões*. These dubious wines, colloquially called *vinho á martelo* ('hammer wine'), have a ready-made market in Lisbon's bars and cafés.

The Ribatejo also makes a small amount of red wine: around 70,000 hectolitres in an average year. Much is rough and astringent, referred to (with a good roll of the 'r's) as *carrascão*, though there are a few reds with better balance and depth of fruit that deserve more praise.

These are the basis for some of Portugal's excellent red *garrafeiras*. Literally, a *garrafeira* is a private reserve wine made only in the very best years with the cream of the crop. But the controlling IVV defines the term rather more precisely. According to the rules, red *garrafeiras* are 'outstanding' wines from a single year, aged for at least two years prior to bottling with a further year in bottle before the wine may be put on sale. The level of alcohol in the wine must also be at least half a degree above the legal minimum for the region.

In practice many *garrafeiras* are aged for considerably longer than the three years required by law. Two of Portugal's larger merchant firms, based on the edge of the Ribatejo, buy heavily from growers and co-operatives in the region. Then they age their wines for ten years or more before they are released for sale.

In the past, few *garrafeira* labels have given away any clues as to the origin of the wine. Most have been bottled with anonymous brand names. This may be about to change. The Ribatejo, traditionally a regional grouping of fairly widespread vineyards, has recently been divided into six tightly delineated IPR regions. As in the adjoining Alentejo and Oeste, these have been drawn around the co-operative *adegas* that make most of the wine.

But there are differences between them. The Atlantic breezes which blow inland over the wide Tagus estuary, known as the *mar menor* or small sea, create cool morning mists which drift up the river valley. Vineyards closest to the estuary, around Azambuja, Salvaterra de Magos and Benavente, are cooler than those upstream. Rainfall is fairly moderate throughout the region, ranging between 700mm on the hills to 500mm further away from the river on the inland plain. Local irrigation networks along the Tagus and its tributaries make up for any shortfall although, by law, irrigation is not permitted in vineyards unless special permission is granted by the IVV.

The Wines from north to south

Ribatejo is Fernão Pires country, which along with the Talia (alias Trebbiano or Ugni Blanc) and the Oeste's Vital grape makes enormous quantities of rather characterless dry white wine. A number of wine-makers have proved that Fernão Pires is capable of better, though it is doubtful if much can be done with the productive but neutral Talia and Vital.

Red wines are made mainly from the João de Santarém grape, which is named after the regional capital. This is none other than the Castelão Francês or Periquita. Where it is not being overcropped it ripens successfully to make good, full-flavoured wines. Other Ribatejo grapes include the red-fleshed Castelão Nacional, Trincadeira Preta and Baga, which in the Ribatejo is referred to by the local unflattering name of Poeirinha (small and dusty). A number of French grape varieties have also arrived in the region. Surprising as it may seem, these are not all newcomers. The Tagus valley has always been an important line of communication between Lisbon and the remainder of Europe, so the plots of Cabernet Sauvignon scattered all over the Ribatejo were probably introduced from France after phylloxera hit Portugal in the latter half of last century. There is also a small but established vineyard planted with Pinot Noir and Cinsaut at Muge near Salvaterra dos Magos. In four out of the six IPR regions French varieties are now 'authorized' (as opposed to 'recommended') by the new governing laws.

The Ribatejo province splits naturally into three zones, the *campo*, the *bairro* and the *charneca*. The *campo* (also called the *lezeria* or *borda d'agua*) is the flood plain alongside the Tagus where the most intensive cultivation is found. The *bairro* on the hills north-west of the river has poor, shallow soils covered with wild shrubs, though olives, figs and grapes are grown wherever an opportunity permits. The *charneca* or heath covers most of the south of the region to the border with the Alentejo. This poor sandy soil sustains only the most extensive farming among the eucalyptus and pine. The dry grassland is referred to as the *mar da palha* ('sea of straw') by locals, who rear herds of cattle there.

Maximum permitted yields are high throughout all three regions. On the *campo* yields of up to 90 hectolitres are allowed for white wines, 80 for red. Here, over-production means that many wines taste thin and washed-out. On the *bairro* or *charneca*, away from the river, yields tend to be considerably lower and wines achieve more character and depth of fruit. Some of the best of the Ribatejo's red wines originate from the *bairro* north of the bull-fighting town of Cartaxo. Starting from the north the wines are:

Tomar
The low limestone hills around the towns of Torres Novas and Tomar used to be renowned for full-flavoured red wines. Today, high-yielding vineyards planted with Castelão Nacional and João de Santarém produce little wine of any quality. Much is used for thin, anonymous blends sold in *garrafões* or returnable litre bottles.

Santarém
Ribatejo's district capital has a commanding view over the Tagus. Vines on the *campo* below the *miradouro* (viewing point) and citadel are awash most winters when the river overflows on to the surrounding plain. Over forty parishes or *freguesias* make up the wine region of Santarém, which extends from the river into the dry limestone hills around Rio Maior. Much of the wine is dull *carrascão* used for filling five-litre *garrafões*. As yet, very little is labelled with the name of the region.

Chamusca
Chamusca adjoins Almeirim on the south side of the Tagus and splits in much the same way between the fertile *borda d'agua* and the dry *charneca*. There are few wines as good as those in the prosperous little town next door. Over two-thirds of the

production is traditional co-operative-made white, and most reds seem to taste lean and lack depth of fruit due to over-production. Very occasionally, Chamusca co-op releases some round, full-flavoured *garrafeiras*.

Almeirim

An iron bridge connects Santarém with the wealthy little agricultural town of Almeirim on the opposite bank of the Tagus. Prosperous looking farmhouses are set well back from the river to guard against the seasonal risk of flooding. More investment has taken place in Almeirim than in the rest of the Ribatejo, both at the local co-operative and at one or two single estates making their own wine. As a result Almeirim is currently producing some of the best wines in the whole region, from local grapes like João de Santarém and Fernão Pires as well as a fair smattering of foreign varieties including Cabernet Sauvignon, Cabernet Franc, Merlot, Pinot Noir, Grenache, Chardonnay, Riesling and Sauvignon. The expanse of sandy *charneca* south of the town known as the Terraços do Tejo tends to produce wines that are lighter and have more character than those produced on the fertile *borda d'agua* vineyards alongside the river.

Cartaxo

Of all the newly defined wine-making districts, the vineyards around Cartaxo are much the best known. An estimated 3,000 growers produce 400,000 hectolitres of wine, amounting to about half the entire output of the Ribatejo. Though somewhat rustic, Cartaxo's red wines can taste round and full and the best are bought to be blended into *garrafeiras*. Most wines are made by the local co-operatives, though a new single estate has recently become a major player.

Coruche

The sandy plains bordering on the parched Alentejo are irrigated by three Tagus tributaries: the Magos, the Sorraia and the Almansor. As yet, few wines bear the name Coruche, but vineyards near Benavente produce a rich, unctuous dessert wine. Fernão Pires grapes on the low-lying plain are susceptible to *Botrytis cinerea* or noble rot in the warm, humid, early morning mists that drift up the Tagus in late summer. This concentrates the sugars in the grape, making wonderfully concentrated, honeyed wine. So far João Pires are the only wine-makers taking advantage of these unique natural conditions (see page 162).

The Wine-makers

Three well-established merchant firms buy in wine made by the co-operatives and sell most of Ribatejo's production under their own brand name, though a few co-ops maintain their own labels as well. More recently, two large single estates have come to the fore with their own distinctive wines.

Adega Co-operativa de Almeirim

Almeirim co-op, the second largest in the whole of Portugal, is also one of the most technically advanced. Most of the wines are fermented at cool temperatures in stainless steel and bottled young before they have had time to oxidize. The whites, which account for most of their output, taste fresh with a tang of grapefruit-like acidity. Only a third of the wines are bottled at the co-op, the best under the Quinta das Varandas label.

Quinta da Cardiga, Golegã

This sprawling property occupies 500 hectares of land on rich alluvial soils near the dusty little railway town of Entroncamento, Portugal's answer to Crewe. The estate was founded by the Knights Templar in the twelfth century and passed into private hands with the abolition of religious orders in 1834. The 60 hectares of vineyard that surround the fanciful, turreted palace grow João de Santarém, Castelão Nacional and Trincadeira grapes. A robust, spicy red aged for a year in 25,000-litre wood *balseiros* is bottled under the brand name of Torre Velha. Butter, cheese and olive oil are also produced at Cardiga and these can be bought, together with the wine, direct from the property.

Carvalho, Ribeiro & Ferreira, Vale do Carregado

CRF have been buying wines from Ribatejo growers since 1895, and are one of the oldest of Portugal's merchant firms. Operating from run-down riverside cellars near Vila Franca da Xíra on the edge of the region, CRF make few wines of their own and therefore have to rely heavily on local co-operatives. Their principal brand is a wine called Serradayres, named after the local Serra de Aire mountains. At one time this was a reliable, soft-flavoured red though recent vintages seem to lack body and depth. Over-stretched production and co-operative wine-making are probably to blame.

But Carvalho, Ribeiro & Ferreira's *garrafeira* wines are some of the best of their type. CRF buy wines from different parts of Portugal depending on the year, but the origin is never disclosed on the label. The 1974 *garrafeira* is a soft, rich wine blended from the Douro, while the 1978 was bought from local producers in the Ribatejo, predominantly around Cartaxo. The style of the wines, however, remains much the same. After long ageing in large wooden vats or *toneis* the wine takes on a smooth, mature, vanilla-like flavour, not dissimilar to a well-aged Rioja.

Besides Ribatejo, Carvalho, Ribeiro & Ferreira have recently expanded their wine interests to include vineyards in Dão, the Oeste and Colares. (See pages 130, 144 and 151.) Like the company's cellars at Vale do Carregado, these enterprises have suffered from a lack of capital investment. Facing mounting financial problems early in 1991, CRF was sold to Costa Pina, a subsidiary of the UK drinks firm Allied Lyons. Indirectly this ties CRF to Port producers Cockburn, one of Portugal's most successful and innovative wine-makers. Carvalho, Ribeiro & Ferreira is a name to look out for in future.

Caves Dom Teodósio, Rio Maior

João Teodósio Barbosa founded an agricultural wholesale company in 1924, and in 1945, seeing the potential market in Portugal's African colonies, he branched out into wine. Until the 1974 revolution which gave independence to Angola and Mozambique, Dom Teodósio was one of the largest exporters of Portuguese wine. More recently they have had to look at other more demanding markets and to make an improvement in the quality of the wines at the same time. With investment in new technology, Dom Teodósio's wines have improved, admittedly from a fairly low base. Topázio, a dry white wine from the hill villages around Rio Maior, tastes fresher than it used to, though Teobar, the company's principal brand, is still stuck in a fairly old-fashioned mode and appeals more to the home market.

Casa Agricola Herdeiros de Dom Luís de Margaride, Almeirim

The Margarides brothers, descended from the Counts of Sobral, own and run two large agricultural estates on the south side of the Tagus. Convento da Serra was established by Dominican friars in 1501 and was bought by the Count of Sobral after the abolition of religious orders in Portugal in 1834. It covers 635 hectares of dry, sandy *charneca* on the Terraços do Tejo that stretch south-east from the town of Almeirim. Thoroughbred horses whip up the dust around 65 hectares of vineyard planted with Fernão Pires and João de Santarém.

Casal do Monteiro, 10 kilometres away, is on the *borda d'agua*. A further 125 hectares of more productive land grows Talia, Vital and Fernão Pires for white wines and João de Santarém, Trincadeira and Poeirinha for reds. Small experimental plots of foreign varieties (Cabernet, Merlot, Chardonnay, Riesling and Sauvignon) have also been planted on different parts of the estate.

Grapes are harvested by machine and delivered to a well-equipped centralized winery. Here Dr Luis Margaride makes around 1,500,000 litres of wine a year, only about a third of which is bottled on the estate, the remainder being sold for blending. His white wines tend to be better than the reds, some of which taste rather too lean and astringent to enjoy, though Convento da Serra is a well-balanced, plummy blend of Cabernet, Merlot and João de Santarém. Casal do Monteiro is a fragrant, dry white with the sherbet and citrus character of early-picked Fernão Pires, and Dom Hermano a fruit salad of a wine with tropical flavours from a blend of indigenous and well-ripened foreign grapes. Margaride also makes good rosé with strawberry fruit character from Poeirinha and Trincadeira.

Madrevinhos, Cartaxo

João Mateus Rosa recently inherited 300 hectares of family-owned riverside land and invested over 1.5 million pounds modernizing four *adegas* on the estate. With the benefit of an up-to-date winery equipped with temperature control and stainless steel, Mateus Rosa is making a range of different wines from local grapes. So far the reds are better than the whites. Três Hastins is a soft, creamy young wine made from a blend of João de Santarém, Castelão Nacional and Trincadeira Preta, while Sesmarias has a peppery, spicy character more in keeping with the Ribatejo.

J. P. Vinhos, Pinhal Novo

João Pires Late Harvest was discovered almost by accident. A truckload of rotten Fernão Pires grapes was about to be thrown away when Peter Bright spotted that the rot was not commonplace grey rot but noble *Botrytis cinerea*. Since 1982, when the wine was first made, Bright has made a botrytis wine whenever he can. The grapes are not harvested until the end of October, when they are 90 per cent covered with noble rot and have a potential alcohol of 20°. The grapes are transported to Pinhal Novo on the Setúbal Peninsula, where they are pressed and the must is fermented in oak barrels at cool temperatures. The wine is then aged for six months in new oak before it is bottled with around 80 grams per litre of unctuous residual sugar.

Caves Velhas, Bucelas

Though based just outside the region, Caves Velhas buy heavily from producers in the Ribatejo. Their wines range from a mean style of red sold in returnable bottles to full-flavoured *garrafeiras*. The best of these is Romeira, named after a village in the hills between Rio Maior and Santarém. João de Santarém and Trincadeira are the grapes making up the blend which give the wine blackcurrant-like depth of flavour. The problem with Romeira is that there is a certain amount of inconsistency from one bottle to another. While most taste round and ripe from long ageing in wood, other bottles from the same vintage can be disappointing.

Caves Velhas are also major producers of Bucelas (see page 153).

Visiting the Ribatejo

The Ribatejo is bullfighting country. On the dry *charneco* south of the river, thousands of hectares of land are given over to raising herds of cattle. *Campinos*, the Ribatejo's own home-grown cowboys, whip up the dust on the plains while prodding herds of unruly black bulls with long poles to keep them under control.

Every small town has a bullring where weekly *corridas* (bullfights) are held in season. Vila Franca da Xira, a small city on the Tagus industrial belt, erupts at the beginning of July with a bullfighting festival. The colourless town centre is transformed by the *colete encarnado*, named after the colourful red and green costumes of the *campinos* who herd bulls around the town.

Bullfighting goes hand-in-hand with a strong equestrian tradition. Agile Lusitano horses are reared all over the Ribatejo, partly for their courage in the bullring but also for their elegant and exacting *haute école* acrobatics. Dressage is performed at the government-run National Stud Farm near Santarém, and an annual horse show is staged every November at Golegã.

A lively wine fair is held after the harvest each year in the town of Cartaxo, where there is also a small museum dedicated to wine-making and rural life in the Ribatejo. The seventeenth-century Solar dos Chavões restaurant just outside the town is a good place to sample the wines, together with regional food.

With so many cattle ranches in the Ribatejo, local dishes tend to make use of large amounts of meat. Most of Portugal's beef is reared on the flat grassland in the southern half of the region, so steaks (*entrecosto*) tend to feature prominently on restaurant menus. At Vila Franca there is even a restaurant, O Redondel, housed underneath the terraces of the bullring. But fish is also popular, especially *sável* (shad), which is caught in the freshwater tributaries of the Tagus.

There are few good hotels in the Ribatejo. Most of the region is readily accessible from Lisbon, though it is worth staying in the extreme north of the region in or around Tomar. Here the Knights Templar built up a monastery over five centuries and finished it off with an ornamental manueline window, perhaps the most fanciful tribute to Portugal's great Age of Discoveries. Nearby, at Castelo de Bode, the River Zêzere has been dammed to create the largest reservoir in the country. A *pousada* and a number of secluded *estalagens* (country hotels) and restaurants have been established here, including one on an island in the middle of the river. Lamprey stewed in its own blood is a local speciality which goes well with the sturdy local red wines.

12

The Setúbal Peninsula: The New World Comes to Portugal

The land between the Tagus and the Sado rivers, south of Lisbon, has agriculture, industry and tourism all scrambling for a place as close as possible to the capital. Until the suspension bridge was built across the Tagus, the opposite bank was separated from the city by a small ferry boat or a 180-kilometre round trip. But since the bridge opened in the mid-1960s, Lisbon has overflowed on to its *outra banda* – the 'other side'.

The port of Setúbal at the mouth of the Sado lends its name to this part of Portugal. In recent years it too has grown from a fishing town into a noisy, industrial city – a Portuguese version of Liverpool. But in between Setúbal and Lisbon there is still a peaceful, largely rural landscape. On the north of the peninsula, tall Lisbon suburbs gave way to a forest of fragrant umbrella pines growing in warm, sandy soils. Around Setúbal to the south, the rugged Arrábida hills rise out of the plain and then shelve steeply to the Atlantic.

This is the setting for some of Portugal's most enterprising and inspired wine-making. Three related companies make wines here, from vineyards as far apart as the Minho and the Alentejo as well as from locally grown grapes. Two confusingly share the name of Fonseca and a third is called João Pires. Between them they probably make a wider range of wines on the Setúbal Peninsula than is made in any other part of Portugal.

The wine-making reputation of the region was established in the last century, when university graduate José Maria da Fonseca came to the region from Coimbra. In 1834 he established a firm bearing his name in the village of Azeitão, on the foothills of the Serra da Arrábida, and set about making the sweet, fortified Muscat wine for which the area was already locally known. The enterprise flourished, and by

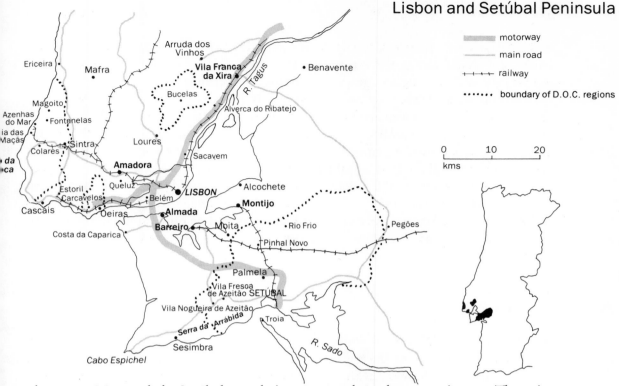

the 1860s Moscatel de Setúbal was being exported to three continents. The wine reached the official statute books when the region was demarcated for its Moscatel wines in 1907.

A second wine from the Setúbal region has certainly found a place in history but has never reached the statute books. Soon after arriving in Azeitão, Fonseca bought a small farm called Quinta da Periquita just outside the village on the way up into the Arrábida hills. With cuttings of Castelão Francês vines brought from the Oeste, he began producing a red wine with the name of Periquita. The success of the wine made other local growers plant Castelão Francês as well. But the name Periquita stuck and now, all over southern Portugal, grapes ennobled by the names Castelão Francês ('French squire') or João de Santarém ('John of Santarém') elsewhere are referred to by the nickname Periquita – 'small parrot'!

This century, Setúbal's fortified Moscatel wines have declined in importance in favour of red and white table wines. The first blow came in the 1930s, when trade restrictions in Brazil wiped away a long-standing slice of the market. Now there are only around 100 hectares of Moscatel vines left on the Setúbal Peninsula, although planting is again on the increase for the dry table wines that are being made from these grapes.

The demarcated area of Setúbal splits into two distinct zones. Behind Azeitão, the north-facing clay-limestone soils of the Serra da Arrábida have traditionally produced the best Moscatel grapes but are now planted with a gamut of Portuguese and foreign vines. A broad, fertile, sandy plain extends eastwards from the fortress town of Palmela along the estuary of the River Sado, and this is planted more extensively with Portuguese grapes, including the Periquita.

Both these areas are now being delimited in their own right for a wide variety of table wines. But the boundary between the two new regions has been drawn to cut straight through the middle of one of the most important properties: the Soares Franco family's Camarate vineyard. You can only blame the authorities if no one, apart from the local co-op, takes the new IPR denominations too seriously (see page 13). Also, with established brand names like Periquita better known both in Portugal and in export markets than the local names of Palmela and Arrábida, it seems unlikely that José Maria da Fonseca and João Pires will be eager to fall into line with the new laws. Many wines will therefore continue to be sold with their labels unchanged.

The Wines

Sweet Fortified Wines

The traditional wine from the region is Moscatel de Setúbal, or just Setúbal, as it must now be labelled if the wine is made from anything less than 85 per cent of Muscat grapes. Local regulations in fact permit Setúbal to be made with a minimum of 70 per cent of either of two different Muscats: the self-styled Moscatel de Setúbal and Moscatel Roxo. The other 30 per cent can be made up of a bevy of local varieties such as Arinto and Fernão Pires, ostensibly to give more acidity. Moscatel de Setúbal is a clone of the Muscat of Alexandria. This crops up all over the Mediterranean and makes the heavy, sweet Moscatel wines of Malaga, Valencia and Lunel. It is a high-yielding variety that still manages to produce grapes with impressively high sugar levels. This makes it a favourite with small growers seeking a good return, but it tends to produce wine that lacks the refinement of the more delicate, perfumed Muscat à Petits Grains, the variety that makes the French Muscat de Beaumes de Venise. This goes some way to explain the unctuous but raisiny style of Setúbal as opposed to the more elegant, scented quality of a good Muscat de Beaumes de Venise, which is perhaps Setúbal's closest commercial rival.

Setúbal starts off being made in much the same way as many other fortified wines. The fermentation is arrested by the addition of grape spirit, which takes the wine up to 18° and leaves a small amount of natural grape sugar. After vinification, pungent Muscat grape skins are left to soak in the wine, imparting a taste of fresh dessert grapes and giving Setúbal its particular intensity of aroma and flavour.

The wine is drained off the skins only after about five months of continuous maceration. At this time the remaining pulp is pressed and the wine is transferred to large oak or mahogany vats. Over a period of three or four years, the wines gain in depth as evaporation, which is high in warm, above-ground cellars, concentrates the sugars. The bulk of Setúbal, by now orange-brown in colour with a spicy, sometimes spirity, raisiny character, is then bottled and sold.

Smaller quantities of wine are kept back and aged further in 600-litre casks, until after twenty years the colour becomes a deep brown and the wine takes on a really rich, grapey intensity.

Older wines are rarely commercially available, but tasting them from casks dating back to the last century at José Maria da Fonseca's cellars shows how Setúbal goes on to lose its grapiness and becomes deliciously but almost undrinkably sticky, treacle-like and caramelized.

A small quantity of Setúbal is made separately from another grape, the Moscatel Roxo. There are only a few hectares left of this rare pink variety of Muscat, so production is tiny. The wine is bottled after spending twenty years in wood, and has a deep amber-red colour and a rich but still remarkably fresh grapey aroma and flavour. Sadly, you have to go all the way to José Maria da Fonseca at Azeitão to find it.

Dry White Wines

A battery of stainless steel has completely transformed the style of the Setúbal Peninsula's dry white wines in the past ten years, putting it several strides ahead of most other parts of Portugal. Whereas ten years ago the region's white wines tended to be dull and often oxidized, the introduction of more interesting grapes together with a complete wine-making overhaul has given them a new lease of life. With the replacement of depressing concrete vats and high fermentation temperatures by gleaming stainless steel and refrigeration plants, this part of Portugal has the capacity to make the kind of squeaky-clean, fresh, fruity, dry white wine that the world is looking for. With classic foreign grapes like Chardonnay and a warm, oceanic climate, the Setúbal Peninsula could soon be making New World style wines on Europe's front doorstep.

But no one has quite reached the New World stage yet. Despite a certain amount of enthusiasm to ape New World wine-making there is an understandable and well-founded resistance to uprooting everything Portuguese and replacing it with foreign imports like Chardonnay. There is no real need. Local grapes like Fernão Pires and Muscat are proving their worth. But a small amount of ripe Chardonnay blended with grapes like Arinto and Esgana Cão has already livened up a few low-key white wines. Varietal wines produced from foreign grapes rarely have the depth of flavour that wine-makers achieve in California and Australia but, as yet, few are beyond an experimental stage.

This so-called 'boutique' wine-making accounts for only a tiny proportion of the region's output, but these are the wines that have probably benefited most from the revolution in wine-making technology. All the Setúbal Peninsula's white wines stand to evolve further as the region's wine-makers gradually become more international in their outlook.

Red Wines

While aware of the need to update wine-making techniques, Setúbal's wine-makers want, on the whole, to retain the national and regional character of their wines. It probably doesn't come as much of a surprise, then, that Periquita continues to dominate the region's red wines. It turns up in a variety of guises, much the best known of which is the wine with the same name from José Maria da Fonseca.

Periquita wine isn't made entirely from the Periquita (Castelão Francês) grape, but it is this that gives the wine a typically firm, raspberryish character. It has the capacity to age well in cask and bottle, taking on a warm, tarry aroma and flavour in older *reservas* and *garrafeiras*.

But Portuguese pride has not stopped foreign grape varieties from coming into the region, and now some good, generously flavoured reds are being made from blends of Portuguese and French grapes. There are wines which successfully combine Periquita and Cabernet Sauvignon to make the sort of vigorous, firm, fruity red with a flavour that crosses international boundaries.

João Pires, the most international of the region's wine-makers, now also makes wines exclusively from French grapes: Merlot and Cabernet. Both grapes ripen well over the peninsula's warm, maritime summer and are able to make full, 'minty' wines with a New World flavour. If other local growers swallowed their pride, foreign grapes could be more widely adopted, but it would be a great shame if the region's red wines were to lose their national character completely.

Rosé Wines

The locally grown Periquita grape crops up in various guises on the Setúbal peninsula, one of which is in the making of a popular rosé. For more information, see Chapter 15, page 202.

Sparkling Wines

Periquita is also used to make sparkling wine or *espumante*. Wines made both by the traditional champagne method and by the new 'Russian Continuous Method' are covered in Chapter 16, page 207.

The Wine-makers

José Maria da Fonseca Sucessores, Azeitão

Descendants of the José Maria da Fonseca who first came to the region in 1834 still own and run the 'Old Winery' on the main street at Azeitão. At first sight, not much seems to have changed for the last 150 years. Behind the imposing nineteenth-century façade is a lobby full of old wine-related paraphernalia which charts the development of one of Portugal's most distinguished wine-making firms. But a look further behind the scenes to the new stainless steel vats that stand above the garden to the rear of the building gives a very different impression of late twentieth-century José Maria da Fonseca.

The company, referred to locally as 'Sucessores', is run today by two young, serious but dynamic brothers. Antonio Soares Franco handles the marketing, sales and administration while his younger brother Domingos looks after their 500 hectares of vineyard and the wine-making. They share the same clear views on the future of the company, seeing the need to steer a course between the traditions of a long-established family business and the necessity to modernize in the face of technology and new tastes in wine.

Domingos Soares Franco is the only wine-maker in Portugal to have been trained at the University of California at Davis, the USA's leading school of viticulture and oenology. Some of this New World training seems to have rubbed off on the wines, which have undergone a significant transformation in recent years.

Take their best-selling white wine, Branco Seco Especial, made from locally grown Vital and Roupeiro grapes. Ten years ago, this was a typically woody and old-fashioned wine lacking in vitality, freshness and fruit. Today 'BSE' is fermented at low temperatures, sees no wood, and is bottled young without any malo-lactic fermentation to retain more badly needed natural acidity. The resulting wine is crisp, clean and fruity; correct and a commercial success.

Other white wines have been altered to give them more character as well as bringing them closer to the Soares Franco view of 'international taste'. The white wine from Quinta da Camarate, between Azeitão and Palmela, was once a traditional Portuguese white. Now it is more like an Alsatian *edelzwicker*: a noble blend of Muscat, Riesling and Gewürztraminer, producing a fresh, fragrant grapey-tasting wine. Likewise the white Pasmados, made from Arinto and Esgana Cão grapes grown locally in Azeitão vineyards, has been livened up with a shot of apple and citrus New-World-style Chardonnay.

A cautious move towards using new oak is improving the standard of the red wines. Ten per cent of José Maria da Fonseca's reds, including the best-selling Periquita, are now matured in new Limousin oak. It is beginning to show. Periquita in the late 1980s is a more consistent, approachable wine than it has been in the past, but it still retains the firm, raspberry character of Arrábida and Palmela-grown grapes. A *garrafeira* wine intriguingly labelled with the code CO is an older, softer Periquita blend.

Quinta da Camarate is the family's own property, where the two Soares Franco brothers live and Domingos keeps a spectacular outdoor aviary for rare birds. The *quinta*'s north-facing vineyards produced a red wine for the first time in 1886, under the name Palmela, and since 1959 under the name Camarate. Periquita and Espadeiro grapes traditionally made a firm but rather hard red which nevertheless aged well. More recently a proportion of Cabernet Sauvignon along with a touch of new oak has given the wine a new dimension: a blackcurrant-fruit character with the mintiness of well-ripened Cabernet grapes. Another *garrafeira*, this time coded TE, is a rich, ripe Quinta da Camarate wine made only from Periquita and Cabernet.

José Maria da Fonseca are still the largest and most important producers of Setúbal, the wine on which the company was founded in the last century. They have traditionally sold their wine as a five-year-old or twenty-five-year-old Moscatel de Setúbal, but more recently, the younger of the two has been given a vintage date. The word Moscatel will soon have to be dropped from the label of Fonseca's wines, as they intend to continue to make them from less than 85 per cent of the Muscat grape.

Deep in the 'Sucessores' cellars, there are also small quantities of wine dating from the 1870s, when casks of Setúbal were shipped, like Madeira, across the Equator and back. These Torna Viagem wines are now dark, rich, and sticky with age and have a heady scent of fresh apricots. They are occasionally bottled for sale, along with a concentrated, syrupy 1900 and an intensely aromatic, ripe, spicy 1934.

These, together with a red and a white Dão and Bairrada and Alentejo reds (see pages 129 and 184), add up to a remarkable range of different styles of wine. 'Portuguese wines that are easy to drink without losing the Portuguese character,' is Domingos Soares Franco's declared aim.

J. M. da Fonseca Internacional, Azeitão

'Internacional', as the locals call it, grew out of the Lancers brand which became too big for 'Successores', the other Fonsecas. Lancers began in the 1940s and was hived off to a newly formed company in 1968. A new state-of-the-art winery was built alongside the old Lisbon-Setúbal road at Azeitão and, although the firm now belongs to Grand Metropolitan, it is still managed by a member of the original family.

Lancers is best known in the United States as a brand of rosé and there is now also a Lancers sparkling wine, made using a continuous method of production adapted from Eastern Europe. The background to both of these may be found on pages 202 and 208.

Adega Co-operativa de Palmela

Originally designated as the Adega Co-operativa da Região do Moscatel de Setúbal, Palmela co-op was given its present name in 1979. Nearly 90 per cent of the production is fairly basic red wine sold in bulk to merchants in and around Lisbon. But a small amount of Setúbal wine is bottled and sold under the co-operative's own label. In spite of some rather heavy-handed wine-making, Palmela's Setúbal is surprisingly good. Underneath a rather maderised aroma is rich, orange-like fruit.

J. P. Vinhos, Pinhal Novo

The dusty little railway town of Pinhal Novo is home base for one of Portugal's most resourceful wine-makers, J.P. Vinhos. João Pires & Filhos, as it used to be called, began producing wine in the early part of the century but was set up in its present form in 1969 to make the enormous quantities of wine needed for the Lancer's brands. It currently belongs to António Avillez, the enterprising, energetic Vice-President of Fonseca International where most of the 15 million litres of wine that the J. P. Vinhos makes each year is supplied under contract. The João Pires brand was sold in 1991 to the UK drinks giant IDV and the firm was consequently renamed.

The million or so litres of wine sold under the J. P. Vinhos and João Pires labels arouse the most interest and this is where Australian wine-maker Peter Bright comes in. Trained at Roseworthy, Australia's leading wine-making school, Bright arrived in Portugal for a look at the vineyards in 1974 and stayed. He's an enthusiast for Portuguese grapes and a firm believer in Portugal's potential for good wine. His no-nonsense attitude to wine-making has already gone a long way towards helping Portugal out of the vinous doldrums since wines like Quinta de Bacalhoa and the João Pires dry Muscat were first released in the early eighties. There seems to be no end to Peter Bright's enthusiasm and experimental thirst which, with the entrepreneurial backing of António Avillez, are bringing a more international look to Portuguese wines.

Peter Bright's enthusiasm for Portugal and Portuguese grapes hasn't stopped him experimenting with foreign varieties like Cabernet, Merlot and Chardonnay. J. P. Vinhos have few vineyards of their own, so nearly all their wines are made from grapes bought in from outside or under contract from single *quintas*. One such property on the Setúbal Peninsula is the American-owned Quinta da Bacalhoa, just outside Azeitão. The Scoville family have led the way in Portugal by planting 4 hectares of north-facing limestone slope with a Bordeaux formula of 90 per cent Cabernet Sauvignon and 10 per cent Merlot vines. The vineyard came into full production in 1979 and early wines tasted rich and minty, with a hint of vanilla from being aged for up to fourteen months in small Portuguese oak casks, a third of which are renewed each year by J. P. Vinhos' own cooperage. It is disappointing to find that as the wine has become more popular, vintages of Bacalhoa in the mid 1980s have lost some of the initial, ripe, New World character to a leaner, more austere style. The 1988 Bacalhoa, however, augmented by production from neighbouring vineyards, is back on form. A more generous, rich-flavoured red made by Peter Bright is made entirely from Merlot vines growing in the small Quinta de Má Partilha vineyard just above Bacalhoa. Here grapes sometimes ripen to 14° of alcohol, making a wine with warm, New World mint, cherry and plum flavours.

Other reds, like the recently launched Meia Pipa and Quinta de Santa Amaro, combine Portuguese and foreign grapes. Meia Pipa is made from locally grown Periquita and Cabernet in a successful 70/30 per cent blend. Aged for two years in

Portuguese oak, it has the firm, blackcurrant and liquorice character of well-ripened fruit. Much less successful, to my mind, is Quinta de Santa Amaro, made with Periquita and Merlot from a 10-hectare vineyard on the Serra da Arrábida, near Azeitão. These ripe grapes don't really seem to benefit much from the Beaujolais treatment of carbonic maceration. Though the wine tastes simple and raspberryish when drunk cool and young, an underlying baked flavour makes it seem a bit clumsy and out-of-place.

Not to be outdone by tradition and the local competition, J. P. Vinhos make a fortified Setúbal wine entirely from Muscat grapes. This is aged in a building like a greenhouse which performs the same role as an *estufa* in Madeira, heating up the wine as it matures.

But Peter Bright's biggest hit is, without doubt, the João Pires dry Muscat. This was first made in 1981 from the surplus of Moscatel grapes. Juice from early picked grapes fermented slowly at cool temperatures makes a squeaky-clean, off-dry white that has proved more popular on overseas markets than in Portugal itself.

More appealing to the Portuguese taste is a fuller, oak-aged wine called Catarina, made mainly from Fernão Pires grapes filled out with a small amount of Chardonnay. Ripe fruit from warm, sandy Palmela vineyards produces a wine that is round but balanced. After six months in Portuguese new oak it takes on the resiny flavour that is more traditional in Portugal's white wines.

One final J. P. Vinhos white that breaks entirely with Portuguese tradition is a newly launched wine made wholly from Chardonnay. This rich, peachy wine from a tiny Azeitão vineyard called Cova de Ursa ('bear hollow') is fermented and aged in new oak casks, where it takes on a toast and butter character. It is probably the nearest both Peter Bright and Portugal get to the New World!

J. P. Vinhos also make two Vinhos Verdes, a sparkling wine and wines from Ribatejo and Alentejo. For information about these see pages 162, 183 and 207.

Herdade do Rio Frio, Montijo

With 1,200 hectares of vines, Rio Frio (cold river) was once the largest single vineyard on the Iberian Peninsula and one of the most extensive in the world. But the future of Rio Frio is now subject to intense speculation. It is likely that Lisbon's desperately needed second airport will be built here, linked to the north side of the river by a new bridge.

Until the cement mixers arrive, Periquita, Boal, Fernão Pires and Moscatel grapes predominate producing 14,000 pipes (over 70,000 hectolitres) of wine a year. The land is flat and sandy, making it easy to mechanize, and Rio Frio is one of the few vineyards in Portugal harvested by machine. But high yields and outdated wine-making combine to produce rather mean red and white wines. A small amount of rather undistinguished Setúbal wine is also made at Rio Frio.

Visiting the Setúbal Peninsula

Provided you avoid the Tagus suspension bridge in the rush hour, Setúbal and the small wine-making town of Azeitão are a short journey from the centre of Lisbon. Both Fonseca wineries welcome visitors and have interesting and well-displayed collections of old wine-making equipment and artefacts. Quinta da Bacalhoa has a small palace, built in the fifteenth century, with beautifully laid-out gardens overlooking the vineyards. It may be visited by contacting the caretaker.

Quinta das Torres, just down the road from Bacalhoa opposite the Fonseca Internacional winery, has been made into a small *estalagem* or inn. The property dates from the sixteenth century, and the bedrooms round the courtyard are full of character with a quaint lack of twentieth-century comfort. Palmela has a *pousada* installed in a fifteenth-century convent, which commands a view over the vineyards and plain, while further away, the *pousada* in the São Filipe castle above Setúbal looks over the city and the busy Sado estuary.

The afforested south side of the Serra da Arrábida is one of Portugal's most beautiful coastlines and has now been designated a national park. Just along the coast, the fishing and resort town of Sesimbra has a seafront full of restaurants. Setúbal's grapey white wines go well with the freshly caught fish. *Espadarte* (swordfish) and shellfish are the local specialities.

13

The Alentejo:
Revolution in the Making

The undulating Alentejo plains extend inland from the Atlantic to the border with Spain, taking up most of the country south of the Tagus. In fact the two provinces that make up the Alentejo (meaning 'beyond the Tagus') cover nearly a third of Portugal's land mass but support only a sixth of the country's population.

In complete contrast to the north, the Alentejo is an area of extensive agriculture. Enormous fields of wheat extend as far as the eye can see over the gently rolling plain. Green in spring, the landscape turns an ever deeper shade of ochre with summer temperatures that frequently soar over 35°C and rainfall that rarely reaches 600mm a year. Umbrella-shaped cork oak and olive trees fleck the heat haze with deep green and provide shade for small nomadic herds of sheep, goats and black pigs. The open country is broken only by the occasional brilliant white *monte* (small farmhouse) or one of the gleaming towns and villages that cap the occasional low hills.

Vineyards are not all that prominent in this expansive landscape. Bush-trained vines are often mixed in with olive groves in a form of dual cropping that is in the process of being outlawed by the European Community. Until fairly recently, the Alentejo's main connection with wine was cork. About half of all the world's cork comes from Portugal, most of it from the Alentejo. Cork oaks, locally known as *sobreiros*, stripped of their thick bark, are a common sight. But the region is being 'discovered', and the Alentejo's wines are now found a long way from the local *tascas* where they were once consumed. The scattered vineyards are starting to show the signs of a revolution in wine-making.

Since the mid 1970s, however, the Alentejo has been on the front line of another revolution, a political one, which has set back the region's already dated farming

Alentejo and the Algarve

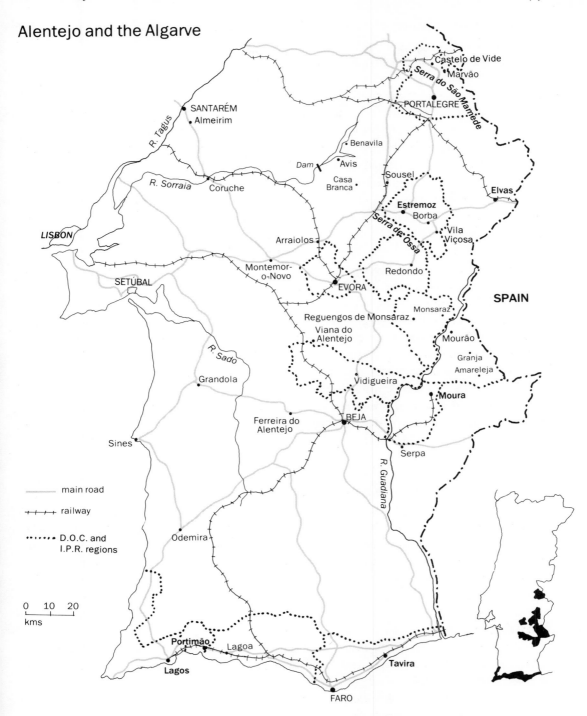

methods. After the military coup which rocked the Lisbon establishment in 1974, the Alentejo became the hot-bed of radical Portuguese politics. Many of the large privately owned estates were occupied by local farm workers who set about running them as co-operatives. These quickly degenerated as many farms went bankrupt and ended up in complete disarray. Cork trees were stripped more frequently than the nine- or ten-year interval that they need to regenerate sufficient thickness of bark, and vineyards were badly pruned and over-cropped. Even though most of the land has now been returned to former owners, it will take time for some of the straggly, unkempt vineyards to return to normal production.

The Alentejo divides into three main vineyard districts, based around the provincial cities of Portalegre, Évora and Beja. Portalegre and Évora lie in the Alto or 'upper' Alentejo, which rises to over 1,000 metres in the north near the Spanish border. Beja is the capital of the Baixo or 'lower' Alentejo, which extends south to the mountains that mark the boundary with the Algarve.

Within the region there are five main vineyard enclaves: Portalegre, Borba, Redondo, Reguengos de Monsaraz and Vidigueira, all of which received their own official IPR denominations in 1988. Three smaller districts, Évora, Granja-Amareleja and Moura, became IPRs in 1991. With the exception of Évora and Moura each Alentejo IPR is centred on a co-operative. Together the co-ops make around 80 per cent of the region's wines. But with technical help from the university at Évora, and money from the European Community, co-ops in the Alentejo are making massive strides to improve the standard of their wine-making. With a slowly increasing number of single estates making as yet untamed wines from high-quality, well-ripened fruit, there are some exciting flavours to be had from the Alentejo in the future.

The Wines from north to south:

In the nineteenth century, the Alentejo was christened *terra de mau pão e mau vinho* ('land of bad bread and bad wine'). Vineyards planted in between cereal crops produce grapes for both red and white wines but, despite a significant improvement in many of the whites, it is the deeply coloured, vigorous reds that hold an exciting future for the region.

Portalegre

The northernmost vineyards in the Alentejo are the highest and therefore the coolest in the province. They cover the granite foot slopes of the Serra de São Mamede around Portalegre, Castelo de Vide ('castle of the vine') and Marvão. The wines are 'lighter' (the term is very much relative), with a little more finesse, than the blockbuster reds that come from the hot plains around Évora. Sadly, though, there are a number of dismal grapes authorized in the area, including the Grand Noir which is 'recommended' by the authorities. Fortunately there are growers who know enough to stop planting productive but dreary grape varieties, and proportions of Castelão Francês, Trincadeira and Aragonez are on the increase. But nearly half of Portalegre's wines are fat, alcoholic whites made by the local co-operative from any grapes that happen to turn up on the doorstep, mainly Fernão Pires, Tamarez and the locally known Alva or Roupeiro.

Borba

Marble quarries surround the bright white-washed towns of Borba, Estremoz and Vila Viçosa. But, away from the dust and the monoliths of pink and grey stone, there are small plots of vines planted in stony, limestone soils. The main grape varieties for the IPR are Roupeiro, Rabo d'Ovelha and Tamarez for white wines and Aragonez, Castelão Francês and Trincadeira for reds, though there is still a large amount of Diagalves, Alicante Bouschet, Carignan and Grand Noir planted in the vineyards. Two-thirds of the production is red, mostly made by Borba Co-op (see page 179).

Redondo

South of Borba, the landscape becomes increasingly featureless apart from the occasional village gleaming in the sun. But a low range of hills, the Serra d'Ossa, marks the edge of a broad vale around the town of Redondo. A single co-operative makes over 90 per cent of the wine although a number of single estates are emerging with their own wines. Castelão Francês, Trincadeira, Aragonez and Moreto are the principal red grapes making big but often baked wines. Roupeiro, Fernão Pires, Tamarez, Rabo d'Ovelha and Manteudo are the main white varieties.

Évora

Until the phylloxera epidemic wiped out swathes of vineyard in the late nineteenth century, Évora was the centre of an important wine-making region. Salazar's campaign to uproot vines and plant cereals in the 1930s left Évora with just one vineyard, Herdade de Cartuxa, on which the new IPR region has been based. Castelão Francês, Trincadeira, Aragonez and Tinta Caiada must account for at least 80 per cent of the blend if a red wine is to be entitled to the IPR and Arinto, Rabo d'Ovelha, Roupeiro and Tamarez must be in the same proportion for white Évora wines.

Reguengos

A tall block of grain silos and a fanciful neo-gothic church are symbols of the agricultural wealth of Reguengos de Monsaraz which has developed into one of the principal wine-making centres in the Alentejo. Monsaraz is an old walled town built on a rocky knoll to defend the River Guadiana from the marauding Spanish. Reguengos is the 'new town', built down on the plain once the threat of invasion had receded. With over 3,000 hours of sunshine a year, the granite-based soils around the town are better suited to growing red grapes than white. Aside from the almost universal Castelão Francês, Moreto and Trincadeira, much the most promising red grape is Aragonez which easily ripens to 13°C under the searing Alentejo sun. One or two fat, honeyed white wines are made with Roupeiro.

Granja-Amareleja

Nudging up to the border with Spain, this IPR surrounding the town of Mourão (not to be confused with Moura immediately to the south) suffers from one of the most extreme climates in Portugal. Annual rainfall frequently less than 400mm leaves the landscape parched in summer as temperatures regularly top 35°C even 40°C. The principal red grapes are Moreto, Castelão Francês and Trincadeira which together must make up at least 80 per cent of a blend destined to meet the conditions of the IPR. Manteudo, Rabo de Ovelha and Roupeiro must amount to 65 per cent in white wines with Antão Vaz, Diagalves Perrum and Tamarez authorized to make up the rest. Production is centred on the Granja co-operative who occasionally, I suspect as much by luck as by design, produce some good, generously flavoured red wines.

Vidigueira

The name 'Vidigueira' derives from the word *videira* meaning grape vine. A low scarp just to the north of the towns of Vidigueira, Cuba and Alvito marks the physical boundary between the Alto Alentejo to the north and the Baixo Alentejo which stretches away to the south. This is one of the hottest and driest parts of Portugal. It therefore comes as something of a surprise that this IPR region makes considerably more white wine than red. Roupeiro is now recognized as much the best white grape but sadly there is far more of the productive Manteudo and Diagalves around to spoil it. The increasing use of stainless steel and temperature control is beginning to help raise quality but with an estimated half of the region's vineyards planted with Diagalves, it will be some time before Vidigueira's wines improve noticeably.

Moura

Until very recently, the little white-washed spa town of Moura was better known for water than for its wine. One of Portugal's most popular mineral waters, Agua de Castelo, is bottled among the cork trees at nearby Pizõs. Moura became an IPR in 1991 after J. P. Vinhos (see below) proved that good wine can be produced on the red clay soils by the River Guadiana. Alfrocheiro, Moreto, Castelão Francês and Trincadeira must together make up at least 80 per cent of any Moura red. Antão Vaz, Fernão Pires, Rabo de Ovelha and Roupeiro are the main white grapes. Chardonnay, Moscatel and Cabernet Sauvignon are authorized perhaps as a sop to Peter Bright, the Australian wine-maker at J. P. Vinhos.

A small amount of sweet fortified wine is also made in the Alentejo, either from Muscat or using the local red grape varieties. These can be quite good when drunk on the spot, but nothing seems to get much farther than the local bars.

Apart from the newly delimited districts of the Alentejo, there are also isolated vineyards in the north of the province around Alter do Chão and Benavila, Sousel north of Estremoz, Montemor-o-Novo west of Évora and Grandola towards the coast further south.

The Wine-makers

Abreu Callado, Benavila

In the broad valley of the Seda, close to an arm of the enormous Maranhão dam north of Avis, is a small, isolated vineyard belonging to the Fundacão Abreu Callado. The foundation was established on the death of Dr Cosme Campos Callado in 1948 to help educate the local agricultural population. A small vineyard was planted as part of the training programme. The *adega* is old-fashioned, equipped with only a vertical press, some cement vats and a few oak casks, but it is clean and well kept. Ripe Castelão Frances, Moreto and Espadeiro grapes make a dark, heady 13° red with remarkable mint and liquorice richness. Maturation in oak helps to soften the dusty, dry tannins. Abreu Callado is clearly a property worth watching.

Adega Co-operativa de Borba

Among the hundred or so down-at-heel co-operative *adegas* in Portugal, Borba sets a shining example. The first co-operative to be established in the Alentejo has been transformed into one of the most modern. With financial help from the European Community, a gleaming new winery has been tacked on to the old utilitarian building with its cement vats. A cool 400,000 contos (£1.6 million) has been spent on equipping the co-operative with the latest technology including the much-needed refrigeration equipment which has helped to reduce fermentation temperatures from over 40°C for red wines down to acceptable, modern levels around 28 degrees. Having the local bank manager as president must have helped but Borba's 300 growers also stumped up some cash.

But as so many Iberian wineries prove, investment on its own is not the only passport to successful wine-making. At Borba the installation of new technology has been accompanied by a change of attitude which has radically improved the wine. It begins with the grapes. The co-op offers incentives to growers for the best varieties. Aragonez, Castelão Francês, Trincadeira and Roupeiro command a premium over other grapes. In keeping with so much of the Alentejo, the winery is kept spotlessly clean.

The quality of the fruit is important to the young oenologists at Borba and the wines are now bottled young to retain primary aromas and flavours. Borba's most immediately appealing wine is its red VQPRD, full of spicy, cherry fruit character. But a second wine, Convento da Vila, made from grapes that are not entitled to the regional IPR, shares the same fresh, sappy hallmark. The whites are fresh and crisp from being fermented at 18°C (compared to 35°C before the improvements) but are rather neutral by comparison.

Quinta do Carmo, Estremoz (Borba)

Within sight of the tall, crennelated keep that overlooks the busy market town of Estremoz is the eighteenth-century Quinta do Carmo, one of the most beautiful houses in the Alentejo. The property used to belong to the Reynolds, who own nearby Herdade de Mouchão (see page 182), and has since been inherited by cousins, the Portuguese Bastos family, who now run the estate.

Quinta do Carmo has produced wine for most of this century but, until recently, very little went further than the family's private cellars. The estate became yet another casualty of the 1974 revolution after it was taken over as a workers' co-operative. When the family regained most of their land in 1977, the vineyards were run down and the vats had been emptied. This left them to start all over again, with the difference that Julio Bastos, who took over the property from his father in 1986, began to offer the wine for sale.

The 70 hectares of vineyard are mainly planted with Alicante Bouschet, one of those productive but dull grapes that do little but lend colour to a wine. It is surprising, then, that the red wines taste as good as they do. The 1987 is concentrated, firm and full, while a 1964, still deep in colour, tastes ripe and cedary. The whites, now that they are cleanly made in stainless steel, are crisp and fruity.

The red wines are made as they have always been: trodden and fermented in cool *lagares* built with the local pink marble and then aged for six months in new Portuguese oak. With a little more investment in the vineyards at Quinta do Carmo, there's no doubt that the red has the potential to be one of the best in the Alentejo. The Rothschild family who are rumoured to be interested in investing in the property may provide the necessary impetus.

Herdade de Cartuxa, Évora

Cartuxa is a former Jesuit monastery close to Évora's city walls. It was founded in 1587 and transformed into a charitable trust, the Fundacão Eugénio de Almeida, in 1975. Even this was insufficient to protect it from the communist tidal wave that followed the revolution, and for six years Cartuxa was occupied by farm workers. According to wine-maker Francisco Pimenta, the 7,000-hectare property was handed back to the foundation in an appallingly neglected state and the cellars and vineyards had to be completely overhauled. Over 200 hectares of vines were replanted and the old heavy-handed autovinification system installed in the 1950s was replaced by modern stainless steel.

The vineyards south of the city on the road to Reguengos currently produce around 2,000 tons of grapes a year but, after rigorous selection, less than a quarter of the total crop is used for making wine under the Cartuxa label. Lack of water keeps yields down and this is evident in the wines. Whites made from a blend of Roupeiro, Antão Vaz and Arinto exhibit an almost tropical weight and richness. A botrytis-affected Colheita Tardia (late harvest) has a heady concentration of peach and apricot fruit in spite of being fermented to dryness. Recent Cartuxa reds have minty concentration reminiscent of the New World in spite of the absence of foreign grapes in the blend. Cartuxa is clearly another Alentejo property to watch.

Herdade do Esporão, Reguengos de Monsaraz

A long, dusty cart track from the edge of Reguengos leads to Esporão, currently one of the largest wine-making properties on the Iberian peninsula. The 2,000-hectare estate was bought by Joaquim Bandeira's agricultural holding company Finagra in 1973 and then snatched away after the revolution a year later. The government returned the estate to private ownership after five years of worker management by which time Esporão was in dire need of investment.

Money flowed in following the stock market flotation of Finagra in 1986 by which time Bandeira had planted 375 hectares of vines. This gave them the green light to spend £3 million on building a new winery modelled on that belonging to Bodegas Torres in Spain. Construction was a prodigious feat. Esporão's cavernous cut and cover cellars were built in just three months to be ready in time for the 1987 vintage.

Esporão's young wine-maker Luis Duarte has seemingly limitless combinations to play with. There are over 50 different grape varieties planted on the estate. Cabernet Sauvignon, Merlot, Pinot Noir, Carignan and Grenache feature prominently among the reds along with indigenous grapes like Castelão Frances, Moreto, Trincadeira and Bastardo. Duarte makes some good but unconventional wines like Alandra, made from a blend of French grapes fermented with carbonic maceration. White wines made from local grapes like Roupeiro, Antão Vaz, Perrum and Rabo d'Ovelha have a ripe, honeyed character. But Esporão's flagship red made from indigenous grapes with a generous shot of Cabernet is more typical of the Alentejo, richly fruity with a tight tannic grip.

Pricing has been a problem at Esporão. Early ex-cellar prices were high to finance the heavy borrowing needed to build the winery. The artistic but unoriginal Mouton-style labels add to the grandeur. Joaquim Bandeira's ideas are big but not always beautiful.

Co-operativa Agricola de Granja

Granja is in a forgotten part of Portugal. It lies close to the border with Spain, cut off from the rest of the country by the river Guadiana. There are 130 members of the Granja co-op, most of whom are farming small plots of old vines yielding tiny quantities of grapes. This may account for the depth of flavour in some of the co-operative-made reds made from locally grown Moreto. Younger *reservas*, aged for a short time in oak, tend to have more fruit than the rather dry *garrafeiras*. Whites made from Manteudo and Roupeiro are old-fashioned and alcoholic.

Horta do Rocio, Borba

Two giant earthenware *talhas*, once used for wine-making, mark the entrance to Horta do Rocio, which lies close to the town of Borba. Alexandre Policarpo makes clean, cold-fermented dry whites and rich, full-flavoured reds from Castelão Frances, Aragonez and Trincadeira grapes grown in vineyards scattered on either side of the main road to Spain. The wines tend to be rather variable, but the red Horta do Rocio 1986 is well balanced, with plenty of fruit and a touch of the vanilla-like flavour of oak.

Montes Claros, Borba

This tiny, ultra-traditional roadside *adega* run by forthright José Mendonça and his sons claims to have Cabernet and Pinot in its vineyards. They have been selling a rather rustic red wine labelled Cabernet for some time and you can just about detect a dollop of blackcurrant fruit when you come to taste it. They also make a sparkling wine by the champagne or traditional method, in which it is more difficult to imagine Pinot Noir.

Morgado de Reguengo, Reguengo (Portalegre)

This property (a *morgado* being the inheritance of the eldest son) belongs to Jorge Avillez, a family shareholder in the Setúbal firm of José Maria da Fonseca (see page 168). It is the best immediate hope for the wines of newly delimited Portalegre, most of which come from the local co-op. Seventy hectares of granite soil have been planted since 1980, principally with Aragonez, Castelão Frances and Trincadeira.

The first wine was made in 1986 and, in the absence of a bottling line, early vintages have been matured and bottled by Fonseca at Azeitão. With a modern *adega* now ready for use and over 100 new casks made of French oak, Morgado de Reguengo will soon be up and running on its own.

Early reds taste good, with ripe, soft flavours and more than a hint of new Limousin oak. A small amount of white wine made from Roupeiro (locally known as Alva) and Arinto is grapey and fresh, but tastes rather of the hot country where it is made.

Herdade de Mouchão, Casa Branca

'Bouncer' Reynolds lost the family property to the revolutionaries in 1974 and unfortunately died before it could be returned. His two daughters now have the task of reviving the property, which, as the '25 April Co-operative', was badly neglected, with ten years of production having been drunk locally as *vinho corrente*.

Like Quinta do Carmo, this is another property that defies the rules. Alicante Bouschet grapes somehow manage to make some good, solid, long-lasting red wines. A 1954 Mouchão, tasted in 1990, is still deep in colour with a big, firm, ripe flavour.

The wine-making is delightfully rustic. Grapes are fermented in *lagares* in a remote but charming little winery until recently without any electricity, let alone any system of temperature control. The wines are then aged in wooden vats made on the estate from mahogany, oak and chestnut, and are bottled by hand. They somehow turn out to be rich and meaty if a little untamed and high in alcohol.

Improvements are on the way at Mouchão, as straggly Alicante vines are uprooted and replaced by more Castelão Francês and Aragonez. Two second wines are sold under the Dom Rafeal and Dona Cristina labels.

Paço dos Infantes, Vidigueira

An administrative wrangle led to José Maria Almodovar breaking away from the local co-op and setting up on his own in 1981. Recruiting João Ramos as wine-maker, he now produces a ripe if rather pruney red from 110 hectares of lush, irrigated vines. The wines are sold under the Serra and Arealva labels as well as Paço dos Infantes.

J. P. Vinhos, Moura

When companies like Setúbal-based J. P. Vinhos (formerly João Pires & Filhos – see page 171) start to make wine in the Alentejo, people sit up and take notice. Australian wine-maker Peter Bright currently makes three wines from Alentejo grapes: two reds and a white. The best known is Tinto da Anfora, a ripe, full-bodied red which has been made since 1978 from Castelão Francês, Trincadeira, Aragonez and Moreto grapes grown around Torrão, Mourão and Ferreira do Alentejo. The flavour is soft and round with a hint of vanilla from ageing in casks of chestnut and new oak.

A second red, Herdade de Santa Marta, comes from a twenty-five-year-old vineyard near Moura in the Baixo Alentejo. A combination of traditional Alentejo grapes together with some inspired New World wine-making produces a big, almost sweet-tasting red. The white Santa Marta, made with a high proportion of early picked Roupeiro, is clean, fairly low in alcohol with crisp, sherbet-like acidity.

Adega Co-operativa de Reguengos de Monsaraz

The co-operative just outside Reguengos was one of the last to be built in Portugal in 1971. It looks just like the others. The utilitarian building on the outskirts of the town resembles a textile factory rather than a place for making wine. But Reguengos does not deal only in grapes. The 500 members who make this the Alentejo's largest co-op also sell olives and sheep.

João Ramos races down from Lisbon to oversee the wine-making here in a new stainless steel winery. The Terras del Rei reds, made for drinking young, taste of well-ripened, sappy fruit, while the older *garrafeiras*, aged for the first time in new oak in 1985, taste slightly cooked although soft and plummy. Unfortunately Ramos is saddled with a load of rather dreary grapes to make his white wines. Still, against all the odds, the Terras del Rei Branco now tastes appley, clean, and fresh if you catch it soon after it has been bottled.

José de Sousa Rosado Fernandes, Reguengos de Monsaraz

Walking down the steps, out of the heat, into the cool Rosado Fernandes cellars is like stepping back in time. Instead of finding shiny stainless steel or even dreary cement vats, you are faced by rows of enormous Ali-Baba-style clay pots, some ten feet and more in height. This is the traditional way of making wine in the Alentejo, and Rosado Fernandes is the last *adega* using these *talhas* or *potes de barro* on a commercial scale.

The *adega* was founded in 1878 and remained until recently in a time warp, with the same family owners. During that time its high-quality, unashamedly traditional red wines became well known in Portugal, but their reputation never travelled any further. Then in 1986, when the last of the family died, the *adega* was scooped up by the Soares Franco brothers of José Maria da Fonseca, who have since set about making more of a name for the wine.

Before they bought the property, the vineyards belonging to the *adega* had been occupied by communist farm workers. The 65 hectares of old but rather dilapidated vines are made up of quality grape varieties traditional in the region: Castelão Francês, Trincadeira, Moreto and Aragonez. All four varieties are planted together in the vineyard, so there is no question of fermenting the different grapes separately when they reach the winery.

Until the *adega* was taken over, all the grapes were trodden in stone *lagares* and then either fermented *in situ* or in clay pots in just the same way as they had been for more than a century. To Domingos Soares Franco, recently back from learning about wine in California, this must have seemed more than just an anachronism. But, ever conscious of the need to safeguard a Portuguese tradition, the Soares Francos have brought the twentieth century into the winery in the form of an automatic press and some stainless steel. Now, steering a characteristic middle way, about half the Tinto Velho is fermented in the traditional clay pots. These are lined on the inside with a laurel resin called *pez* and cooled on the outside by a shower of cold water. Only the *garrafeira*, made in the best years, is trodden in *lagares* and fermented entirely in clay pots or *talhas*.

Ageing takes place for a year in wooden vats and in 600-litre oak casks, 10 per cent of which are now renewed each year. The resulting wines are rich and concentrated, with a spicy, tar-like character that resembles an Italian Barolo. A wine from 1945, sold in 1986 by London auctioneers Christie's, tasted ripe but soft and warm – an indication of just how well these powerful wines can age. The 1986 *garrafeira*, still tough and spicy with 13.5° of alcohol, could well age in much the same way.

Tapada do Chaves, Frangoneiro (Portalegre)

Vines grow side by side with olive trees in this small, traditional vineyard set in the hills just to the east of Portalegre. Little seems to have changed since the family of the present owner, Gertrudes Fino, began making wine here in the early part of the century. In that time Tapada do Chaves has built up a reputation inside Portugal, and the wine fetches a high price when it can be found for sale.

The original vineyard is planted with vines over seventy years old, which include Castelão Francês, Trincadeira and Aragonez as well as a grape they call the 'Tinta Francesa'. I suspect this is nothing more than the Grand Noir, which gives little to a wine except colour. The wines are vinified in large clay *talhas* or *anforas* and in the same type of auto-vinification tanks that are used for making Port in the Douro. They are certainly deep in colour. The problem is that in the absence of efficient temperature control, the wines tend to taste cooked and some bottles can be heavily flawed by volatile acidity that gives the wine an acetic taste. Levels of alcohol in the reds can be as high as 14°, with 13° common in the old-fashioned, heady whites.

Improvements are on the way now that this ultra-traditional *adega* has taken on a young wine-maker with the patriotic-sounding name of João Portugal Ramos. Ramos has tried to take the Alentejo by storm since he took on wine-making at the Reguengos de Monsaraz co-op (see page 177), and Tapada do Chaves is one of a lengthening list of properties he is overseeing. He has already installed some stainless steel and brought the temperature of the white fermentation down to a level that can just about be called 'cool'. He still has some way to go before Tapada do Chaves really lives up to its price and reputation.

Adega Co-operativa da Vidigueira

Two-thirds of the wine produced at this co-op in the heart of the Alentejo is white, made from the productive Manteudo, Perrum and Antão Vaz grapes with some Roupeiro. This suits the local farmers, who are able to see the wine sold early after the harvest and therefore achieve a quick return on their money. Until recently, all the co-op's white wines tasted typically old-fashioned, flat and heady, lacking in freshness and fruit. A new winery, used for the first time in 1988, has altered the style of some of Vidigueira's whites, making them taste clean, crisp and appley when young.

Pinheiro da Cruz, Grandola

One of the world's most laudable but bizarre wine-makers is a prison near Grandola on the Alentejo's western, Atlantic flank. Inmates of the Establecimento Prisonal de Pinheiro da Cruz tend 13 hectares of vines planted in sandy soils in the 1940s. Production is small and the wines are highly sought after. They are mostly sold at Pabe, one of Lisbon's best restaurants.

Adega Co-operativa de Portalegre

Quality comes in small quantities at Portalegre. To date just 54 hectares of vines have been granted IPR status, 11 of which are farmed by members of the local co-op. Portalegre's wine-makers have clearly concentrated all their efforts on the red VQPRD wine made from Aragonez, Castelão Francês, Trinadeira and Grand Noir grapes grown on the granite slopes around the town. Aged in casks of new oak, the wine has a deliciously savoury, toasty character along with firm, ripe fruit. It is expensive. Most of Portalegre's wine is bottled under a second label, Terra de Baco.

Roquevale, Redondo

Maria Clara Roque do Vale has a mission. As the first president of the newly formed Comissão Vitivinicola Regional Alentejana, she is responsible for promoting the wines of the Alentejo's newly delimited IPR regions as well as ensuring fair play among wine-makers. She is a wine-maker herself. In 1983 the Roque do Vales planted their own vineyard at Herdade da Madeira near Redondo. For the first six years the grapes were delivered to the local co-operative but in 1989 the Roque do Vales broke free and set up their own winery. There are currently 120 hectares of vines at Herdade de Madeira planted mainly with traditional red varieties. Three different wines are made. The best, Tinto da Talha, is full flavoured and concentrated having been fermented in large earthenware *anforas* or *talhas*. A second wine, Vinho Redondo, produced in larger quantities, is smooth and supple if rather rustic in style. A third wine, Terras do Xisto, falls outside the regional IPR.

Visiting the Alentejo

The brightly coloured, larger-than-life landscape, open roads and dazzling whitewashed towns and villages make the Alentejo one of the most beautiful parts of Portugal. The best time to visit is in the spring or late summer, when the heat is bearable and the colours are at their most vivid. The walled city of Évora, at the centre of the province, is a good base from which to see the outlying towns and vineyards. Among the most attractive and historic are Estremoz, Castelo de Vide and Marvão to the north, the hill town of Monsaraz near Reguengos to the east, and Beja in the south.

Évora itself is the Alentejo's largest city, with a roman temple and a Gothic cathedral for a skyline. There is a *pousada* installed in the former Lóios Monastery, where today's bedrooms were at one time cells for the monks, and a small, simple *residencia*, the Solar Eborense, in a manor house below the cathedral. Évora has a number of good restaurants. The Cozinha de Santo Humberto, in the street leading up to the cathedral, is well known for its hearty soups and *migas*: a tasty fry-up of pork, garlic and crumbs of yesterday's dry bread. The Fialho, one of Portugal's best-known provincial restaurants, is also famous for its Alentejano pork dishes.

There are small hotels or *pousadas* in Castelo de Vide, Marvão, Portalegre, Elvas, Serpa, Beja and the old spa town of Moura. More lavish accommodation can be found at the *pousada* at Estremoz, which is installed in the castle that overlooks the town and the surrounding plain, pitted with marble quarries. A good restaurant is the Águias d'Ouro ('golden eagles') in the enormous market square in the lower town.

14

Other Regions: Waiting in the Wings

There are pockets of viticulture all over the map of Portugal. Only the very highest peaks of the central and northern mountain ranges are unable to support vines. Most of the wine from these smaller vineyard regions is made to be drunk by the locals, but a few labels from more enterprising growers are being found outside rural bars and *tascas*. Some of Portugal's 'country wines' have now found official recognition, having been awarded IPR (Indicação de Proveniência Regulamentada) status in 1989. Thirty-one new regions have recently joined the ranks of the European Community's VQPRDs (Vinho de Qualidade Produzido em Região Determinada) to coin the Euro-jargon for 'quality wine produced in a specific region'.

Most of the new IPRs are in the south of the country encompassing the vineyards left out of earlier legislation (see page 8). For some, IPR status is no more than a stepping stone towards becoming a fully fledged Denominacão de Origen Controlada or DOC. In order to qualify for promotion the growers and wine makers must establish regional commissions. Some regions (the Alentejo IPRs for example) have been quick off the mark and already have the necessary bureaucracy in place. Others will probably never make it to being DOCs and will fade quietly into insignificance.

The most important IPR regions in the Alentejo, Ribatejo, Oeste and on the Setúbal Peninsula are covered in earlier chapters. These are the areas that are more likely to achieve fame and fortune than the more remote wine-making districts away from the coasts. This chapter covers wines from six such regions, as well as the archipelago of the Azores, the four Algarve DOCs and the legendary, one-off wines bottled at the Buçaco Palace Hotel.

Trás-os-Montes

The north east corner of Portugal is remote country locked in on one side by mountains and on the other by the border with Spain. Four mountain ranges, the Serrass de Barroso, Cabreira, Alvão and Marão, separate this high, barren country from the densely populated coastal strip earning it the provincial name of Trás-os-Montes; 'Behind the Mountains'. An old saying, 'Para cá do Marão mandam os que cá estão' ('This side of Marão belongs to those who are here') is quoted frequently by the local Trásmontanos who pride themselves on their independence from the rest of Portugal. But, over the last twenty years Trás-os-Montes has suffered from depopulation as many inhabitants have been forced to leave their region to find profitable work. Some villages are now almost deserted, while others are left with a largely old, illiterate population as the young migrate to the coastal cities, or overseas.

The mountains that isolate Trás-os-Montes from the rest of Portugal cast a rain shadow over the region, making it progressively drier and hotter the further you travel inland towards Spain. Rainfall totals decline sharply from over 2,000mm on the highest peaks of the Serra de Alvão to as low as 500mm on the plateau to the east. The locals divide the region into two zones. The 'Terra Quente' or 'hot land' to the south includes the deeply incised Douro valley and the high schist hills around it. The 'Terra Fria' or 'cold land' to the north takes in the higher granite country with a continental climate. The summer is often baking, with temperatures reaching 35°C or more, and the winters are cold with snow covering the mountains and temperatures falling to well below freezing. These climatic extremes make cultivation difficult and life hard for the predominantly agricultural population left behind to farm frequently poor, shallow soils. But in 1985 (a year before Portugal joined the European Community) a scheme was drawn up by the World Bank to help the region's beleaguered farmers in an attempt to stem emigration. The World Bank Project, as it has become known, offers low-interest loans to anyone seeking to invest in specific sectors of Trásmontano agriculture, including viticulture. The fund has helped the larger, prosperous growers in the Douro valley (see page 67) considerably more than the small farmer scratching a living for himself on the high lands to the north. But limited benefits are being felt and, with a new road under construction linking Trás-os-Montes with Oporto and Spain, development is beginning to take place.

Three IPR regions have recently been designated for table wines in Trás-os-Montes. They border on the Douro Demarcated Region and extend north across the high plateau to the border with Spain (see map on page 12).

The Wines from west to east:

Chaves

This, the westerly of the three IPR zones, spans the broad upper reaches of the Tamega valley around the city of Chaves. The region is more famous for cured hams (*presunto*) and health-giving waters than it is for wines, which are often light and acidic. To qualify for the new rules, whites must be made from grapes similar to those used in the Douro, though many wines have more in common with Vinhos Verdes. The locally named Boal, along with Códega, Gouveio and Malvasia Fina, must account for at least 70 per cent of the blend. Reds are made mainly from Bastardo, Tinta Carvalha and Tinta Amarela. Red wines from the town of Boticas, 20 kilometres to the west of Chaves, are called *vinhos dos mortos* ('wines of the dead'), due to the fact that the bottles were buried in the ground for up to two years to mature. But the wines might be called *morto* because the tradition is almost dead. Most is now *vinho corrente*, made from American hybrid grapes.

Valpaços

The co-operative in the town of Valpaços makes better wine than the other rather primitive establishments in Trás-os-Montes. Grapes grown on the granite slopes of the upper reaches of the River Tua make some firm, alcoholic reds with ripe cherry-fruit flavours. Grapes are similar to those permitted in the Douro, with Tinta Amarela, Tinta Roriz, Touriga Francesa and Touriga Nacional among the quality varieties recommended for making red wine. Whites made from Códega, Fernão Pires, Gouveio and Malvasia Fina are less good and suffer from old-fashioned co-operative wine-making. The co-op also produces rosé and a sweet red *jeropiga*. this is made from unfermented Tinta Amarela and Bastardo must, fortified to 18° with *aguardente* and aged in oak for three years.

Planalto-Mirandês

This is the most easterly of the Trásmontano wine regions, extending to where the River Douro forms the border with Spain. It is hot, wild country where annual rainfall totals are often below 600mm. A few scrubby vineyards around the towns of Mogadouro, Vimioso and Miranda do Douro make big, alcoholic wines. Nothing much is seen outside the area.

The Wine-makers

Nearly all Trás-os-Montes wine-making is in the hands of local co-operatives, around which the new IPR regions have been built. A substantial amount of rosé is still made in Trás-os-Montes, most of which is bought by merchants for their anonymous, sweet, carbonated brands. But there is one grower seriously attempting to make good wine on a single estate on the edge of the Valpaços region.

Sogrape, Vila Real

Mateus producers Sogrape began buying grapes in the Trás-os-Montes region after the launch of their brand of rosé in the 1940s (see page 201). Their well-equipped plant close to the baroque palace of Mateus now makes other wines from the Douro and the surrounding Trás-os-Montes vineyards. One of their greatest successes in recent years has been Planalto, a wine made from Viosinho grapes with a little Malvasia Fina and Gouveio grown on the high plains above the Douro (hence the name Planalto). The grapes now come from vineyards in the demarcated Douro region (see page 111), and with the new Trás-os-Montes IPR of Planalto-Mirandês, Sogrape are fighting to keep the name.

Unamontes

Five co-operatives at Chaves, Boticas, Mirandela, Sendim and Macedo de Cavaleiros have grouped together under the heading of the União das Adegas Co-operativas de Trás-os-Montes – Unamontes for short. The co-operatives share the facilities of a bottling line at Macedo de Cavaleiros but the best wines come from Chaves. Old-fashioned white wines bottled under the S. Neutel label are made from Códega, Gouveio and Boal. Red wines, made from Douro grapes Tinta Amarela and Bastardo, tend to be light and low in alcohol. A small amount of *reserva* wine bottled under the Unamontes label lacks sufficient depth and body to age.

Valle Pradinhos

One of Portugal's most competent wine-makers, João Nicolau de Almeida of the Port house Ramos Pinto, is a great believer in the future of the country to the north of the Douro. On high, barren land not far from the town of Macedo de Cavaleiros, he looks after 45 hectares of vines belonging to Maria da Conceição Pinto de Azevedo, widow of an Oporto industrialist and a dynamic woman with an insatiable love of work. Her age has not stopped her from establishing a luxury hotel, the Estalagem do Caçador, in Macedo de Cavaleiros, as well as planting 10 hectares of experimental vines. Cabernet Sauvignon, Riesling, Chenin Blanc and Sauvignon now grow successfully along with traditional grapes like Tinta Amarela, Roriz and Bastardo. João Nicolau de Almeida carries out the wine-making at the *quinta*, where he has been experimenting with fermenting and ageing the reds in new French, Portuguese and American oak. It is released as Valle Pradinhos only in the best years, and wine from the lesser 1984 and 1988 vintages has been bottled under the property's second label: Porta Velha. Wines from both 1986 and 1987 are deep in colour, well balanced with deliciously minty, ripe fruit and tannins from new oak. They should keep and age well. The white wines, made with the benefit of temperature control, have fresh fruit salad flavours from a mixture of grapes. They certainly show that there is potential in Trás-os-Montes to make excellent wines.

Visiting Trás-os-Montes

Not long ago, a trip 'behind the mountains' was a journey for travellers rather than tourists. Now, with new roads and hotels in all the main towns, visiting one of the most remote parts of Portugal has become much easier, even though it may have lost some of its excitement and charm. Around Chaves the spa towns of Vidago and Pedras Salgadas have grand, *belle époque* hotels that seem at once to be both in another age and out of place in Trás-os-Montes. They are still well patronized by people from Lisbon and Oporto, who come to take the waters in the summer season.

Bragança, in the very north-east of the region, is an old city with a well-preserved walled town commanded by a tall keep. The arcaded Domus Municipalis, at one time the town's meeting place, is a rare example of Romanesque civic architecture. A *pousada* and a modern hotel make Bragança, the district capital, a good place to stay.

Miranda do Douro, perched high above the river gorge that forms the border with Spain, has been turned into a gaudy entrepôt by visiting Spanish, who come to buy up cheap textiles and ugly gold-painted ornaments. The city is famous for its statue of a good-living Jesus Christ dressed in an opera hat and white bow tie. A *pousada* overlooks the dark grey-green waters of the Douro and the dam that links Portugal to Spain.

Trásmontano food tends to be plain and homespun. Offal is eaten widely in peasant communities, either in a rich casserole with beans or in sausages. With communities having been isolated from each other for so long, every locality seems to have its own dish. The town of Mirandela is famous for *alheiras*: spicy pork sausages, deep-fried and usually served with turnip tops. Valpaços is known for *bexigas*: smoked pigs' bladders stuffed with a mixture of pork, bread, red wine, blood and garlic. Chaves has *presunto* or cured ham, which you can smell hanging in dark doorways as you walk along the narrow streets in the town. A good restaurant, worth the journey for its food, is the Maria Rita in the village of Romeu, between Mirandela and Macedo de Cavaleiros. You are unlikely to be the only one speaking English there, as British Port shippers come all the way up by train from the vineyards around Pinhão to try Maria Rita's Trásmontano dishes.

Beira Alta and Beira Baixa

The Beira provinces make up the central part of Portugal south of the Douro. Beira Litoral is the coastal zone and includes the wine-making district of Bairrada (see page 133), while Beira Alta and Beira Baixa span the interior as far as the Spanish border.

This is the highest and much the most mountainous part of the country, rising to nearly 2,000 metres (over 6,500 feet) at Torre on the Serra da Estrela. The steep, granite slopes and cool, damp summers account for the few blank spaces on Portugal's otherwise crowded viticultural map. As the land rises, Dão vineyards (see page 126) give way to forest and pasture where ewes graze, producing the milk for Queijo da Serra, Portugal's most highly prized cheese. But on the high plains to the north and the hills to the south, vineyards are an important part of the rural economy. Three large districts have been designated IPRs.

The Wines from north to south:

Varosa
The high land above the Douro and the city of Lamego is planted predominantly with white Malvasia making acidic dry wines for the production of *espumante* (see page 205). The Adega Co-operativa de Vale de Varosa at Castanheira do Ouro produces most of the region's wine, the best of which is bottled under the Terras D. Tarejas label.

Encostas da Nave
Centred on the town of Moimenta da Beira, vineyards along the upper reaches of the River Tavora run from the southern margins of the Douro to the edge of Dão. The Co-operativa Agricola do Tavora makes most of the region's wines, mainly light, inconsequential red.

Lafões
High-trained vines like those growing grapes for Vinho Verde make similarly acidic wines sometimes called *verdascos*. One property, Quinta da Comenda, is making an organic dry white from Arinto, Donna Branca and Cerceal grapes. Considerably more red is produced than white, and most is drunk locally. Lafões adjoins Dão around Vouzela and the spa town of São Pedro do Sul in the valley of the River Vouga. It has recently been designated an IPR but there is talk of it being included in the Vinho Verde region.

Pinhel
The upper reaches of the Coa valley around the city of Pinhel are farmed by around 1,500 small growers, most of whom deliver their grapes to two large co-operatives. Red wines, made mainly from Bastardo, Marufo, Rufete and Touriga Nacional, can taste full and fruity. The co-op in Pinhel bottles a *reserva* under the royalist D. Manuel I label. Whites are made mainly from a number of Malvasias. Few are cleanly made and much goes into producing rather poor sparkling wine.

Castelo Rodrigo

A primitive co-operative at Figueira de Castelo Rodrigo makes wines from grapes grown in the right bank of the River Coa and the broad valley of the River Seca close to Spain. The extreme climate and shallow sandy soils make viticulture difficult. The grape varieties authorized for making wines under the new IPR are the same as those in neighbouring Pinhel. Reds, whites and rosés are sold mainly for blending and bottling by merchants based outside the area. One single estate, Quinta do Cardo, makes an ebullient, spicy red wine.

Cova da Beira

This is the largest of all the new IPRs, stretching from the eastern slopes of the Serra da Estrela all the way south to the Tagus at Vila Velha de Rodão, a distance of nearly 100 kilometres. The region covers most of Beira Baixa. It is hard to find much homogeneity about the wines from a zone which takes in cool, alpine mountains and hot, dusty plains. The better wines are light reds from thousands of smallholdings in the north around the towns of Covilhã, Belmonte and Fundão. Covilhã co-operative, the best known outside the region, has around 1,000 members and makes rather inconsistent reds, mainly from Rufete, Jaen, Marufo and Castelão Francês grapes.

The Wine-makers

This is co-operative country. Around 80 per cent of all wine from Beira Alta and Beira Baixa is made in out-dated co-ops built in the 1950s. Fermentation takes place in cement vats, and few *adegas* have any way of controlling temperatures. White wine fermenting at 25 or 30°C is a common occurrence around harvest time. Many of these wines are then bought by merchants outside the region. For example, Carvalho, Ribeiro & Ferreira buy their white *reserva* from Figueira da Castelo Rodrigo. João Serra's branded whites are from Moimento da Beira, and Ouro Velho, a red bottled by Vinho Verde producers Caves Casalinho, is a blend of wines from the Beiras.

Visiting Beira Alta and Beira Baixa

Centuries of cross-border conflict with Spain has left the Beiras with a string of heavily fortified towns staring bleakly towards Portugal's hostile neighbour. The gargoyles facing east on Guarda's strong, granite cathedral are shaped like cannons, in a gesture to ward off invaders. Apart from the unwelcome Spanish, few tourists have ever ventured over the mountains into this inaccessible part of Portugal, and towns like Pinhel, Trancoso, Castelo Rodrigo and Almeida are largely undisturbed. Few tourists also means few places to stay, and accommodation is confined to Beira

Alta's district capital, Guarda, or a new *pousada* in the elaborately defended town of Almeida.

Food, rather like the local wine, tends to be rough and ready. Thick soups, kid cooked over charcoal and creamy goat's cheese from the Serra da Estrela are good local staples.

Buçaco

The Serra do Buçaco rises out of the coastal plain, separating Bairrada on the *litoral* from Dão inland. Set in the forest, just below the ridge where Wellington fought one of the most decisive battles of the Peninsular War, is an extraordinary building: a Portuguese architectural fantasy concocted as a palace for Portugal's penultimate king, Carlos I. He was shot by assassins in 1908, and before the palace was completely finished Portugal had been declared a republic.

In 1910 it became a hotel, one of the few Palace Hotels around the world really to deserve the name. It was leased by the state to hotelier Alexandre de Almeida, who began making wine to serve exclusively to guests in the dining-room. Buçaco is still leased by the Alexandre de Almeida hotel group, and the wine continues to be served in the restaurant. The label is unchanged since it was first used in 1917.

The wine-making today is carried out by Buçaco's fastidious manager, José Rodrigues dos Santos. Sr Santos, as he is called with respect by guests and staff alike, began working in the hotel as a bellboy in 1934. He rose through the ranks and made his first Buçaco wine in 1952. It comes from 9 hectares of vines, some close to the Hotel das Termas nearby at Curia, the rest from vineyards just outside the Bairrada region. Baga, the small, dark grape that produces tough, tannic Bairrada wine, accounts for over half of red Buçaco, with Tinta Pinheiria and Bastardo making up the remainder of the blend. According to Sr Santos, the grapes are trodden by foot and fermented in *lagares*. The wine is then taken to cool cellars underneath the hotel, where it ages in large vats or *toneis* made from oak grown in the surrounding forests.

After three years in wood, the wine is bottled by hand without any fining or filtration. Each year 40,000 litres of red are bottled and sealed with a beeswax resin made by the hotel. As Buçaco is outside a demarcated wine region, it is not bound by official legislation and Sr Santos is able to buy in wines from other producers to make up shortfall in his own production. He has contacts all over the region, and buys regularly from Quinta de Santos Lima at Silgueiros in Dão, the same property that supplies Caves São João with their solid Porta dos Cavaleiros reds.

Stocks in the immaculate cellars underneath the hotel amount to 60,000 bottles. The list goes back to 1927, and most vintages since 1945 are still available to order in the hotel dining-room. I have had the pleasure of tasting Buçaco's wines on a number of occasions with both Sr Santos and Bairrada wine-maker Luís Pato. Providing that you sometimes suspend your disbelief in the typed vintage date on the label and reject some rather inconsistent bottles, there are some very impressive wines to be drunk from the Palace Hotel's wine list. Among the best are:

1982: Mid-deep purple-ruby colour; vanilla-cask aroma; lean, austere flavour with dry, spicy length. Needs time to soften.

1978: Dark ruby colour; closed, slightly cooked baga-berry fruit on the nose; rather lean spicy flavour with a warm though astringent finish.

1970: Slightly paler, still deep ruby; again closed and tight on the nose with underlying ripe blackcurrant aromas; rich, concentrated lasting flavour with an explosively tannic finish.

1963: Still very dark, thin brown rim; closed initially and perhaps a touch volatile; firm, rather woody flavour though still retaining good fruit and finesse on the finish.

1962: Massive colour, just beginning to brown on the rim; wonderfully rich mulberry fruit aroma; big, ripe, intense flavour. Long tannic finish. This is one of the very best Buçaco wines that I have tried and was apparently the favourite of Américo Tomás, the President of Portugal deposed in the 1974 revolution.

1959: Deep brick-red colour, amber-brown rim; still incredibly closed on the nose with a cedarwood aroma underneath; good, ripe claret-like concentration of flavour with a full, oaky finish. Watch out for inconsistent or corky bottles.

1953: The oldest Buçaco that I have tried; retaining a deep black hue, thin brown rim; tobacco-box nose; still plenty of fruit, fading rather on dusty, dry, tannic finish. Showing signs of age.

Some of Buçaco's white wines are as remarkable as the reds, if not more so. Sr Santos bottles about 20,000 litres of white Buçaco annually, after ageing it for a year in wood. The wine is made from locally grown Maria Gomes, Bical and Arinto grapes blended with a tiny amount of Moscatel. They are dry but age in a most extraordinary way, gaining an apricot and peach-like depth and concentration in bottle. The hotel lists wines dating back to 1944. Of these, the best that I have tasted are:

1985: Pale straw colour; developing an unusual aroma of dried fruit; tastes clean; apple flavours from cold fermentation combine with apricots and almonds which linger on the finish.

1984: Slightly deeper straw-yellow colour; richer than the 1985 with a more intense, complex aroma and flavour; peaches, honey and almonds.

1966: Deep gold, no trace of brown; remarkably fresh aroma with the complexity similar to a Condrieu; clean lemony-tasting fruit with an underlying oily richness and a touch of oak. Fresh, fruity acidity lingering on the finish.

1956: Deep brown-gold; smoky, buttery aroma; losing its freshness, still tastes rich though slightly oxidized, woody, smoky length.

Buçaco wines are sold only to guests dining at the Palace Hotel and the other hotels run by Alexandre de Almeida: the Termas at Curia, the Astoria in Coimbra and the Praia Mar in Carcavelos near Lisbon. 'Off' sales are not allowed, although very occasionally a few old wines reach the auction rooms. In 1986, at a sale held to commemorate 600 years of the Anglo-Portuguese alliance, Christies sold four bottles of 1929 Buçaco. But if you want to taste some of Sr Santos's remarkable wines, it is well worth going to stay for a few days at Buçaco's bizarre Palace Hotel.

Algarve

Portugal's southern coast is better known for its beaches than for its wine. The thousands of tourists who flock there each year must come away with thousands of bad headaches from drinking the bland, alcoholic local hooch. Algarvean wines come from four co-operatives spread along the coast from Tavira in the east to Lagos in the west. For some inexplicable reason (one suspects local politics), the Algarve was elevated to a Demarcated Region in 1980. It has since been split into four DOC districts: Lagos, Portimão, Lagoa and Tavira. A discussion is under way to demote them to IPRs.

The hot Mediterranean climate in Algarve may be perfect for tourists but it is not good for wine. A small amount of fat, blowsy white is made from a gamut of dreary grapes including Perrum, Manteudo and Diagalves. Thin-tasting reds are produced from the productive Negra Mole, though this is thought to be different from the grape with the same name that is planted extensively in Madeira. Some Trincadeira and Castelão Francês vines produce wines that make up in alcohol (around 13°) what they lack in acidity. There is, however, evidence of a long wine-making tradition in Algarve. H. Warner Allen in his book *The Wines of Portugal* contends that Osey, a fortified wine popular in England in the fourteenth and fifteenth centuries, originated in Algarve. The Adega Co-operativa de Lagoa continues to make a small amount of dry, fortified wine from the locally grown Crato Branco grape. It ages in a solera under a film of flor yeast which lends the wine a nutty character resembling a coarse Montilla or fino Sherry.

The Azores

Vines were introduced to the Azores by Portuguese settlers colonizing these remote volcanic islands in the fifteenth century. Having built churches, wines were needed to celebrate mass. Two islands, Pico and Graciosa, exported fortified wines made from Verdelho grapes in the last century, but these were all but wiped out by oidium and phylloxera. Like Madeira (see page 209), productive American hybrid vines replaced *Vitis vinifera* varieties, and now two *V. labrusca* varieties, Isabella and Seibel Jacques, make thin, acid wines drunk by the locals. Two co-operatives, at Madalena on the island of Pico and Santa Cruz on Graciosa, are trying to save Açorean wine from complete extinction.

15

Portugal's Rosé Wines: Decline and Fall

It is easy to be dismissive about commercial brands, and Portugal's rosés, rather like Italy's Lambrusco and Germany's Liebfraumilch, are wines that enthusiasts love to hate. But throughout the 1980s, Portugal has kept up exports of rosé wine. Over 20 million litres are produced each year, which adds up to more than all the wine made in the demarcated regions. For this reason alone, the twentieth-century rosé phenomenon merits consideration in a chapter all of its own.

Portugal does not have a tradition for rosé wine. Unlike Spain, where deliciously fruity, dry *rosados* are drunk country-wide, pink wines have never really caught on. Portuguese rosé is the creation of entrepreneurs who saw its potential in overseas markets emerging after the war. After a slow start in the lean 1940s, rosé took off. Lancers, packaged imaginatively in a terracotta-coloured crock, took the United States market by storm. Mateus, bottled in the familiar flagon that made a thousand table lamps, brought the taste of wine to an army of British consumers for the first time. Both were early and outstandingly successful exercises in launching and developing a brand.

Grapes for the first of Portugal's pink wines came from the districts where they were made. For Mateus this was the area around Vila Real in Trás-os-Montes, and for Lancers, the Setúbal Peninsula. But as demand increased and the wines were imitated by a number of look-alike brands, producers had to cast around to find more raw material. In 1979 the government made an attempt to impose some sort of order on the burgeoning demand for grapes, and defined extensive and therefore rather meaningless areas all over Portugal for the production of rosé wines. Today Bairrada, Beira Alta, Oeste, the Ribatejo and Algarve are all permitted to make rosé wine from a long list of specified grapes.

In reality, Portugal's style of rosé could be produced just about anywhere from just about any grapes. More important than the raw material is the technology behind the wine-making. The plants producing Mateus and Lancers are some of the most up-to-date in Portugal. From start to finish hygiene is of the utmost importance, and from the grape reception to the bottling line everything is decked out in stainless steel. The wine-making procedure differs little between the two main producers and is covered in detail on page 48. The manufacture of other brands of rosé wine often takes place in less than hygienic co-operatives, and vinification methods are much more crude. None of them have benefited from the same levels of investment as the two main brands, so they lack both the skill and the technology to make wines that are clean and consistent. Like so many commercial brands of Vinho Verde, too many rosés are badly flawed by unhygienic wine-making combined with lavish doses of sulphur dioxide.

But after years of success backed by heavy investment in production, promotion and advertising, the fortunes of Portugal's major brands of rosé have gone into decline. Consumers in Britain and the United States are starting to shy away from simple 'pop' flavours that first weaned many of them on to wine. Although both Italy and Japan have grown in importance as markets, it seems doubtful if there is the potential in the future to maintain rosé as anything other than a 'stable' brand. The producers of Mateus and Lancers have seen that the writing is on the wall and are currently busy diversifying into other products. Sogrape, the company making Mateus, have invested heavily in the Douro, Dão, Bairrada and Minho, while J. M. da Fonseca have come up with a new Lancers sparkling wine.

The Wines

In spite of their image, Portuguese rosés are far from standardized. They are tailor-made to suit the requirements of particular markets. Both Mateus and Lancers are sold as still wines in the United States, without the carbon dioxide fizz that is injected into their European equivalents. Market research has concluded that some countries prefer sweeter wines, so rosés are adjusted and blended to order. In general, though, Portugal's pinks are fermented to 10° of alcohol, 40 grams per litre of largely residual sugar and five atmospheres of pressure from injected CO_2. If well made, they taste clean though sugary and confected.

The Wine-makers

Sogrape, Vila Real, Anadia and Avintes
The Mateus story began in 1942, when a group of friends sitting round a dining-table decided to set up a company to export Portuguese wine. One of the party was

Fernando van Zeller Guedes, whose family owned Quinta da Aveleda, a well-known Vinho Verde property at Penafiel to the north of Oporto. Inspired by these *pétillant* wines which were already popular in both Portugal and Brazil, Guedes had the idea of creating a new wine, still with the same sparkle but pink and slightly sweet, making it easier to drink.

Production began at Vila Real in a plant built close to the Baroque palace of Mateus. The property had never belonged to the Guedes family, so the owners were offered payment for the use of the name and a picture of the palace on the label. Faced with the choice of a lump sum or a royalty on each bottle sold, the hapless owners played safe and opted for a one-off payment.

Mateus Rosé took some time to achieve success. The Brazilian market had collapsed in 1946 and Europe was still in the grip of post-war austerity. It was only in the early fifties that Mateus reached England. Sacheverell Sitwell, writing in *The Times* in 1951 after a visit to Portugal, is credited with the discovery of 'this most delicious vin rosé'. Soon after, it was being drunk by royalty at the Savoy, setting off a band-wagon which is only just beginning to slow down.

Mateus is now sold in over 100 countries, and in 1988 accounted for 42 per cent of all Portugal's table wine exports. Of the 3.25 million cases sold annually, most is now destined for the United States. Only a tiny amount stays at home, mainly for the benefit of visiting tourists. The Portuguese themselves have always been disdainful about their single biggest wine export and Mateus has never really attracted a following.

Mateus continues to be made at Vila Real, but over the years more and more production has been moved to a newer plant at Anadia in Bairrada. The grapes that go into Mateus are those grown locally: principally Baga along with Bastardo, Alvarelhão, Tinta Roriz, Tinta Pinheira and Touriga Nacional. At vintage time the two plants are able to handle 1,700,000 kilos of grapes a day and have the capacity to store 43 million litres of wine. Bottling takes place in an immaculate factory at Avintes close to Oporto, where the very first bottle of Mateus rosé, looking much the same as those on the off-licence shelves today, stands yellowing with age in a glass case.

After nearly fifty years, Sogrape remains in family hands. Fernando van Zeller Guedes became the majority shareholder in 1981. He died in 1987, the same year that Sogrape bought the Port house Ferreira. The group is now run by his son, also called Fernando, and grandsons. It survived Portugal's 1974 revolution almost unscathed after the company's 500 employees bucked the trend and voted against worker occupation. As a result, Sogrape in the 1990s is in a much stronger position than many Portuguese-owned companies and continues to set the pace among Portugal's leading wine-makers. The profits made from Mateus have allowed Sogrape to diversify into other areas including the Douro, Dão, Bairrada and Vinho Verde. (See relevant chapters.) They are also considering investing in wine-making in the

Alentejo. Among the wines recently launched by Sogrape is a good dry but fruity rosé called Nobilis, made predominantly from the Baga grape at the firm's Anadia winery.

J. M. da Fonseca Internacional, Azeitão

While Mateus has always been proudly Portuguese, Portugal's other rosé superstar, Lancers, is much more international. It began at about the same time as Mateus, when a certain Mr Behar, owner of a company called Vintage Wines in New York, saw that American GIs returning from the war in Europe had developed a taste for wine. At the time, France, Germany and Italy were at war and Spain was in complete disarray after the civil war that had torn the country apart in the 1930s. Portugal, on the other hand, had stayed neutral and so, in 1944, Mr Behar set off on a ferry across the Tagus in search of wine on the Setúbal Peninsula. At José Maria da Fonseca he found the wine that he had been looking for, and by Christmas, the first 100 cases of a new rosé arrived in the United States. Behar christened it Lancers after one of his favourite paintings: *Las Lanzas* by Velázquez. The wine, packaged in rustic clay crocks, was an instant success. By the end of the 1960s it had outgrown the production capacity at José Maria da Fonseca's *adega*, and a new company called J. M. da Fonseca International was formed just to produce Lancers. With help from the US drinks firm Heublein, which had bought Behar's Vintage Wines a few years earlier, a brand new winery was built alongside the Lisbon-to-Setúbal road at Azeitão in 1970.

'Internacional', as it is called for short to distinguish it from the old firm, was subsequently bought by Heublein, who have in turn been taken over by the British Grand Metropolitan group. It is now run as a subsidiary of IDV, but a descendant of the family who launched Lancers, António Avillez, heads the firm and runs it day-to-day.

Avillez is an energetic company man, full of ideas and always on his feet directing operations from inside 'Internacional's' glass-fronted, air-conditioned offices. He has put himself in a powerful position for, besides running one of Portugal's most advanced wineries, he also owns João Pires e Filhos at nearby Pinhal Novo. It is João Pires and wine-maker Peter Bright who supply 'Internacional' with all the base wine for Lancers Rosé (see page 199).

Lancers is made predominantly from Castelão Francês (Periquita) grapes, grown on the Setúbal Peninsula and in the Ribatejo and the Oeste. One and a half million cases are exported each year, mainly to the United States, where Lancers is the single best-selling brand of rosé.

If imitation is the sincerest form of flattery, then the people at Sogrape must be smiling at the same time that they are gritting their teeth. Mateus has spawned numerous Portuguese look-alikes, right down to the shape of the bottle and the design on the label. Other than the own-label wines to be found on supermarket shelves in Britain, these are the most common in Portugal:

Trovador (Borges & Irmão)
Acácio (Caves Acácio)
Casalinho (Caves do Casalinho)
Três Cavaleiros (Gonçalves Monteiro)

With the image that these and other Portuguese brands of rosé have created, it is not surprising that few serious, dry rosé wines are made in Portugal. But, apart from Sogrape's Nobilis, there are just two worthy of mention.

The Margarides Estate, Almeirim
One of the Ribatejo's most enterprising wine-makers, Dom Luís Margaride, makes a good, full-flavoured *rosado* from Trincadeira, João de Santarém and Poeirinha grapes growing on a 1,300-hectare estate near Almeirim. The wine has a deep purple-pink colour and a ripe soft fruit aroma and flavour. (See page 161.)

Buçaco
The Palace Hotel at Buçaco, which makes legendary red and white wines, also sells a small amount of own-label *rosado*. The 1984 (tasted in 1990) is dry, with more than a touch of oak to the flavour. Like all Buçaco's wines, it is sold only in the hotel restaurant and, to my mind, you would be better off choosing one of the other wines. A full guide may be found on page 195.

Visiting Rosé Wine-makers

Both the Mateus plant at Avintes and Lancers at Azeitão are geared up to receiving visitors. The Lancers winery is the more interesting. Side by side with gleaming high technology is a small museum, full of equipment and artefacts relating to wine. In the cellars underneath, António Avillez keeps his personal collection of old *azulejos*, the decorative tiles that adorn so many of Portugal's houses and public buildings.

16

Portugal's Sparkling Wines

Lamego, high above the vineyards of the Douro, is a cheerful, country town. Every September it comes alive as people travel from all over the north to take part in one of Portugal's most colourful celebrations: the Romaria of Nossa Senhora dos Remédios. A few pilgrims still climb the geometric flights of steps (one or two on their knees) to the 'wedding cake' church at the top of a thickly wooded hill. Most stay down in the town, chewing at pieces of the local smoked ham while popping the corks from bottles of Lamego's own *espumante*.

This is the home of Portugal's first and most popular sparkling wine. The 'champagne' method was introduced here just over 100 years ago and, as production has increased, an ever larger network of cellars has been dug into the hill underneath the Remédios church. But Lamego is no longer the only place making *espumante*. The traditional method that puts the sparkle into champagne has spread to other parts of the country. There are now some good sparkling wines being made in Bairrada and on the Setúbal Peninsula, but few of these wines are drunk by anyone outside Portugal and Brazil. Perhaps because exports have been so limited, the authorities have not yet made an attempt to demarcate regions for sparkling wine. Unlike neighbouring Spain, there is not even a Cava-type denomination which lays down rules telling producers what they must or must not do. This has left Portugal's wine-makers with a free hand, enabling them to buy grapes or wine from just about any part of the country. Much of the base wine used to make the major proprietary brands of *espumante* comes from vineyards on the high margins of the Douro and Beira Alta (see page 192). The grapes growing in these cooler vineyards retain good levels of acidity and are well suited to making sparkling wine. But old-fashioned co-operatives, lacking equipment and know-how, frequently turn out large amounts of flat, badly oxidized white. This is then bought by producers all over the north of Portugal, who transform it into their own brands of *espumante*.

The potential for making good sparkling wine in Portugal is being recognized by a few wine-makers who, with one eye on export markets, are making significant improvements in their production methods. One or two outsiders are beginning to take notice as well. At one end of the sparkling spectrum, Californian producers Schramsberg have been looking at making a sparkling wine from native Portuguese grapes growing on the high lands around the Douro. At the other end, IDV, part of the Grand Metropolitan group, have chosen Portugal as the place to adapt and update a continuous method of sparkling wine production which has not previously been used outside Eastern Europe. This is explained more fully on pages 49-51 and in the section on J. M. da Fonseca on page 207.

The Wines

Portugal's principal brands of sparkling wine are made by the traditional 'champagne' method. The process is much the same in Portugal as in other countries, and is covered in some detail on page 49. The best *espumante* is produced by those companies who also make their own base wine. They can be clean and crisp when drunk young but few have the staying power to age. Many companies make the mistake of leaving the wines on the lees for too long prior to remuage and disgorgement. A year, in most cases, is more than enough.

The grapes used for making *espumante* vary in different parts of the country. Around Moimento da Beira, Castelo Rodrigo and Pinhel, in the north, Malvasias, Códega, Viosinho, Arinto and Cerceal are capable of producing attractively fresh-tasting wines if cleanly made. Around Lamego, a small amount of Pinot Noir and Chardonnay has been planted to add more character to wines made from local grapes. Down in the coastal vineyards of Bairrada, white grapes are in short supply. Here, Maria Gomes (alias Fernão Pires) is the most planted variety but tends to make fairly neutral dry white wine. Bical and Cerceal make wines with a more aromatic, grapefruit-like character. South of Lisbon on the Setúbal Peninsula, early picked red Castelão Francês (Periquita) grapes yield a good, acidic *blanc de noir* base for J. M. da Fonseca's continuous method wine.

The Wine-makers

Caves Raposeira, Lamego

Along the road that winds out of Lamego towards the hill town of Castro Daire are Caves Raposeira. *Raposo* is the Portuguese word for fox, and the thickly wooded slope where Raposeira have built their cellars was once a foxes' den. Today a labyrinth of underground tunnels turn out 2.5 million bottles of *espumante* a year, making Caves Raposeira Portugal's largest producers of sparkling wine.

Until 1980, Raposeira belonged to brandy producers Macieira. It suffered from under-investment, and when Seagram (owners of Sandeman) took over the firm they stripped out all the old wooden vats that had been used to make the base wine and replaced them with stainless steel. Now Raposeira buys in grapes from around 100 small growers who farm the high land between Lamego, Tarouca and Castro Daire. They also have two properties of their own. Quinta do Valprado and Quinta da Racheca are both just above the 600-metre boundary where the demarcated Douro region ends and the wilderness begins. They have been planted with Chardonnay, Pinot Blanc and Pinot Noir and produced their first crop in 1986. Raposeira use the grapes in conjunction with the local Malvasias, Códega and Cerceal to make a range of *espumantes*, while the Chardonnay is used on its own for a still wine sold under the Quinta do Valprado label.

The grapes for Raposeira are gathered and packed in small plastic boxes to prevent them being crushed before they are loaded into a horizontal vaslin press. The juice from different pressings is then separated and each *cuvée* is inoculated with strains of yeasts brought from France. Fermentation takes place at cool temperatures (around 18°C), producing a clean, fresh-tasting, dry base wine to turn into sparkling wine.

Raposeira sell three different *espumantes*. The Reserva is the youngest and is made from native grapes. It spends a year ageing on the yeast sediment created by the secondary fermentation and is bottled as a brut (*bruto*) and a dry (*seco*). Brut Super Reserva is made mainly from Chardonnay, Pinot Blanc and Pinot Noir. This spends two years on its lees, rather too long for this style of wine, before disgorgement and dosage. Pinot Noir, together with other indigenous grape varieties, goes into a pale pink rosé *espumante* with a good strawberry-fruit aroma and a clean dry flavour.

All Raposeira's wines still undergo *remuage* by hand in wooden *pupitres*, although they are soon to experiment with mechanical *remuage* in automatic gyropalettes. A small quantity of Super Reserva is now being exported to Belgium under a beguilingly French 'Renoir' label, and with plans to increase production to 4 million bottles, Raposeira's wines could soon be appearing in other European markets. They will provide serious competition for the best of Spain's Cavas and many smaller regions in France where wine is made by the traditional champagne method.

Luís Pato, Óis de Bairro

Luís Pato (Louis Duck in English) is a one-man grower-producer of some of the Bairrada's most innovative wines. One of the wines that I most enjoy is a pink sparkling wine made entirely from Baga grapes. The wine began as a mistake when

Pato, experimenting with a red, found that he was not getting the colour that he needed and decided to turn it into *espumante*. The wine was so well received that he now makes a *bruto* rosé most years. The 1988 has a deep pink-purple colour and a wonderfully ripe, creamy aroma and flavour.

The Bairrada's white *espumantes* are made mostly from the Maria Gomes grape, though Pato adds wine from two other local varieties, Bical and Cercealinho. Bical wines are scented and grapey, while Cerceal has good fruit and acidity but suffers from rot in Bairrada's damp oceanic climate. Cercealinho is an attempt to combine the best of two worlds: the fruit of the Cerceal and the aroma and resistance to disease of the Alvarinho. Certainly Pato's white *espumante* is clean and has more fruit than the others made in the Bairrada region. A duck on the label distinguishes it from the rest.

Messias, Mealhada

One of the larger producers of *espumante* for the national market, Messias make as much base wine as they can from grapes growing in vineyards close to their Bairrada cellars. A severe shortage of white grapes in the region forces them to look elsewhere and Messias, like so many other *espumante* producers, are forced to buy in ready-made wine from co-operatives in the Beiras. This is a shame, as it takes the edge off their own cleanly made white wines.

A single-*quinta espumante*, Quinta de São Miguel, is soon to be launched from a 7-hectare vineyard belonging to the Messias family.

J. P. Vinhos (formerly João Pires), Pinhal Novo

There seems to be no limit to the different wines that are being made in Setúbal. Peter Bright produces all the base wine for J. M. da Fonseca's Lancers rosé and sparkling wines (see page 171). But João Pires also keep back some wine for themselves. Their *espumante* comes from a blend of locally grown and red Castelão Francês (Periquita) and white Fernão Pires. The varieties are fermented separately, blended, and then aged in small oak casks until bottling with the addition of yeasts for the second fermentation. The wine is matured on the yeasts for three years and then disgorged without dosage. It is therefore completely dry but tastes soft and honeyed from well-ripened fruit.

J. M. da Fonseca Internacional, Azeitão

'Internacional' has relied on Lancers rosé since the company was hived off from the other Fonsecas ('Sucessores') in 1968. Seeing the dangers of relying on one mega-brand, they have recently begun to diversify. Miller Guerra, the company's oenologist, has developed a new sparkling wine plant which has been adapted from a system used extensively in Russia and Eastern Europe. The production of sparkling wine in bulk by the *cuve close* method is much faster than the traditional method used for champagne but makes wine of inferior quality. One of the main problems is that contact between the wine and the yeast sediment is much more limited when the secondary fermentation takes place in a tank than it is when it takes place in a bottle. As a result you get none of the biscuity complexity in the wine. The theory behind the Russian continuous method at Fonseca is that it combines the speed and ease of the *cuve close* process while turning out a better-tasting wine. In short, wine entering at one end of a series of eight pressurized stainless steel tanks is injected with active yeast and a dose of sweet liqueur to ferment in bulk. From there the wine moves slowly through the interlinking tanks which are packed with wood shavings. These support the dead yeast cells that are left behind after the secondary fermentation so that they are always in contact with the wine. After approximately twenty-one days in the system, the wine emerges in a continuous stream at a rate of 50 litres an hour, ready for the addition of *liqueur d'expedition* and bottling. The whole process is described in more detail on pages 49–51.

Lancers Brut is produced by this method. Wine from early-picked Castelão Francês grapes makes a lively, fresh-tasting base for a good clean sparkling wine with a persistent *mousse* and just a touch of the yeasty quality of a champagne. But champagne producers need have no cause for concern. To be fair, the quality of Lancers is some way off but then so is the price!

Visiting Makers of Sparkling Wine

Although somewhat off the beaten track, Caves Raposeira welcome passers-by in working hours. They have a small centre for visitors where you can taste the wines. The Lancers plant at Azeitão is rather more accessible and is only a short drive from Lisbon. A small museum full of artefacts charts the history of wine-making.

17

Madeira:
Bananas and Vines

Few vineyards are as spectacular as those on the island of Madeira. Rising sheer from the Atlantic, nearly 1,000 kilometres from the Portuguese mainland and 700 kilometres off the Moroccan coast, Madeira's sub-tropical shores are fringed with palms, banana plants, avocado trees and an abundance of exotic flowers and shrubs. Above them, tiny shelf-like vineyards are stacked up the hillsides until they seem to disappear from view in the forests and clouds that almost always cover the island peaks. the seclusion of the island, the steep volcanic terrain and the warm, humid climate make this an unlikely place to find such an exciting and individual wine.

But few vineyards have endured as many difficulties as those on Madeira. Since Madeira wine first became fashionable at the end of the eighteenth century, the island's vineyards have suffered a chequered history, lurching from a periodic boom to recurring crises. But with the sort of resilience shared by these long-lasting wines, Madeira's fragmented wine industry has managed to survive.

Madeira began as a strong, unfortified wine. It was known to Shakespeare, who implies that by the end of the sixteenth century, less than 200 years after the discovery of the island, Madeira was already a commonplace drink. Noel Cossart, in his book *Madeira – the Island Vineyard*, notes that by the end of the seventeenth century there were around thirty wine shippers, including ten British traders who had set up firms. This compares with a total of eight exporters operating on the island today.

Madeira's boom period began about a century later, and in 1800, with shipments at over 16,000 pipes (668,000 litres) of by now predominantly fortified wine, demand had outstripped supply. The fashion for Madeira both in Britain and in the United States continued unabated through the brief British occupation of the island until

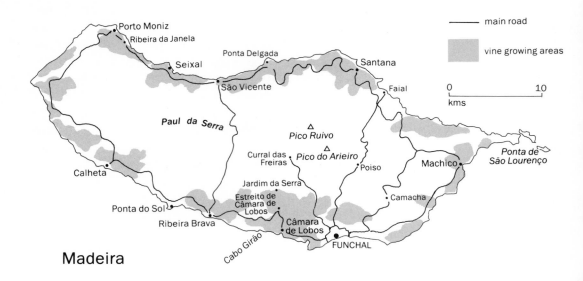

Madeira

1851, when the first of a series of crises struck. Oidium or downy mildew reached Madeira and quickly ravaged the dense, tightly packed vineyards, reducing output by as much as 98 per cent in three years. This devastated the island's monocrop economy and many established wine shippers simply packed up and left, releasing large quantities of old wines for those who had the courage to stay behind.

Worse was to come. Soon after a prevention for oidium had been found (sulphur dusting of the vine leaves), phylloxera struck, once more reducing the island's vineyard economy to ruins. From the mid-1870s vines all over Madeira were uprooted and replaced by sugar cane. Replanting began a decade later but with repercussions that have lasted until the present day. Thousands of phylloxera-resistant American vines were imported, ostensibly as rootstocks on which to graft Madeira's traditional European grapes. But many peasant farmers, seeking a quick return to normal production, planted *Vitis labrusca*, *V. riparia* and *V. rupestris* vines without grafting *Vitis vinifera* varieties. This has left Madeira with chaotic vineyards full of a hodge-podge of vines with odd names like Jacquet, Cunningham and Isabella (see page 34). There is currently a move to reduce the number of so-called 'direct producers' with a view to eliminating them altogether by 1997, though with half the island's production still emanating from these vines it will be an agonizingly slow process. But money talks loudest to small farmers, and European Community grants and price incentives are beginning to help now that hybrid grapes are no longer allowed to make Madeira wine.

With a return to normal harvests around the turn of the century, Madeira resumed shipments to its traditional markets, including Britain and the United States. But with the upheaval of the Russian Revolution and prohibition in the United States, Madeira lost two important markets and many firms were forced to amalgamate or close. Since the 1900s France, Germany and the Benelux countries have taken an important role, shipping enormous quantities of Madeira wine for cooking. Little attention was paid to quality when the wine was destined from the start to make *sauce madère*, so large bulk shipments of rather dreary wines have been the 'bread and butter' that has kept Madeira's wine trade going. Britain has now fallen back to third in the league, taking 11 per cent of Madeira's exports as opposed to the 40 per cent that is sent in bulk to France. The United States is a long way behind, only just making it into the top ten with 5 per cent, but Britain, the US and Japan are much the most important markets for Madeira's high-quality wines.

More recently three other dramatic changes have taken place which are certain to affect the future production of Madeira's vineyards and wines. The first of these, which put paid to an integrated island economy, was the abolition (in the late 1960s) of the use of spirit distilled from locally grown sugar cane to fortify Madeira's wines. The government, which controlled the sale of *aguardente*, forced producers to buy grape spirit distilled to 95 per cent alcoholic strength from their own monopoly instead. Then came the 25 April Revolution in mainland Portugal (or the *continente* as the islanders call it), which brought both inflation and mild social unrest to the previously isolated island economy. Finally, Portugal's entry into the European Community in 1986 has led to some sharp words about the state of Madeira's vineyards and the labelling of Madeira wine. All this has served to increase production costs for Madeira at a time when many small farmers have already found it more profitable to grow bananas than vines.

None of this cultivation would be possible at all were it not for the complex labyrinth of irrigation channels that criss-crosses the island. Madeira at its summit rises to over 1,800 metres (6,000 feet). Annual rainfall here reaches nearly 3,000mm, more than three times the predominantly seasonal rainfall that falls in Funchal down on the coast. Water falling on the mountains is diverted into small channels or *levadas*, which cascade down the hillsides irrigating crops and now generating hydro-electricity at the same time. The first *levadas* were built at the end of the sixteenth century, and by 1900 there were over 200 of them extending 1,000 kilometres around the island. After a government construction scheme in the 1930s and 1940s there are now over 2,000 kilometres of *levadas*, carefully regulated to ensure an even distribution of water to every tiny property. Without the *levadas* it would be difficult for Madeira's intensive agriculture to survive.

At the present time, Madeira has around 4,000 small growers farming 1,800 hectares of vines. Simple mathematics determine that the average vineyard holding is less than half a hectare in size. With the largest single vineyard less than 4 hectares in extent, growers talk about their plots in terms of square metres rather than acres or hectares of vines.

Nearly all Madeira's vineyards are perched on tiny terraces or *poios*, hacked out of the red or grey basalt that makes up the island. Vines are trellised or *latada* in a similar way to that practised in Vinho Verde country (see page 114). This raises the grapes above the ground, making them less vulnerable to the fungal diseases that thrive in Madeira's warm, damp climate. With a mean annual temperature in Funchal of 19°C and rainfall of about 750mm, oidium and botrytis are a real threat against which every farmer takes precautions. Unlike Vinho Verde country, though, few vines are trellised more than 2 metres above the ground, making vineyard work back-breaking as labourers duck in between a lattice of straggly interconnected vines to apply treatments or pick the grapes. Because of this structure, in most vineyards, mechanization is clearly an even more remote possibility than in the Port vineyards of the Douro (see page 66).

Add to this Madeira's dense population, and the use of cultivatable land (restricted to the coastal belt) is under the most enormous pressure. The best crop wins. Recently the best crop has been bananas. In future it is to be hoped it will be wine.

The Wines

Madeira's wines have traditionally been named after the grapes from which they were made, and range in style from dry to rich and sweet. Degrees of residual sugar in each case are given in brackets. There are four principal styles of Madeira wine.

Sercial

This is usually grown in the coolest vineyards, at heights of up to 1,000 metres or on the north side of the island. There are large plots of Sercial at Jardim da Serra ('mountain garden'), about 900 metres above Câmara de Lobos on the south coast, and at Porto Moniz and São Vicente in the north. Many growers still think that Sercial is the same grape as the German Riesling when it is in fact the Esgana Cão ('dog-strangler') growing on the mainland. At high altitudes, it ripens with difficulty to make an 11° wine, which is high in acidity and tastes rough and tart when young. With ten years or more a good Sercial wine develops a high-toned almond-like aroma and a delicate, nervy taste with a searingly dry finish. High-quality vintage Sercial wines last for 100 years. A 1910 Sercial from Blandy's still tastes astringent and spicy with an exploding finish. Such wines are wonderful as an aperitif. (0.5-1.5° Baume.)

Verdelho

Found growing predominantly on the north side of the island around Porto Moniz, Ribeira da Janela and Santana, Verdelho ripens to give more sugar than Sercial, making a more balanced, high-quality, nutty, peachy base wine. Old Verdelho wines are sweeter than Sercial yet retain a tang of acidity. There are still some extraordinary wines around, like Barbeito's smoky 1839. They are drunk either as an aperitif or with a clear soup or consommé. (1.5-2.5° Baume.)

Bual (Boal)

Bual is grown in warmer locations on the south side of the island, around Calheta, Câmara de Lobos and Funchal. Achieving higher levels of sugar than either Sercial or Verdelho, Bual makes rich, sweet, dark wines which retain their spicy verve with age. A Bual like Blandy's 1920 is rich and round with an aroma and flavour of almonds and raisins, while an 1837 Bual from the Acciaioli cellars, auctioned at Christie's in London in 1989, still has a long tangy finish. Buals are usually drunk at the end of a meal. (2.5-3.5° Baume.)

Malvasia (Malmsey)

Malvasia grapes are grown mostly in the warmest vineyards at low altitudes along the south coast, especially around Câmara de Lobos, although there is still a considerable amount produced at São Jorge in the north. Two types of Malvasia, Malvasia Candida and Malvasia Babosa, ripen to make the very sweetest and darkest of Madeira wines, which have always been the most sought after in Britain. A wine like Blandy's ten-year-old tastes rich and concentrated, while the Acciaioli 1836 is intensely sweet and almost syrupy with wonderfully concentrated length. Old Malmseys should be drunk like Port at the end of a meal. (3.5-6.2° Baume.)

Three other styles of Madeira, now rarely seen, are also based on individual grapes.

Terrantez

Terrantez is almost extinct in Madeira's vineyards but old wines made from this once highly esteemed grape still turn up. They tend to be medium sweet, between a Bual and a Verdelho in style. Acciaioli's 1802 Special Reserve Terrantez, auctioned at Christie's in June 1989, is wonderfully powerful yet fragrant, with searingly fresh acidity right to the end. Barbeito have a quantity of 1795 Terrantez which is still fresh if tasting slightly of cask with vanilla-flavoured length.

Bastardo

Bastardo (meaning bastard) is Madeira's most highly thought-of red grape which now, like Terrantez, is almost extinct. It is rarely found bottled on its own as a style of wine these days, but casks of old Bastardo wine lie around in old lodges and are occasionally used for blending. The grape is not thought by the islanders to be the same as the Bastardo (see page 26) on the Portuguese mainland.

Moscatel

This always seems to crop up where fortified wines are made, if only for sweetening. Most are now eaten as table grapes, though old wines made exclusively from three types of Moscatel growing on Madeira can still be found. The Madeira Wine Company have bottles of 1900 Moscatel. The wine is deep black-brown in colour and tastes of treacle and molasses, rather like old Setúbal (see page 26).

The grape varieties listed above are, with the notable exception of Moscatel, officially classified as *nobre* (noble). Since phylloxera ravaged the vineyards in the last century these grapes have accounted for no more than 20 per cent of the total amount of Madeira wine that has been made. Direct producers or hybrid vines and a red grape called Tinta Negra Mole made up the difference in wines variously labelled Sercial, Verdelho, Bual and Malmsey according to their style and sweetness. The law has now been tightened up, and since 1990 wine from hybrid grapes may no longer be made into Madeira wine. But Tinta Negra Mole is much the most widely planted variety. It is classified as *boa* or good rather than noble, and makes all but the very finest Madeira.

The European Community have had something to say about naming wines after one variety and making them with another. So from the beginning of 1993, all Madeira labelled with the accepted names Sercial, Verdelho, Bual and Malmsey must be made with at least 85 per cent of the grape stated on the label. Wines made from the versatile Negra Mole will be restricted to being labelled dry (*seco*), medium dry (*meio seco*), medium sweet (*meio doce*) and sweet (*doce*).

Wine-making on Madeira is covered in detail on pages 57–60. It is worth remembering, however, that production methods differ according to the company and the style and quantity of wine being made. All but the best Madeiras undergo *estufagem*: heating in large epoxy-lined concrete tanks to temperatures between 40° and 50°C for a minimum period of three months. This serves to accelerate the maturation of the wine in much the same way as long sea voyages used to in the eighteenth and nineteenth centuries. It is now the cheapest way of producing wines with the accepted maderized aroma and taste.

The generally accepted hierarchy of Madeira wines from the youngest and most basic to the oldest and most distinguished is as follows:

Granel: Granel (bulk) wine undergoes rapid *estufagem* in tanks and ages in bulk. Much is shipped after two years, having been coloured and sweetened with caramel. Most goes to France for cooking, so quality is not a prime consideration. *Vinho de granel* accounts for between 30 and 40 per cent of all Madeira produced. For many companies it is a staple wine.

'Finest': These are three-year-old wines, made from Negra Mole base wine and bottled after *estufagem* in tank and ageing in bulk, rarely in wood. Again some are sweetened and coloured with caramel. These are the most basic Madeiras bottled on the island and tend to taste and smell baked. Synthetic cheese frequently comes to mind when describing the aroma.

Reserve: These are made from a blend of five-year-old wines, some of which will have undergone *estufagem* in tank, while others will have been aged in cask. Most, if not all, of the base wine will be Negra Mole. Wines that have spent time in an *estufa* typically smell and taste stewed.

Special Reserve: This is where the excitement begins! These are blends of wines where the youngest wine is ten years old, having aged without any bulk *estufagem*. The base wine should contain a high proportion of the grape stated on the label. Blandy's ten-year-old Special Reserve wines are excellent examples.

Extra Reserve: This category is rarely used but denotes high-quality wines made from the stated grape and aged for at least fifteen years in cask.

Vintage: These are wines of the very highest quality from a single year, hence the name. Unlike vintage Port, which is bottled young, Vintage Madeira must age for a minimum of twenty years in cask and two years in bottle. Most wines are bottled after spending considerably more time ageing on *canteiros* (scantles or racks) in the warm eaves of a shipper's lodge, and sometimes in twenty-litre glass *garrafões*. Once in bottle, vintage Madeiras develop little but may be kept almost for ever, such is their resistance to oxidation. Firms with stocks of old vintage wine like the Madeira Wine Company and Pereira d'Oliveira keep the bottles standing up so that there is no risk of a poor cork spoiling the wine. They are then periodically recorked.

Solera: The *solera* system, used in Spain to age and blend sherry, has also been used for Madeira. Some firms, in particular Henriques & Henriques, still pride themselves on their old dated *solera* wines. But sadly, after a number of past frauds, this category of Madeira wine is soon to be wound up. Firms with established *soleras* will eventually be forced to blend their wines with other old stocks.

Rainwater: The legend behind the name goes like this. Casks of Madeira being sent to Savannah in the United States were left on the beach for too long and rainwater seeped in. The American buyer noticed the difference in taste but found he rather liked the style. Since then it has been used by some exporters to denote a lighter style of medium dry Madeira.

The Wine-makers

The structure of the Madeira wine industry is complicated by the large number of tiny growers and the *partidistas* who often act as middle-men or *armazénistas*, holding stocks of old wines. At one time there were numerous *partidistas* ageing wines in and around Funchal. Now they number less than ten, though they still perform an important function for some of the smaller exporters who hold few old stocks of their own. The exporters are the well-known names found on the labels and there are currently eight of them, all with lodges in Funchal. Six well-known wine-makers are listed here. The Instituto do Vinho da Madeira (Madeira Wine Institute) operates the system of quality control.

The Madeira Wine Company

The redoubtable Madeira Wine Company is by far the largest producer of Madeira on the island. It began in 1913 as the Madeira Wine Association when two shippers, Welsh & Cunha and Henriques & Camara, joined forces in the wake of the phylloxera crisis. Other companies facing difficulties joined, and for a time with the collapse of the Russian market it became known rather cruelly as the 'shippers' cemetery'!

After a difficult period, Blandy & Leacock, seeing the economies that could be made by centralizing production, amalgamated their interests with a Portuguese firm, Viuva Abudarham, and joined the association in 1925. From that time the Blandys, who have interests in shipping and tourism all over the island (they own Reid's Hotel), have taken a leading role. John Blandy, the grandfather of present chairman, Richard, became the new enlarged association's first chairman and appointed Thomas Mullins, then in charge of Blandy's wines, as managing director. Subsequently, other famous Madeira names facing problems in a changing market also joined the Association. Rutherford & Miles became a partner in 1951 and Cossart Gordon followed in 1953.

A total of twenty-seven different Madeira wine houses now make up the organization, which since 1981 has been renamed the Madeira Wine Company. Together they account for around 40 per cent of Madeira's wine exports, most of which are shipped under the names of Blandy, Cossart, Leacock and Miles. A further list of names under which wines are still sometimes found includes:

Barros Almeida
Bianchi
F. Martins Caldeira
Donaldson
F. F. Ferraz
Luís Gomes

Henriques & Camara
Krohn Bros
Lomelino
Power & Drury
Royal Madeira Company
Shortridge Lawton
Viuva Abudarham
Welsh Bros

The Madeira Wine Company currently operates from two lodges in the centre of Funchal. The São Francisco Lodge, housed in a former monastery next to the tourist office on the Avenida Arriaga, is their showpiece. It is open to visitors. Brass nameplates by the door testify to the many different companies that have joined forces. Above, rickety wooden attics house *canteiros* of old wines ageing slowly in sub-tropical warmth, the best wines being kept in the eaves of the roof. Casks of American oak store 70,000 litres of the very highest-quality wines, while downstairs a dusty vinotheque contains 50,000 bottles of vintage wine.

The real work is done at a much less picturesque but rather more practical Mercês lodge above the city centre on the Rua dos Ferreiros. Here, grapes from the company's own 4-hectare vineyard at Santana as well as from around 2,000 growers (about half the total number on the island) arrive for fermentation in a battery of stainless steel autovinification tanks. Young Negra Mole wines destined to be sold in bulk or as three-year-old finest and five-year-old reserve wines undergo *estufagem* in concrete vats, while better wines for blending age in cask in warm rooms around the *estufas*.

The Madeira Wine Company is now at pains to maintain the 'house styles' of each firm, though in the past, with so many different brands, this has been a near impossible task. The best wines are now bottled under the Blandy and Cossart Gordon labels and their ten-year-old Special Reserve wines are of a very high standard. Blandy's wines tend to be richer than the slightly drier, lighter-coloured Cossart Gordon style. Dry, nervy Lomelino wines are also well worth searching out. Stocks of vintage wines date back to 1822. Bottles of Cossart, Blandy and Shortridge Lawton from late last century and the early 1900s are some of the most exciting Madeiras still to be found.

The Madeira Wine Company has rarely stood still, and since the 1974 revolution which shook Madeira in much the same way as the rest of Portugal, the Company has been taking a long hard look at itself. In the period of rationalization that followed the revolution, the Leacocks sold their share in the company to the Blandys, who then took control. But in 1988, looking to the future, the Madeira Wine Company went public and the Symington family of Dow, Graham and Warre Port fame took a 46 per cent stake in the firm, putting them on an equal footing with the Blandys.

Since 1989, the first vintage in which the Symingtons became involved, wine-making practices have been thoroughly overhauled. The company has reverted to the traditional methods of stopping the fermentation to leave natural grape sugar and is looking to reduce the amount of *estufagem*. The Symingtons also intend to re-establish the individuality of the Madeira Wine Company's chief brands, keeping Blandy and Cossart Gordon for high-quality wines and using Leacock and Miles for supermarket blends. With this investment in technology and marketing now coming from Oporto, the future of the Madeira Wine Company as the largest Madeira wine-maker now looks assured.

Barbeito
Mario Vasconcelos Barbeito used to work for H. M. Borges until 1946, when he set up on his own. In a lodge on the Estrada Monumental, close to Reid's Hotel, his daughter Manuela now looks after the firm's substantial exports. Japan is their most important market. Around half their wines are bottled, the remainder being bulk wine destined mainly for France.

The family own no vineyards but buy in grapes and wines from local growers and *partidistas*. They retain substantial quantities of excellent vintage wines, going back to a delicious 1795 Terrantez.

Mario Vasconcelos Barbeito was a great historian, with a special interest in Christopher Columbus. His collection of books, maps and documents is now beautifully displayed in a small museum adjoining the family's wine shop on the Avenida Arriaga in Funchal.

H. M. Borges
This small family firm, founded in 1877, operates from a rather chaotic lodge facing the Madeira Wine Institute in the centre of Funchal. They buy grapes from small estates around Estreito de Camara de Lobos and have a shareholder who owns a Sercial vineyard high up at Jardim da Serra. Japan, Italy and the United States are important markets for bottled Madeiras, with Scandinavia the destination for most of the firm's bulk wine. They are honest enough to admit that only their vintage wines are made from noble grapes. The remainder come from Tinta Negra Mole.

Henriques & Henriques
Founded in 1850, Henriques & Henriques began as a *partidista*, making and supplying wines to other exporters from extensive vineyards at Belém, Camara de Lobos. The company began exporting under its own name only in 1925, and today it is established as one of the larger producers on the island outside the fold of the Madeira Wine Company. The last member of the Henriques family died in 1968, and now three partners including the Cossart family direct the firm from rather cramped

premises in the centre of Funchal. The company still owns 6 hectares of vineyard near Camara de Lobos and has a project to move there from Funchal.

The firm's young wines include a dry wine called Monte Seco, made largely from Listrão grapes grown on the island of Porto Santo. Three-year-old wines tend to taste typically baked from *estufagem*. They are also bottled under both the Harvey and the Sandeman labels. The firm is proud of its excellent *solera* wines, based upon wines laid down in the last century, which taste dense and smoky through age. Unfortunately, it looks as though this style of wine will have to come to an end, as *soleras* no longer fit into Madeira's legislation.

Wines are also sold under the names of Carmo Vinhos, Casa dos Vinhos da Madeira, António Eduardo Henriques and Belém's Madeira Wine. All are companies that have been incorporated into Henriques & Henriques.

Pereira d'Oliveira

This tiny family firm with a showpiece lodge in the heart of Funchal turns out some high-quality wines. The company makes nothing for export in bulk, its youngest wines being five-year-olds bottled from oak without any *estufagem*. There are no synthetic cheese smells here! Their own vines provide them with 70 pipes of Madeira each year (about 38,000 litres), and grapes bought in from other growers in the Estreito de Câmara de Lobos district make up the rest.

D'Oliveira still have vintage wines dating back to 1850, including a deliciously complex 1907 Malvasia and a revealing 1957 'Old Wine' made from Negra Mole.

Sadly, few Pereira d'Oliveira wines reach the United Kingdom. Many high-quality wines go to the United States.

Veiga França

A relative newcomer to the Madeira scene, Veiga França was established in 1944 and is still family-owned. By the church at Estreito de Camara de Lobos, Veiga França have a small winery where they ferment grapes from their own vines as well as from local growers. At their lodge, now surrounded by holiday accommodation on the Estrada Monumental outside Funchal, they prepare and ship large quantities of *granel* or bulk Madeira principally for France. Of their 1,300,000-litre production, 60 per cent is *vinho de granel*. Nearly all of their wines undergo *estufagem* at 50°C and it shows!

Instituto do Vinho da Madeira (Madeira Wine Institute)

A striking building in the centre of Funchal (formerly the British Consulate) now houses the Madeira Wine Institute. It was founded in 1980 to take a more active role in controlling quality, after hybrid grapes had been forbidden for Madeira wine. Today well-equipped laboratories analyse all wines for traces of malvina, an anthocyanin found in high concentrations in the skins of ungrafted American vines.

Madeira's seal of origin is granted to a wine only after it has passed a series of analyses and been tasted by the institute's panel of tasters. Since 1982, the Madeira Wine Institute has had the power to buy and age Madeira wines. It now holds substantial stocks of old wines, which are sometimes sold to exporters requiring wine for blending. A small museum (open to passing visitors) charts the story of Madeira wine.

Visiting Madeira

Madeira has been a resort since the end of the last century, when travellers came to realize the benefits of the island's mild winter climate. Reid's Hotel opened to guests in 1891 and lives on as a legend. In spite of many changes, it is still *the* place to stay.

Funchal, with a population of 100,000, is the capital and much the largest town on Madeira. Behind the waterfront and the impressive basalt black and white buildings in the hectic city centre, houses have piled up the hillside overlooking the broad sweep of the bay. Most of the wine lodges are crammed into the noisy 'downtown' area. They all welcome visitors and are within walking distance of the city's main hotels.

It is by travelling outside Funchal that you get an impression of the real Madeira. Câmara de Lobos to the west is a poor but picturesque fishing village, where children beg for money and old ladies with wizened hands embroider linen in the streets. Câmara de Lobos used to be at the centre of some of Madeira's best vineyards, but now terraces adjacent to the town grow bananas rather than vines.

To see vineyards you really have to go to Estreito de Câmara de Lobos, 500 metres above the coast. Around the scruffy village, vines are packed on to terraces overlooking the sea.

The most spectacular vineyards on Madeira are on the north side of the island. The road between Porto Moniz and Ponta Delgada is cut out of the cliff, with waterfalls crashing off the mountains into the sea. On either side, vineyards cling to near-vertical slopes with windbreaks made from bamboo and broom protecting them from the sometimes fierce northerlies.

Higher up, black volcanic peaks jut out above the *capacete* or almost permanent cloud cover. A road leads to the Pico do Arieiro, which at over 1,800 metres above sea level is a good place to survey the island.

Food on Madeira is made from local produce. *Espada* (scabbard fish) is cooked in a number of ways, usually grilled on a spit or fried with banana. Tuna (*atum*) is excellent served with a sauce made from tomatoes, carrots, peppers, coriander and wine. Most of the restaurants are concentrated in Funchal, but there are good places to eat by the beach in Câmara de Lobos, Camacha and on top of the mountains at Poiso. Wines other than Madeira are imported from the mainland. The local reds, made from hybrid grapes, are best left for the locals.

18

The Future For Portuguese Wines:
A Personal View

Among the wine-making countries in western Europe, Portugal probably has more untapped potential than any other. The maritime climate in conjunction with the wealth of indigenous grape varieties offers countless opportunities for wine-makers seeking to develop exciting, new flavours. Since the country settled down from the political upheaval of the mid-1970s considerable headway has been achieved. A new generation of wine-makers have shed their ancestral blinkers and started to think about a market for their wines outside Portugal. Year by year, an increasing number of wines is released on to the market bearing the clean, fresh hallmark of up-to-date wine-making.

But change has been slow; painfully slow if you compare the developments in Portugal with those that have taken place over the same period in South America or elsewhere in the New World. Portugal is a conservative nation and, at the present time, only a handful of wine-makers seem to have either the will or the wherewithal to change their production methods. Parochial attitudes will persist while many Portuguese wine drinkers continue to accept and even take pride in old-fashioned, alcoholic, often flawed, flat-tasting wines.

The pace is likely to speed up in future. Money from Brussels is pouring in as Portugal enjoys a long honeymoon after being hitched on to the EC. There are signs that the domestic market is becoming more discerning. Per capita consumption is falling as the growing middle class in Lisbon and Oporto sits up and takes an interest in better wine.

Port, which has enjoyed a boom in the 1980s, is unlikely to be as successful in the 1990s. Alcohol has become an issue and fortified wines will sadly bear the brunt of the health lobby as people count wine in calories and degrees of alcohol. Just as

2,500 hectares of new vines come on stream, the consumption of Port has begun to decline. The new vineyards are unlikely to suffer as there will always be a demand for high-quality wine. It is the smaller growers with vineyards in the Baixo Corgo (page 62) who will suffer as sales of inexpensive bulk Port tail off. Wine-makers in the Douro should therefore be adapting *adegas* to improve their table wines.

With the odds stacked against fortified wines, it looks as though Madeira could be facing terminal decline. Heavy investment in both the vineyards and wineries is the only way that the island's wine industry can be salvaged from the price-cutting spiral that many shippers have inflicted on themselves. The recent injection of capital into the Madeira Wine Company by the Symington family (page 217) is one of the few rays of hope if Madeira is to avoid following Setúbal and Carcavelos down the path to near extinction.

Ironically it is Portugal's resistance to change that will equip the country for the future. While other parts of the world leapfrog over regions like the Douro, Dão and Bairrada bowing to the latest international trend, Portugal's wine-makers are hanging on to their heritage. The country is a custodian of who knows how many unique grape varieties. With a little more foresight on the part of growers and some initiative from the producers, the twenty-first century could prove to be a renaissance or *renascença* for Portugal's wines and wine-makers.

Glossary

Portuguese Wine-making Terms

Every wine-producing country has its own wine-making and tasting vocabulary. Most modern terms are used internationally and have been adapted from the French equivalent, though in Portugal there are also a large number of words that have developed in line with local traditions. This glossary is far from being exhaustive but explains the meaning of all those most commonly used by Portugal's wine-makers.

Abafado: a generic term for fortified wines where the fermentation has been arrested by the addition of alcohol leaving residual sugar.

Adega: Winery.

Adamado: A rather sexist term meaning 'sweet'. *Dama* means 'dame' or 'woman'.

Afrutado: Fruity.

Agrafo: The wire or metal clip used to hold the cork of a bottle of *espumante*.

Agua pé: Literally 'foot water'. *Agua pé* is obtained by fermenting grape skins and stems macerated in water. It is often drunk by vineyard workers.

Aguardente: Grape spirit or brandy used to fortify wine.

Almude: A Port measurement. One *almude* equals 25.44 litres. 21 *almudes* make up a pipe.

Aloirado: A term used to describe the amber colour of a tawny Port. In Portugal, back-labels on a bottle of tawny Port describe the wine as *aloirado doce*, literally 'blond' and 'sweet'.

Amargo: Bitter.

Anfora: Amphora or clay pot originally used by the Greeks and Romans to transport and keep wine. Large *anforas* or *potes de barro* are still used in parts of the Alentejo for making wine (see page 184).

Apagado: A descriptive term for a wine that is dried out, finished.

Armazém: Literally a 'warehouse', an *armazém* is also a lodge where wine (especially Port) is kept and matured.

Bagaço: Stems, pips and skins left over after pressing.

Bagaceira: A distillation of the skins and stems. *Bagaceira* is a powerful, usually colourless spirit drunk in cafés all over Portugal.

Balseiro: A large wooden vat used for fermenting or storing wine.

Barril: Barrel.

Bica aberta: White wine vinification where the must is separated from the skins before the start of fermentation.

Borras: Lees or sediment left behind after fermentation.

Bruto: *Brut* – the driest style of *espumante* with less than 1.5 grams per litre of residual sugar.

Calcário: Calcareous.

Canada: A traditional measurement for Port. A *canada* is 2.12 litres, making 12 to an *almude* (q.v.).

Canteiro: Rack used for stacking casks or pipes. The word assumes greater significance in Madeira, where *vinho do canteiro* is high-quality wine which is aged in cask without heating in an *estufa* (q.v.). See page 215.

Carrascão: Rough, astringent red wine like red Vinho Verde.

Carvalho: Oak.

Casco: Cask. *Casco de carvalho*: an oak cask used for ageing wine.

Casta: Grape variety.

Cepa: Vine plant.

Chapeu: Literally, the 'hat' of floating skins and/or stems forced to the surface by carbon dioxide in a fermenting vat of wine. The *chapeu* is more commonly referred to as the *manta*.

Clarete: Term occasionally used to describe a light red wine.

Colagem: Fining to clarify a wine with sediment remaining in solution.

Colheita: Vintage.

Cor: Colour.

Corpo: Body.

Cruzeta: Form of pruning used in the north-west of Portugal for Vinho Verde; so named because the supporting stakes are shaped like crosses. See also page 114.

Cuba: Vat made out of wood or cement. If wood, it may also be called a *balseiro*.

Curto: Short; descriptive term for a wine lacking length of flavour.

Degustacão: Tasting.

Desavinho: Uneven development on individual berries within a bunch of grapes provoked by cold or wet weather at the time of flowering. *Millerandage* in French.

Desequilibrado: Unbalanced.

Desengaçar: Destemming bunches of grapes prior to fermentation.

Doce: Sweet (see also **Adamado**).

Duro: Descriptive term for a wine that is tough or hard.

Encepamento: Composition of a wine by grape variety. *Cépage* in French.

Enforcado: System of training vines up trees used in the north-west of Portugal (see page 114).

Engaço: Stems or stalks.

Enologia: Oenology, the science of wine-making.

Enxertia: Grafting of native *Vitis vinifera* vines on to American rootstock.

Equilibrado: Descriptive term for a wine that is well-balanced.

Escolha: Choice, selection.

Escuro: Dark.

Esmagamento: The mechanical crushing of grapes prior to fermentation.

Espumante: Naturally sparkling wine made by the traditional champagne, *cuve close* or continuous method (see page 49).

Espumoso: Artificially carbonated sparkling wine (see also **Gasificado**).

Estágio: Period of ageing.

Estufagem: The heating process used to age Madeira wine (see page 58).

Extra-seco: A category of *espumante* with between 12 and 20 grams per litre of residual sugar. Not as dry as *bruto*.

Fermentação Alcoolica: The fermentation that transforms sugar into alcohol, sometimes referred to as the *fermentação tumultuosa* or tumultuous fermentation.

Fermentação Malolactica: The secondary fermentation that transforms harsh malic acid into softer lactic acid (see page 42).

Filoxera: *Phylloxera vastatrix*, the aphid imported from North America that devastated European vineyards in the mid nineteenth century.

Fim da boca: Finish or length of flavour.

Floração: Flowering.

Forte: Descriptive term for a strong wine.

Fraco: A wine that is thin and weak.

Garfo: The *Vitis vinifera* scion used to graft on to American rootstock in order to resist phylloxera.

Garrafa: Bottle.

Garrafão: A 5-litre demijohn used for *vinho corrente* or basic table wine.

Garrafeira: A red wine from an exceptional year that has been matured in bulk for at least two years prior to bottling, followed by a further year in bottle before sale. White wines must age at least six months in bulk followed by a further six months in bottle to qualify. Both must have an alcoholic strength at least 0.5° above the legal minimum.

Gasificado: Sparkling wine made with an injection of carbon dioxide (see also **Espumoso**).

Generoso: Descriptive term for generously flavoured wine (see also **Vinho generoso**).

Granel: Bulk. *Vinho de granel*: wine sold in bulk.

Grau: Degree of temperature, alcohol or sugar.

Guyot: Method of pruning widely used in Portugal, adapted from France.

Hectare: 10,000 square metres of land, equivalent

to 2.471 acres.

Hectolitre: 100 litres.

Híbrido: Hybrid. In Portugal this is generally taken to mean an ungrafted, direct-producing American vine.

Idade: Age.

Inox: Stainless steel. Short for *aco inoxidavel*.

Jeropiga: Grape must prevented from fermenting by the addition of *aguardente*.

Jovem: Young. *Vinho jovem*: a young, fruity wine.

Lagar: Low-sided stone trough where grapes are trodden and fermented. Most have been replaced by fermentation vats except in the Douro, where some of the best Ports are still made in *lagares* (see page 52).

Lagrima: Literally 'tears'; *mosto lagrima* is the free-run juice released from the grapes after crushing but before pressing.

Latada: System of high training and pruning used in the north-west of Portugal and on Madeira.

Leve: Light; in the Oeste a few producers label their light, low-alcohol white wines as *vinho leve*.

Levadura: Yeast.

Licor de expedição: The same as the French *liqueur d'expedition*; the liqueur of wine and sugar added to sparkling wine after disgorging.

Ligeiro: A descriptive term for a wine (usually red) that is light, low in alcohol and tannin.

Limpo: Clean.

Lodge: A term used by British Port and Madeira shippers to mean a building where wine is stored and matured. The Portuguese prefer to use the term *armazem* (q.v.).

Lote: A parcel of wine used in blending. A Port or Madeira will be made up from a number of different *lotes*.

Maceração carbonica: Carbonic maceration – the fermentation of whole, uncrushed red grapes producing a distinctive fruity style of wine similar in style to a Beaujolais.

Maceração pelicular: Skin maceration; a few wine-makers macerate the skins of white grapes for up to twelve hours before fermentation starts, to make more aromatic wines.

Macaco: The pronged stick used in some wineries to punch down the cap or *manta* of floating grape skins during fermentation. *Macaco* also means 'monkey'.

Macio: Descriptive term for a red wine that is soft and smooth.

Magro: Almost the opposite of *macio*: lean and thin.

Manta: Literally the 'blanket' of red grape skins that floats to the top of a vat during fermentation.

Míldio: Mildew.

Morto: A wine that is dead, having reached the end of its life.

Mosto: Must or grape juice.

Nobre: Noble, e.g. *casta noble* – noble grape variety.

Oídio: Oidium.

Pelicula: Grape skin.

Pesado: Heavy – a descriptive term for a wine with plenty of alcohol and extract.

Picado: Literally 'sting'; used to describe a wine with excess volatile acidity.

Pinga: A drop; some wine-makers will refer colloquially to a good wine as a *boa pinga*.

Pintar: The same as *véraison* in French, when red grapes begin to develop colour.

Pipa: A pipe; the Portuguese for a cask or barrel. It is also commonly used as a unit of measurement, but this varies all over Portugal. In the Douro the yield of each vineyard is measured in pipes of 550 litres, while a pipe in Gaia Port lodge varies in size between 580 and 630 litres. For shipping purposes, however, a Port pipe has a precise measurement: 534.24 litres, while in Madeira a shipping pipe contains 418 litres.

Pipe: See **Pipa**.

Pisa a pé: Trodden by foot.

Poda: Pruning.

Podridão: Rot.

Porta-enxerto: Literally 'graft carrier'; the American rootstock on to which European *Vitis vinifera* vines are grafted. Also called the *barcelo* or *cavalo*.

Prensa: Press.

Prova: Tasting.

Quinta: A farm or vineyard.

Ramada: High-trained vines, sometimes also referred to as *latada* (q.v.).

Redondo: Round; a descriptive term for a wine with no hard, tannic edges that fills the mouth.

Região demarcada: Demarcated region.

Remontagem: Pumping over to macerate and extract colour and tannin from the skins in red wine-making.

Remuagem: Remuage; the riddling of bottles of sparkling wine made by the traditional Champagne method.

Rolha: Cork.

Saca-rolhas: Corkscrew.

Seco: Dry; a wine with less than 4 grams per litre of residual sugar.

Solar: Literally, a Portuguese mansion sometimes used to designate a wine in much the same way as *château* is used in France.

Solera: A system of fractional blending much used in Jerez and occasionally used in Madeira. Since Portugal's entry to the European Community, *solera* wines are no longer permitted.

Suave: A descriptive term for a wine that is soft and smooth.

Sulfroso: The smell of sulphur dioxide in a wine, common in cheap, sweetened Vinhos Verdes.

Surdo: Especially sweet wine fortified with *aguardente* (q.v.), used on Madeira for blending with other wines.

Tanino: Tannin.

Tanoeiro: Cooperage.

Tataro: Tartrate sediment encrusted on the side of vats and casks after fermentation and maturation; also called *sarro*.

Tasca: A small street bar selling wine by the glass or by the bottle.

Termovinificação: Thermovinification; the heating of fermenting must to between 70 and 75°C. This destroys dangerous oxidases when the grapes arrive at the winery in poor condition. Thermovinification may also be used to extract colour rather than tannin from the skins of red grapes; however, it tends to make wine with rather bland, cooked flavours.

Tinto: Red, as in Vinho Tinto.

Tonel: A large vat made from wood (usually oak), ranging between 1,000 and 25,000 litres in size.

Torna viagem: Literally, 'return trip'. Casks of Madeira and Setúbal were stowed in the hulls of ships crossing the tropics as ballast, and the change of temperature made the wine develop more rapidly. The practice has now died out (see page 170).

Trasfega: Racking.

Uva: Grape.

Vinho generoso: Fortified wine.

Abbreviations

The Portuguese have an enormous number of abbreviations. They need them to refer to all the bureaucratic organizations that flex their muscles in so many walks of everyday life. This is a list of the most common in the wine-world.

ADVID: Associação para o Desenvolvimento da Viticultura Durense.
DOC: Denominação de Origem Controlada.
IPR: Indicação de Proveniência Regulamentada.
IVM: Instituto do Vinho da Madeira.
IVP: Instituto do Vinho do Porto.
IVV: Instituto da Vinha e do Vinho.
JNV: Junta Nacional do Vinho; precursor of the IVV and now extinct.
RD: Região Demarcada.
VQPRD: Vinho da Qualidade Produzido em Região Determinada.

Select Bibliography

Andrade Martins, Conceição. *Memoria do Vinho do Porto*. Instituto de Ciencias Sociais da Universidade de Lisboa, Lisbon, 1990.

Bradford, Sarah. *The Story of Port*. Christies Wine Publications, London, 1983.

Bravo, P., and Oliveira, Duarte de. *Viticultura Moderna*. Officinas do Commercio do Porto, Porto, 1916.

Carvalho, Bento de, and Correira, Lopes. *Vinhos do Nosso País*. Junta Nacional do Vinho, Lisbon, 1978.

Cincinato da Costa, Bernardino Camilo and de Castro, Luis Filippe. *Le Portugal au Point de Vue Agricole*. Imprimeri Nationale, Lisbonne, 1900.

Cossart, Noel. *Madeira: the Island Vineyard*. Christies Wine Publications, London, 1984.

Fletcher, Wyndham. *Port: an Introduction to its History and Delights*. Sotheby Parke Bernet, London, 1978.

Fonseca, Álvaro Morreira de, Galhano, Amândio, Serpa Pimentel, Eduardo, and Rosas, José, R-P. *Port Wine: Notes on its History, Production and Technology*. Instituto do Vinho do Porto, Oporto, 1981.

Galhano, Amândio. *Vinho Verde*. Comissão de Viticultura da Região dos Vinhos Verdes, Oporto, 1986.

Gonçalves, Franco Esteves. *Dicionário do Vinho*. Lisbon, 1986.

Gonçalves, Francisco Esteves. *Portugal: A Wine Country*. Editora Portuguesa de Livros Tecnicos e Cientificos, Lisbon, 1984.

Howkins, Ben. *Rich, Rare and Red*. William Heinemann, London, 1982.

Jefford, Andrew. *Port: An Essential Guide to the Classic Drink*. Merehurst Press, London 1988.

Lopes Vieira, Antonio. *Os Meus 50 Melhores Vinhos*. Chaves Ferreira Publicacões. Lisbon, 1990.

Metcalfe, Charles, and McWhirter, Kathryn. *The Wines of Spain and Portugal*. Salamander, London, 1988.

Oliveira Marques, A. H. de. *History of Portugal*. Second Edition. Columbia University Press, New York, 1976.

Postgate, Raymond. *Portuguese Wine*. J. M. Dent & Sons, London, 1969.

Read, Jan. *The Wines of Portugal*. Third Edition. Faber and Faber, London, 1987.

Robertson, George. *Port*. Faber and Faber, London, 1978.

Robinson, Jancis. *Vines, Grapes and Wines*. Mitchell Beazley, London, 1986.

Roque do Vale, Clara, and Madeira, Joaquim. *Os Vinhos do Alentejo*. Aventur, Évora, 1991.

Salvador, José A. *O Livro dos Vinhos*. Lisbon, 1989.

Suckling, James. *Vintage Port*. Wine Spectator Press, San Francisco, 1990.

Truel, P. *Notes sur les Cepages du Portugal et leur Synonymie*. I.N.R.A. – Montpelier, 1983–1985.

Vizetelly, Henry. *Facts about Port and Madeira*. Ward Lock, London, 1880.

Warner Allen, H. *The Wines of Portugal*. George Rainbird, London, 1963.

Index